free

as in speech
and beer

Open Source, Peer-to-Peer

and the Economics

of the Online Revolution

Darren Wershler-Henry

FINANCIAL TIMES
Prentice Hall

A Pearson Company
London · New York · San Francisco · Toronto · Sydney · Tokyo · Singapore · Hong Kong
Cape Town · Madrid · Paris · Milan · Munich · Amsterdam

Canadian Cataloguing in Publication Data

Wershler-Henry, Darren S. (Darren Sean), 1966–
  Free as in speech and beer : open source, peer-to-peer and the economics of the online revolution

ISBN 0-13-094429-7

1. Intellectual property. 2. Internet (Computer network). I. Title.

K1401.W47 2001   346.04'8   C2001-901235-7

Editorial Director, Trade Division: Andrea Crozier
Acquisitions Editor: Susan Folkins
Managing Editor: Tracy Bordian
Copy Editor: Karen Alliston
Proofreader: Tara Tovell
Art Direction: Mary Opper
Cover Design: Sputnik Art and Design Inc.
Interior Design: Julia Hall
Author Photograph: Lucas Mulder
Production Manager: Kathrine Pummell
Page Layout: B.J. Weckerle

1 2 3 4 5   WEB   06 05 04 03 02
Printed and bound in Canada.

ATTENTION: CORPORATIONS

Books are available at quantity discounts with bulk purchase for educational, business, or sales promotional use. For information, please email or write to: Pearson PTR Canada, Special Sales, PTR Division, 26 Prince Andrew Place, Don Mills, Ontario, M3C 2T8. Email ss.corp@pearsoned.com. Please supply: title of book, ISBN, quantity, how the book will be used, date needed.

Visit the Pearson PTR Canada Web site! Send us your comments, browse our catalogues, and more. **www.pearsonptr.ca**

A Pearson Company

for the Ubu Boys and Girls

ACKNOWLEDGMENTS

It was only possible to write this book because of generous gifts of time and patience from many people. I would like to thank all the editors who helped to shape these words: Karen Alliston, Tracy Bordian, Susan Folkins and Jennifer MacTaggart; thanks also to Andrea Crozier, Ed Carson and everyone else at Prentice Hall Canada for their support of this project.

Thanks to Stuart Baird and ICLEI for showing me around the office, and letting me use them as a case study.

Kenny Goldsmith, Bryce Johnson, Bill Kennedy, Graeme Lennon, Lucas Mulder, Brian Kim Stefans, Mark Surman and Tonya Surman all know more about computers than is strictly healthy for normal human beings. Thank you all for your insights and occasional skepticisms. Christian Bök, as always, was a sounding board for many of the ideas in these pages.

Thanks to the following people and organizations for graciously providing images for this book: Cédric <www.freeoldies.com>, Michael Colton <www.modernhumorist.com>, Tim Macinta <www.kmfms.com>, Kirk McKusick <www.mckusick.com>, the Nevrax Design Team and the FSF <www.gnu.org>; it's very encouraging to meet artists who aren't motivated solely by the bottom line.

Special thanks to Alana Wilcox and Jason McBride for forgiving the unforgivable, and picking up my slack at Coach House while I wrote this, and to Liz, for helping me hold it all together.

CONTENTS

INTRODUCTION:
NOTHING EXCEEDS LIKE EXCESS

Everybody has to find his own way to be free.

—BOB DYLAN

This is not a techno-anarchist manifesto advocating the destruction of the copyright system as we know it. As entertaining as that might be, this is a book for grownups.

This is not a starry-eyed paean to the wonders of e-business, nor is it a smug, self-congratulatory dismissal of the possibilities of dot-coms.

This book is an executive summary about the fraught relationship that networked society has to one word: FREE.

As Richard M. Stallman (the originator of the Free Software Foundation) has famously noted, in the context of Internet politics and ethics, the word 'free' has two very different but related meanings. On the one hand, people like to get useful and entertaining things, such as software, without expending any energy or resources to do so. In the hacker community, the shorthand for this truism is that 'software should be **free as in beer**.' On the other, more complex, hand is the philosophical belief that it is morally wrong to charge people for software—or even other forms of intellectual property. This is what GNU/Linux hackers mean when they say 'software should be **free as in speech**.'

The primary example of 'free as in speech'—the one that is currently rocking the computer industry as no other force ever has —is GNU/Linux software. Stallman began the GNU project as a clone of the powerful Unix operating system (hence the acronym 'GNU,' for 'GNU's not Unix'), and was soon joined by a small but dedicated horde of volunteer hackers ... including Linus Torvalds, who famously invented the eponymous 'Linux' kernel, the key component of the operating system. Other than the inception of the GNU project, Stallman's other major contribution to the free software world, which is at least as important as the OS kernel itself, is the 'copyleft,' the underlying principle of GNU/Linux's unique licensing system. Briefly, the copyleft ensures that Free Software stays free (as in speech), and is not co-opted into any company or individual's intellectual property.

As a culture, we confuse the two meanings of 'free' all the time. Sometimes this confusion is the result of cynical marketing, such as Apple's

'Rip.Burn.Mix' campaign, a 'free-beer' effort that presents the downloading and swapping of MP3 files on peer-to-peer (P2P) networks as some sort of bleeding-edge countercultural gesture when it's really the latest and most efficient form of rampant consumerism. Even the humor that has sprung up around MP3 file-sharing is aware of the dubiousness of its revolutionary rhetoric. The Modern Humorist's fake 'red scare' poster depicting a Leninist devil looking over the shoulder of a young man clearly using his iMac to rip, burn and/or mix is typical in its mixture of revolutionary chic, consumer culture and misunderstood threat. 'WHEN YOU PIRATE MP3S, YOU'RE DOWNLOADING COMMUNISM,' it warns, adding the sentiment that purchasing this image for one's home is the perfect way to say 'I recognize that stealing music is unethical, but I'm protected by my sense of irony.'[1]

... Which moves us directly to the first of many qualifications in this book. While downloading MP3s may not be revolutionary per se (most of the stuff that you can download for free off the Net can be obtained more quickly and easily for 10 bucks at the corner store), P2P technology itself is. For reasons that will become evident later in this book, the recording industry's vendetta against Napster and other P2P networks is a classic shortsighted instance of attempting to throw the baby out with the bathwater—and may have cost them one of the largest established customer bases in the history of the Internet. As it turns out, things that appear to be 'free as in beer' may have a lot to do with 'free as in speech' after all; the fact that business is playing catch-up with technological innovation is no reason to create laws favoring business at the expense of fundamental rights to use and share information.

Another reason why confusion sometimes arises between the two meanings of 'free' is that there are actually a surprising number of things that are **free as in speech *and*beer**. Although there's nothing in the copyleft specifying that free-speech software can't have a price tag, most GNU/Linux software is available on the Net for nothing.

... Which moves us along to our next qualifier. Despite what you'd expect, the existence of free-as-in-speech-and-beer software hasn't stopped many viable businesses from springing up that produce commercial distributions of GNU/Linux software, or sell support for it, or use it in conjunction with proprietary software or make money off of it in some other way. This turn of events seems to annoy Richard Stallman to no end, but pretty much everybody else is extraordinarily pleased. The mix of

Modern Humorist's <www.modernhumorist.com> apt summary of the Fear, Uncertainty and Doubt that surrounds the act of downloading music.

GNU/Linux and commercial software that's commonly referred to as the 'open source'[2] movement has been so successful that it's even made some inroads against Microsoft itself, probably because it plays by entirely different rules. (Even stodgy old IBM has shown new signs of life with its 'Love, Peace & Linux' campaign; Big Blue has gone so far as to hire an ad agency to stencil elaborate stencil graffiti featuring three icons—a peace symbol, a heart and a penguin [Tux, the Linux mascot]—onto the sidewalks of New York and San Francisco.[3])

Those rules—which describe the erratic ebb and flow between the moments of excessive generosity and the tedium of the corporate grind that together define the two extremes of the online environment—are the other subject of this book. Both free-speech and free-beer phenomena tend to behave according to the patterns of a gift economy, or potlatch. Unlike our regular economy, which derives profits from restricting the flow of goods to market, gift economies are defined by a constant, fluid exchange of wealth, with only a vague expectation that others will also contribute freely to that flow. But one of the key tenets of this book is that the gift economy and the regular economy are opposite sides of the same coin—one can't ever entirely replace the other. Most of the time, the regular 'restricted' economy keeps the gift economy in check, but every now and then the gift economy seizes control and embarks on a brief but nearly unstoppable rampage.

While gift economies have been around for a very long time, they seem particularly suited to the medium of the Internet, because digital commodities are far, far easier to replicate and circulate than their physical counterparts. The digital realization of the potential of gift economics has had real, startling and often unpredictable effects on contemporary business and culture. The combined impact of phenomena that function according to gift economics (most notably peer-to-peer networking and GNU/Linux) pose a direct challenge to the notions of authorship, copyright laws, licensing systems, distribution systems, pricing schemes and the other trappings of intellectual property management that our society has carefully tended for the last century.

Broadly, there are three possible responses to this situation: the scorched-earth approach typical of the entertainment industry and other aggressive proponents of the DMCA (Digital Millennium Copyright Act), who would legislate away the technology that they don't understand; the techno-anarchist contention that the Internet is inimical to commerce;

The gift economy and the regular economy are opposite sides of the same coin— one can't ever entirely replace the other.

or a synthesis of the two: an adventurous—even playful—attitude that is allowing many individuals, companies, not-for-profit organizations and even governments around the world to mix the benefits of a digital economy based on excess with garden-variety capitalism. This 'third way' isn't so much an advocacy of moderation as a recognition of the inherent unpredictability of networked culture. Neither the capitalist market nor the gift economy is about to disappear any time soon; if anything, the interactions between them may well become more violent and pitched over the next decade.

What follows is the story of how we got into this glorious mess ... along with a few ideas about how to enjoy it, and even make—or lose, if you prefer—some money in the process. Nothing exceeds like excess.

PART 1

free

When will you people learn? In America we stopped using corporal punishment and things have never been better. The streets are safe, old people strut confidently through the darkest alleys and the weak and nerdy are admired for their computer programming abilities. So, like us, let your children run wild and free, for as the old saying goes, 'Let your children run wild and free.'

—HOMER SIMPSON

Give it away now: A brief history of gift economies

Rich gifts wax poor when givers prove unkind.

—WILLIAM SHAKESPEARE, *HAMLET*

Before computers, before the Internet, before Usenet, FTP and Napster, for as long as people have been buying things from and selling things to each other (and that's a long-ass time), there has always been a counter-tradition of grandly and excessively giving stuff away—for free.

An environment where the predominant form of exchange is the circulation of gifts is called, as you might expect, a *gift economy*. Gift economies (sometimes called 'general economies,' 'potlatch economies' or 'reverse markets') are based on the excessive, free circulation of goods, with a general, intangible expectation of reciprocity from the broader community.

The opposite of a gift economy is a *restricted economy*, which derives value from real or artificial scarcity. This category includes our own society's economy. 'Restricted' isn't a value judgment so much as a description of function; in a restricted economy, the people or companies that control access to valuable goods meter them out to consumers in order to make a profit.

The important thing to understand from the outset is that these two types of economy *aren't really opposites*. A contemporary society can't really choose to operate according to the tenets of one to the exclusion of the other, because the gift economy and restricted economy function more as the interchangeable personalities of Dr. Jekyll and Mr. Hyde, jostling for control of the same body. The gift economy quietly percolates along 'underneath' the everyday transactions of a restricted economy, occasionally erupting in wild and unpredictable moments of largesse and excess (and occasionally, senseless destruction). Think west-coast First Nations potlatch. Think Mardi Gras in New Orleans. Think Woodstock. Think the rave scene in England during the early 90s. Think Free Software and GNU/Linux. Think Napster, Morpheus and Gnutella. Think 'fun' for some and 'a massive headache' for others.

Historically, gift economies have been marginal to Western society. When they *have* occurred, we've done everything in our power to ruthlessly stomp them out of existence, or, at the very least, circumscribe them to the point that they become innocuous curiosities. The rapid expansion of the Internet, in conjunction with the emergence of technology that allows anyone to cheaply and easily produce digital goods that other people actually want, has placed both the desire and the means to share those goods with a vast number of people. There are two ways to proceed: either we lace up our jackboots and start stomping (and a large number of big, important organizations have already begun to do so), or we take a slightly riskier but more interesting approach, and try to find ways to make the alter-ego of our economy work *for* us.

Ayn Rand vs. the geeks, round 2

Mark Surman and I discuss this phenomenon at some length in our book *Commonspace*, but it's nicely encapsulated in a little homily we call 'Bring Me the Head of Ayn Rand'[1]:

Garrett Hardin's 'Tragedy of the Commons,'[2] which first appeared in 1968, describes the problem of sharing in an atom-based world. We'll summarize it here, spiced up slightly to reflect the wonderful world of the new millennium:

A village of farmers holds one field in common, which they use to feed their herds. Each farmer has a herd of equal size, and together, the herds eat exactly all of the fodder that the field produces. One day, one farmer, while thumbing through his dog-eared copy of *The Fountainhead*, gets the brilliant idea that he should exploit the other farmers by adding another cow to his herd. After all, he'd only be paying the same as everyone else for his grazing rights, even if he had more cattle. While all the animals will be a little skinnier when they go to market because of the overuse of the pasture, he'll still make a few extra bucks. And what the hell, he deserves it. Selfishness is a virtue. Ayn says so.

Meanwhile, the other farmers are losing money to their Objectivist buddy because their cows go to market with slightly less meat on them, and they have fewer animals to sell. What to do? Inevitably, they all decide that they too have to buy more cattle to stay competitive. The cycle repeats itself. The field becomes muddy and rank and bare of grass; the increasingly scrawny cattle are packed in like sardines. Eventually, all the grass is gone, and one of the farmers (probably that bastard with the copy of *The Fountainhead*) decides that the only thing to do is to feed the living but scrawny cattle on the ground-up remains of the cattle who've died of starvation. Everyone gets Mad Cow Disease and dies a horrible, foaming, gibbering death. Not a pretty picture.

Eric Raymond to the rescue. In 'The Magic Cauldron,'[3] he uses the example of open source to demonstrate how 'The Tragedy of the Commons' disappears in commonspace. The self-interest vs. common good dilemma flips upside-down in an economy driven by bits.

Say you have a custom program for managing your farm. If you are willing to open the source code and share this software with your 'community' (the other farmers), you'll definitely build goodwill. But will it cost you anything? No! Will it make the software less usable for your business? No! In fact, sharing it (and contributing to the common good) may even make the software more valuable, because the farmers you share it with may have geeky kids who improve the software and then share the improvements with you. Instead of falling under a despotic communist dictator or being broken up into tiny little capitalist freeholds, the commons continues to expand. Freaky but true.

The Internet was built on open standards, and its rapid-fire growth to date is largely due to people sharing the resources (free software, donated server space on corporate, university and institutional mainframes, cheap and occasionally free connections for remote users) that permitted the speedy and efficient expansion of the Net's boundaries.

Further, the dot-com boom—and bust—was due to a fundamental misunderstanding on the part of many people (and companies) about the nature of the current Internet. As I just noted, the Net exists in the first place because of the generosity of others. Its basic structural feature is massive redundancy; if a computer can't find a resource it needs (or its user wants) in one area of the Net, it reroutes until it locates a new path to that resource or an identical copy of that resource in another location. Thus both the existing culture and structure of the Internet are inimical to attempts to meter the flow of information for profit.

Many of the dot-coms that went belly-up over the last two years used business models predicated on the notion that people would pay for content or services that they could get for free elsewhere. Others assumed that attaching ads to free content would allow them to pay for the content. But slapping a few banner ads on a Web site does not a revenue stream make, because the content on the site remains essentially free, no matter how much screen real estate the ads occupy ... and there are an infinite number

The Net exists in the first place because of the generosity of others.

of paths to that content other than by clicking through a banner ad. Jason McCabe Calacanis, the editor and CEO of Silicon Alley Reporter, finally said the unsayable late in 2000, calling banner ads 'an absolute, complete, unmitigated failure,' and lamenting that 'we standardized a failed concept. That's how stupid we are in the Internet industry.'[4] The alternative that Calacanis suggests is 'disruptive' advertising that inserts itself between the reader and the content, not unlike a TV commercial ... or a tollbooth.

This *might* work ... but then again it might not. Banner ads are the most innocuous manifestation of a gated system—anything that serves to limit access to online content to paid users. Creating more aggressive versions of such systems may result in a few people paying the toll, but mostly it means that people go elsewhere, as long as there's a free alternative. Since people have already been educated to expect that what they find online is theirs to keep for free, the only way to ensure that people pay for all the content and services they consume online would be to change the fundamental structure of the Net itself.

Increasingly, large software companies like Microsoft and AOL/Time Warner, in conjunction with the largest publishers of commercial content— the major record labels and the Hollywood movie studios (both individually and as represented by blanket industry organizations such as the Recording Industry Association of America [RIAA] and the Motion Picture Association of America [MPAA])—are considering how to make the free part go away for good. Establishing digital 'walled suburbs' like AOL or Microsoft's .Net, where every aspect of the handling of content can be controlled, is one way to establish a successful online business model, but it's definitely of the 'we had to burn down the village in order to save it' school of thought.

At the same time, an increasing number of people think and behave as though the free Internet works just fine, thankyouverymuch, and moreover, see the death of the current system of managing intellectual property online as a good and laudable turn of events.

These people aren't just college kids swapping MP3s or pimply teenage hackers sweating over a few minutes of downloaded digital pornography (though such people number in the millions). And they're not just businesspeople using bootleg copies of astronomically expensive software suites and operating systems, or designers using unlicensed fonts, or moms and dads saving a few bucks by sneaking disks home from the office to copy onto their kids' hard drives (though these people also number in the millions).

They're also people who are willing to invest copious amounts of time and effort into the creation of software, music, literature and art ... and then give it away. Sometimes they do this for ideological reasons, to guarantee that some things remain outside the provenance of corporate licensing. Sometimes they do it in order to establish a reputation for themselves, which, after all, is a marketable commodity. Sometimes they do it in order to create interest in other parts of their businesses, which involve paid services. And sometimes they do it simply for the pleasure of giving.

Outrageous as it may seem, these kinds of thoughts and actions are not unprecedented.

A warning

To paraphrase Ezra Pound, we are about to enter the 'longish dull stretch' that appears shortly after the beginning of most nonfiction books in order to establish some historical and philosophical context. By avoiding ambiguity now, I'm hoping to save you time later. Nevertheless, if you find the notion of history and philosophy too horrible to contemplate, you can skip this part, because I'll be back to discussing computers soon enough. What follows is a highly condensed, occasionally reductive backgrounder on the concept of the gift economy. Like many good hacks, this section compromises precision for functionality; it won't leave you with enough knowledge to do a PhD on the subject, but it will nevertheless provide you with the basic goods.

Mauss and the gift

Gift economies have existed in many cultures around the world for centuries, but it took a French anthropologist named Marcel Mauss to draw this to the attention of contemporary European and North American society in 1950. Mauss's book, *The Gift: The Form and Reason for Exchange in Archaic Societies*, describes the practice of giving in many cultures, chiefly in Melanesia, Polynesia, and North American west coast First Nations such as the Tlingit and Haida. To describe this system of gift exchange, he uses the word *potlatch* (Chinook jargon from the Nootka *p'achitl*—'to make a potlatch gift'). *The American Heritage Dictionary of the English Language* defines potlatch as follows:

A ceremonial feast among certain Native American peoples of the northwest Pacific coast, as in celebration of a marriage or accession, at which the host distributes gifts according to each guest's rank or status. Between rival groups the potlatch could involve extravagant or competitive giving and destruction by the host of valued items as a display of superior wealth.[5]

In Mauss's formulation, potlatch gifts circulate through a community with a guarantee of reciprocity. That is, something inherent to the value of the gift itself compels the recipient to respond in kind within a particular time limit.[6]

Jacques Derrida, in his book *Given Time: I. Counterfeit Money,* carries Mauss's analysis a step further, explicitly identifying the gift as a gift of time itself: 'What it gives, the gift, is time, but this gift of time is also a demand of time. The thing must not be restituted immediately and right away. There must be time, it must last, there must be waiting—without forgetting.'[7] Derrida's formulation is particularly appropriate to the digital milieu, where a gift of software is, if nothing else, a gift of the programmer's time in highly concentrated form, a gift that either saves time for the user by increasing productivity, or wastes time (in the positive sense of the word) by providing amusement.

Mauss draws an explicitly moral conclusion from his study of potlatch, suggesting that contemporary society should itself adopt potlatch traditions. 'It is essential ... that the rich return, freely or by obligation, to considering themselves as the financial guardians, as it were, of their fellow citizens.'[8] Mauss isn't advocating freeloading; rather, he desires a more humane world, where the needs of an individual are better looked after, and contracts are handled with greater generosity and an overall good faith.

Is this simply the longing of some tweedy academic for a mythical golden age? Derrida doesn't think so. He suggests that the ethics underpinning Mauss's study of potlatch isn't nostalgia for a lost utopia, but an impetus for revolution. If potlatch is a system of circular exchange, a cyclical ebb and flow of generosity based on boom, bust and (after a re-accumulation of goods) boom again, then it is possible to pass through late capitalism to 'a non-Marxist socialism, a liberal anti-capitalism or anti-mercantilism.'[9]

But Mauss isn't the only significant theorist of potlatch. Before we draw any conclusions, let's expand the notion a bit.

Bataille and the general economy

Surrealism wasn't all melting clocks and giant eyeballs, and it's left more of a legacy than Pink Floyd album covers and fish jokes. Some of the most knobby and irreducibly weird aspects of Surrealism, its most provocative ideas, haven't really been widely disseminated. One of these ideas is Georges Bataille's notion of the 'general economy.'

Bataille (1897–1962), librarian by trade, philosopher and writer by avocation, was a major influence on today's French philosophy and theory. While the writers that gathered around his early journal *Documents* (1930) presented a kind of internal opposition to André Breton, the Pope of Surrealism, Bataille and Breton later reconciled their differences to launch a mutual attack on fascism and its ideals. Bataille's later journals, *Acephale* (1936) and *Critique* (1943), were even more influential; *Critique* published the early work of many of the philosophers who would later champion his ideas (including Roland Barthes, Jacques Derrida, Michel Foucault and Maurice Blanchot).

Bataille describes his theory of the general economy in a sprawling, ambitious three-volume work called *The Accursed Share*. The crux of his argument is that conventional economics is flawed in its analysis because it always focuses on particular systems, and never considers economic activity as a whole.

As a corrective, Bataille proposes an economics that considers the energy of living matter in general—hence, a 'general' economics. 'On the surface of the globe, for living matter in general, energy is always in excess; the question is always posed in terms of extravagance. The choice is limited to how the wealth is to be squandered.'[10] In other words, it's possible to conceive of an economics based on plenitude rather than scarcity ... a possibility with some startling implications.

Accumulation, Bataille suggests, cannot continue indefinitely. At some point, all wealth has to be squandered. And ignoring this dictum has results that range from unfortunate to horrifying:

Incomprehension does not change the final outcome in the slightest. We can ignore or forget the fact that the ground we live on is little other than a field of multiple destructions. Our ignorance only has this incontestable effect: it causes us to undergo what we could bring about in our own way, if we understood. . . . For if we do not have the force to destroy the surplus energy ourselves, it cannot be used, and, like an unbroken animal that cannot be trained, it is this energy that destroys us; it is we who pay the price.[11]

While Bataille's thought was very much informed by the two World Wars that raged during his lifetime—war was for him one of the major mechanisms that the world has developed for dealing with excess energy—he was not a nihilist or an anarchist. In fact, he saw a change in perspective

It's possible to conceive of an economics based on plenitude rather than scarcity.

to accommodate the notion of a general economy as necessary for the development of a post-industrial, postwar economy, especially in North America. 'The industrial development of the entire world demands of Americans that they lucidly grasp the necessity, for an economy such as theirs, of having a margin of profitless operations.'[12] Bataille predicted the development of an economic network whose complexity greatly exceeded the old mechanical paradigms, and warned that it would develop its own laws and energies ... energies that could not be regulated from within the mindset of the old industrial economy.

Bataille also foresaw the transformation of the safety valve of warfare into something very much like the boom-and-bust of the 1995–2000 Internet economy: a 'vast economic competition' that would require expenditures from the participants comparable to those in wartime ... without any real hope of recovering those costs.[13]

While Bataille's vision goes a long way toward explaining the NASDAQ carnage of early 2001, the former employees of the dot-com sector may take small comfort in the explanation.

What Bataille leaves his reader with is not exactly reassurance, but it is, nevertheless, pertinent and useful. While gift economies don't really do anything to call into question the benefits of growth, they do provide 'a strange, exuberant, simultaneously beneficent and disastrous sense of wealth' as an alternative to wilful ignorance and nihilism. It is only possible to develop this sense in an environment where selfishness has ceased to dominate; further, Bataille suggests that it provides an alternative to the constant anxiety that accompanies greed and selfishness.[14]

This is the overall mood of the new economy: success and disaster rolled up into one chaotic, amorphous mass. So your startup is on the front page of Fucked Company <www.fuckedcompany.com>. Big deal. Put down your Nerf dartguns, sell your Aeron chairs, lay off your employees, file Chapter 11—and get back to work, for yourself or someone else. What drives people to do this? A sense, perhaps, that something is happening on the Internet that transcends us as individuals ... and the giddy possibility that the next killer app is right around the corner, sitting on top of a hayrack full of money.

Circulation and process

In his essay 'Writing as a General Economy,' poet, critic and professor Steve McCaffery expands Bataille's notions further in a direction that's useful for our purposes here. McCaffery points to a dichotomy that exists between the general or gift economy and our restricted economy, which operates according to the rules of 'restraint, conservation, investment, profit, accumulation and cautious proceduralities in risk taking.'[15]

McCaffery's major contribution to the development of this idea is that a general economy is not an alternative to a restricted economy—the two always coexist in an unequal but symbiotic relationship. (Derrida's discussion of the gift is similar in that it suggests that while gifts circulate through the economy, they maintain a 'relation of foreignness' to economic circulation, insisting on their separateness from the process of circulation and exhaustion that typifies commodities.[16]) In most instances, the general economy is held in check by the restricted economy, but is still percolating away, and occasionally 'ruptures' the restricted economy to manifest itself for a brief period of time before it is once again suppressed, subverted or rechanneled.

Think of Mardi Gras as an example of this process of containment. On Fat Tuesday in New Orleans, pretty much anything goes. But the free-for-all is highly localized both spatially and temporally; outside of specific areas within the city, and after midnight strikes, it's all over.

In this conceptualization, the general economy can't present itself as an equal-but-opposite 'alternative' to the restricted economy because it doesn't create value; its only concern is pure expenditure and dispersal. In a general economy, the process of gift-giving isn't like a regular economic transaction with two parties and some expectation of recompense. The gift itself is often fractured into smaller parts to facilitate its own circulation. The general economy functions more as an ongoing process of consumption and expulsion, with no real structure except continual movement.[17]

Further, a general economy doesn't offer a critique of the restricted economy's notion of value so much as it 'risks its loss' and subsequently casts doubt on all of the economic and political positions that we normally consider 'tried and true.' This does interesting things to the roles that status and rank play. In a general economy, status doesn't derive from the accumulation of wealth, but from the act of circulating it, or perpetuating its circulation.

Parts of the experience of the general economy *can* be capitalized on, in a literal sense. To continue with the Mardi Gras example, the New Orleans tourist board has developed a huge industry based on selling this temporary freedom as a consumable experience. And, for those intrigued

In a general economy, status doesn't derive from the accumulation of wealth, but from the act of circulating it, or perpetuating its circulation.

with the possibility of riding the whirlwind (there *is* a certain amount of risk involved), there are a number of other, indirect ways that productivity and power can be derived from gift economies in operation.

Potlatch, egoboo and the GPL

This doesn't mean that status derived from activities in a general economy isn't useful or tangible. Ask Linus Torvalds, inventor of the Linux kernel (the central component of the operating system), or Shawn Fanning, the creator of Napster. The reputation that results from circulating, or facilitating the circulation of, free digital commodities can build powerful careers and sometimes even financial empires.

After you've donated copious amounts of your time and energy to a project, the rush of energy and inspiration that results from your burgeoning reputation is something that science fiction fans refer to as 'egoboo' (short for *ego boost*). The notion of egoboo has become a useful tool in partially explaining the success of online gift economies of many types, from the Free Software and open source communities to consumer opinion aggregation sites such as ePinions <www.epinions.com>. While there have been several recent articles that foreground the role of egoboo in community-building, including Mark Frauenfelder's 'Revenge of the Know-It-Alls' in Wired <www.wired.com/wired/archive/8.07/egoboo.html>, the most significant examination of its usefulness remains Eric Raymond's *The Cathedral and the Bazaar* <www.tuxedo.org/~esr/writings/cathedral-paper-10.html>. Raymond argues that, using little fuel other than highly refined egoboo, the open source movement has rechanneled the selfishness of individual hackers to focus on difficult goals that can only be achieved by sustained cooperation. Bataille's discussion of the gift goes to support Raymond's argument: 'the gift would be senseless (and so we would never decide to give) if it did not take on the meaning of an acquisition. Hence giving must become *acquiring a power*.'[18]

The value of the egoboo-stature that the act of giving creates is so great that in many instances it actually compels the recipient to respond in kind. 'In order to get even,' Bataille writes, 'the giver must not only redeem himself, but he must also impose "the power of the gift" on his rival in turn ... Thus the gift is the opposite of what it seemed to be: To give is obviously to lose, but the loss apparently brings a profit to the one who sustains it.'[19]

The act of receiving the gift creates a very real obligation—just as the use of software code under a Free Software license places an obligation on the coder to return his work to the public code base. (I'll discuss Free Software licenses in detail in Part 2 of this book.)

According to Bataille, the paradoxical wish to profit or benefit in any way from gift economies is a contradiction that underlies 'man's entire existence.'[20] In his view, the only people who can truly benefit from the feeling of true wealth that potlatch creates are the hackers, slackers and anarcho-libertarians.[21]

For a librarian, Bataille was a man of extremes. There is some speculation that in his quest to explore the outer limits of waste and excess, he and the other members of Acéphale, his creepy but fascinating secret society, may have committed a (willing) human sacrifice (see Alastair Brotchie's introduction to the amazing *Encyclopedia Acephalica*, page 15). Bataille's goal was to perform actions powerful enough to create a new mythology, one that would accrete a community around it with different values from the society of the time. The Acéphale disbanded in part because its members came to the realization that new myths can't be synthesized from scratch; they have to arise spontaneously and haphazardly from real events and trends (*Encyclopedia Acephalica*, page 16). With the advent of Free Software and peer-to-peer networking has come several powerful new myths, and, although there may be destructive aspects to those myths, nobody had to be sacrificed to bring them into being.

Though gift economies function according to a paradox that is for the most part alien to our conventional mode of thought—how can anyone profit from excess and waste?—they are nevertheless a real means of acquiring stuff *and* ensuring that the goods remain in circulation, outside of the control of those who would hoard them and make the rest of us pay through the nose for them. Free Software and file-sharing technologies aren't just for the geeks anymore; they're important because they allow real people from all walks of life to accomplish desirable goals ranging from creating powerful but affordable large-scale computer systems to sharing music with their friends. And there's no reason that these technologies and their underlying philosophies can't be used in tandem with conventional business strategies, because, in addition to power, economy and convenience, they supply something that can be difficult to acquire through conventional channels: the respect of a sophisticated group of power users who are normally contemptuous of corporate methods and ideologies.

Free Software and file-sharing technologies aren't just for the geeks anymore.

The main purpose of the rest of this book is to explore these five related propositions:

1. *It's Not Just a Theory Anymore:* The digitization of information and the interconnecting of the planet with networks such as the Internet make gift economies a viable and vital part of contemporary life. While gift economies have thrived briefly at other times and in other places, right here and right now they are changing our society significantly, whether we like it or not.

2. *Easy Come, Easy Go:* The emergence of a gift economy is always localized and limited in time and space. Spaces for circulating digital commodities come and go erratically: Napster, FTP sites and Web sites crammed with illegal or semi-legal copies of software, copies of (or even links to) programs like DeCSS which fall into legal gray areas, and maybe even the entire dot-com boom itself demonstrate the evanescence of gift economies. People who are interested, take heed: get while the getting's good.

3. *The Incredible Hulk Analogy:* Because of their very nature, gift economies will never entirely replace capitalist economies. Gift economies are to capitalism what the Hulk is to Bruce Banner.

4. *Don't Piss into the Wind:* Despite their brief life spans and frequent disappearances, gift economies can't ever be eliminated entirely, and no one should waste their efforts in trying.

5. *If You Can't Beat 'em, Join 'em:* In fact, more people and corporations should be trying to figure out how to incorporate the energy and movement of gift economies into their practices. Exploring the possibilities that gift economies offer is necessary to further develop the floundering 'new economy.'

For the most part, I'll be looking at two broad sectors of online activity that are fueled by gift economies: Free Software (GNU/Linux) and peer-to-peer file-sharing. While the former is free as in 'speech,' and the latter is free as in 'beer,' the categories aren't always that cut and dried, and a discussion of one type of freedom frequently leads to the other. Such are the messy inevitabilities of a networked society.

2

The road to copyleft

> Share and Enjoy!, *imp. 1. Commonly found at the end of software*
> *release announcements and README files, this phrase indicates*
> *allegiance to the hacker ethic of free information sharing (see*
> *hacker ethic, sense 1). 2. The motto of the complaints division of*
> *Sirius Cybernetics Corporation (the ultimate gaggle of*
> *incompetent suits) in Douglas Adams's* Hitch Hiker's Guide to the
> Galaxy. *The irony of using this as a cultural recognition signal*
> *appeals to hackers.*[1]
>
> —THE HACKER'S DICTIONARY

Many people don't realize that the Internet is crammed to bursting with free
software. (Of course, when I told my friends that I was writing a book
about free software, many of them gave me a slightly contemptuous look,
because they haven't paid a dime in their entire lives for *anything* on their
computers.) Some of it is pirated commercial software ('warcz') being
circulated through the digital backwaters by script kiddies. Some of it,
called 'freeware,' circulates without cost, though a donation may be
suggested. Some of it, called 'abandonware,' is obsolete and unimportant
to all but a few collectors and hobbyists. Some of it (called 'shareware') is
free for a trial period, or only usable in a reduced capacity until you pay for
and register it. And some of it (called, predictably enough, 'Free Software'—
throughout this book I'll be using 'Free Software' with caps to indicate
software that circulates under the General Public License or one of its
variants) is really and truly free of cost or restriction *and* licensed to ensure

that (a) it stays that way and (b) people can access its source code as well as executable versions of the files.

Surprising as it may seem, commercial software is the new kid on the block. What follows is a brief introduction to the alternatives.

Abandonware: Rogue librarians

Abandonware is software that is not currently sold or supported by its publisher. And it's free ... sort of. The Home of the Underdogs, a venerable site for enthusiasts of underappreciated games, claims that the word 'abandonware' was coined around 1997 by gamers to designate video games that have been, well, *abandoned* by their original publishers. Abandonware is distinct from warez—pirated commercial software that is still being developed. Both abandonware and warez are illegal, but the circulation of the former is motivated by enthusiasm and a curatorial impulse rather than a desire to avoid paying for a commercial product.[2]

In the United States, software copyrights are valid for 70 years from the date of publication, whether or not they're enforced. In other words, just because a program is no longer in commercial circulation doesn't mean that it's in the public domain.

Section 302 of the US copyright law, which details the duration of copyright, is quite clear on the subject. In the case of works produced later than 1978, copyright endures for the life of the creator plus an additional 50 years. Copyright duration in the case of works done for hire and anonymous and pseudonymous works is either 75 years from the year of first publication or 100 years from the year of creation, whichever ends first. Copyright law does not in any way require copyright owners to make their creation public in any way, or for any length of time. Therefore, the notion of the abandonment of a copyright due to a lack of distribution, technical support or even the copyright holder's going out of business is false.[3]

Documents such as the Paris 1971 Berne Convention <www.law.cornell.edu/treaties/berne/overview.html>, signed by 96 countries including the US, and the WIPO Copyright Treaty <www.law.cornell.edu/treaties/berne/overview.html> make similar provisions uniform over many international borders.

However, there is a vast chunk of the Internet-using population that either is ignorant of or ignores this fact outright. C|Net estimates that there are over 100 abandonware sites in existence, circulating somewhere in the vicinity of 1,000 software titles, mostly games but also some

The Free Oldies abandonware search engine <www.freeoldies.com>—a helpful tool for rogue librarians, retrogamers and those yearning to frag Nazi zombies at low resolution.

Unlike books and other traditional forms of media with durable physical formats and universal interfaces, old computer games and other types of programs are much more susceptible to disappearing forever.

applications and operating systems,[4] some of them even ranging back into the days of the early 80s.[5] Check it out: the Google Web Directory's Abandonware page <directory.google.com/Top/Computers/Software/Abandonware/> is one of many such pages that lead to entire networks of abandonware enthusiasts, not just single users, or even single sites. Or go straight to a site like the original Abandonware Ring <www.abandonwarering.com> or the Home of the Underdogs <www.theunderdogs.org>, or, if you have a specific title in mind, the Free Oldies search engine <www.freeoldies.com>. You'll find sites loaded with abandonware, plus a series of lively discussion forums filled with people looking for versions of their old favorite arcade games, asking for help and generally arsing around.

Many of the people who maintain abandonware sites see themselves in a curatorial role. Jeremiah Kauffman of the Adventure Collective argues that, unlike books and other traditional forms of media with durable physical formats and universal interfaces, old computer games and other types of programs are much more susceptible to disappearing forever. Books can be canonized and reprinted, but even the 'bad' or obscure ones stand a chance of turning up in some musty old corner, and can be read immediately. Because hardware and software platforms change so regularly, older games are in danger of vanishing entirely unless voluntary collectors store them and design emulation software that allows such games to be played on more recent systems.[6] From this perspective, abandonware users are rogue librarians for posterity.

Most abandonware sites state that if they were requested to do so, they would take down disputed software titles immediately. Some go a step further, actively seeking permission to publish obsolete games, or even encouraging publishers to re-release titles as freeware or, failing that, commercial software.[7]

There are also several projects afoot to legitimize the notion of abandonware entirely, such as the Abandonware Petition, which proposes that software that is wholly discontinued, more than seven years old or two 'versions' older than its previous incarnation should be released into the public domain. Such software would presumably circulate without warranty or support; the sole purpose would be to ensure that a particular cultural artifact continued to exist.[8]

As an example of abandonware as a positive practice the maintainers of the petition cite the Apple Corporation, which makes old versions of its software, including some versions of the Mac OS, available for free download <www.info.apple.com/support/oldersoftwarelist.html>—and has developed an increase in customer loyalty (and no visible loss of interest in its new products) as a result.

Many corporations remain unconvinced, to say the least. When contacted by a ClNet journalist, Microsoft's anti-piracy manager Diana Piquette was quick to categorically state that 'if you haven't paid for it, it isn't right,' even though she'd never heard of the concept of abandonware before the interview.[9] (So much for open minds, never mind open source.)

Enforcement is erratic. The Underdogs site, for example, is still going strong, though other sites, like Flashback Abandonware <www.flashback-aw. net/>, haven't been as able to avoid the long arm of the law. As of August 13, 2001, the first item on Flashback's front page reads 'Flashback Abandonware is currently offline, due to the IDSA having a few problems with the downloads that are offered here. All downloads will be down until I can get a chance to take a look over all the games and work out what downloads need to be removed etc.' This is likely how things will remain in the world of abandonware—seesawing back and forth, like the larger gift economy itself. One site goes down, another appears; the range and nature of what's available is constantly in flux.

Salvaging someone else's cast-off software isn't the only way to get something for nothing online, and beachcombing the Net certainly isn't a very efficient way of locating software that might actually be useful to you. From the other side of the fence, 'abandoning' software to the public domain doesn't provide any real incentive for people to use it unless they're collectors or obsessives, nor does it do much to guarantee that your product will remain available for posterity. But there are other ways of circulating software for zero cost, or next to zero cost for both producer and consumer ... *and* making a tidy profit for the producer in the process.

Shareware: Buttons to dollars

When a good idea finally has its time, it often occurs to several people at once. Such was the case with *shareware*, the software revolution of the 80s that started with the birth of the personal computer.

Shareware is software that circulates on a 'try before you buy' basis. Shareware is usually copyrighted, but its minimal license allows users to continue to circulate it. Typically, shareware manufacturers rely on the honor system for payment, and they've traditionally done very well, as we'll see shortly. (A subspecies of shareware known by the tasteless moniker 'crippleware' stops working after a certain time, or has major features locked out until payment is made.) Those users who do register their software and pay a minimal fee (usually somewhere in the vicinity of $25) receive some combination of support, extra features or regular updates.

So where did the shareware idea originate? In 1982, a Seattle-based IBM employee and Apple computer hobbyist named Jim Knopf had a problem. He needed to create a program to print mailing labels for a local church congregation. Like most hackers, when it came to problem-solving Knopf was prone to overkill. Instead of coding a program limited strictly to printing mailing addresses, he wrote a full-blown database in Applesoft BASIC and dubbed it 'Easy File.'

When Knopf bought his first IBM PC he converted his homebrewed database to IBM BASIC. His friends and colleagues at work also began to buy PCs and he shared Easy File with them. As the user base began to grow beyond the confines of Knopf's friends at IBM, and eventually, Seattle itself, Knopf resorted to using the program itself to manage its own user list. But he was running out of admin time, and mailing costs were becoming prohibitive. He needed to come up with a system that would identify the serious users of the software for him—the ones who really needed the bug

There are ways of circulating software for zero cost, or next to zero cost for both producer and consumer ... and making a tidy profit for the producer in the process.

fixes and the upgrades—and maybe generate a little operating revenue, without compromising the ability to circulate the software for free.

The simple solution Knopf created changed software distribution forever. Knopf placed a note in the software asking its users to voluntarily send a modest $10 donation to help defray costs, while still encouraging people to continue to use and share the program. People who sent in the donation were added to the mailing list; everyone else was on their own.

The first person who received the version of Knopf's database with this note attached phoned him immediately with a stunning piece of news. He had also received a piece of modem software written by Andrew Flugelman, called PC-Talk, *and PC-Talk bore an almost identical shareware license to the one that Knopf had devised.* Knopf called Flugelman right away, and the two decided to standardize their idea. Knopf renamed his program PC-File, and changed his suggested payment amount to $25 to match Flugelman's. Thus the first shareware business model was born. (Initially, Knopf and Flugelman called their programs 'freeware,' but eventually settled on the more accurate term 'shareware.' Freeware has since come to refer to copyrighted software that the creator circulates without any expectation of payment.)

Before long, Knopf was receiving mail by the bagful. Within two years, revenues from voluntary payments for his software amounted to more than 10 times his IBM salary. Jim quit his job and started Buttonware ('Jim Button' was his *nom de programming*; 'knopf' is German for 'button'), a company that, at its peak, employed 35 people and had annual revenues of $4.5 million. Not bad for a giveaway.[10]

Today, there is more shareware than ever. Web sites like Tucows <www.tucows.com> continue to sort, store and evaluate the plethora of shareware programs that perform all sorts of mundane but crucial tasks, such as compressing files, enabling all manner of Internet actions (file transfers, browsing, chat, telnetting), managing images and much more. You may not even realize it (most people never think about software licenses of any sort), but you probably use some shareware on a regular basis, maybe even every day.

Of course, not everyone who subsequently adopted a shareware model for their business was as lucky as Jim Knopf. The other major figure in the history of the development of the shareware concept, Phil Katz, had a business that was arguably even more successful than Knopf's, but it destroyed his personal life in the process.

Phil Katz comes unzipped

On April 14, 2001, Phil Katz, the founder of PKWare Inc., a software firm worth millions, was found dead in a hotel room in his underwear, cradling an empty peppermint schnapps bottle. Cause of death: acute pancreatic bleeding caused by chronic alcohol abuse.

Katz was the creator of the standard Internet 'zip' file compression format. File compression software does two very important tasks: it aggregates large numbers of fiddly little files into one manageable package, and it compresses individual files down to a fraction of their normal size. Both of these functions are extremely useful when attempting to send large, complex software packages over the Internet—and were even more useful when a 28.8 modem connection was considered to be smokingly fast. The ability to distribute software directly, without packaging in any physical form, was an enormous boon to online commerce, particularly at the smaller end of the spectrum. Zip wasn't the first file compression format for the PC, but it was the first wildly popular one ... and its ubiquity dramatically and demonstrably changed the way people use the Internet.

Katz's life had been on the skids for some time. In August 1997, neighbors complained about the stench coming from Katz's condo until officials obtained a search warrant and entered the home. They were confronted by mountains of insect-infested garbage, half-eaten food, and a colorful assortment of sex toys, credit cards, porno mags and videos, money, computer equipment, and jewelry still in its boxes. Katz, a longtime alcoholic, became increasingly paranoid after the raid, and kept all pieces of paper with any financial information on them in a huge heap in the back of his 1991 Nissan Pathfinder.

Life was always somewhat rocky for Katz. The death of his father while he was still an undergrad was a key factor in the development of his textbook-geek/misanthrope personality. After graduation, he spent his days programming for software companies and his evenings hacking his own code.

What those evening hacking sessions produced was the first version of the archiving software that would eventually make Katz rich. The program, called PKArc, was a direct competitor to the then-standard archiving package, called Arc. Before long, PKArc was starting to threaten the business of System Enhancement, the makers of Arc.

In 1987, shareware did for Katz what it had already done for Knopf. With his income from his shareware program far greater than his salary, he left his job to start PKWare in his mother's house. In exchange for filling her living room with cables and ugly putty-colored boxes, Katz gave his mother a 25% equity share in the business.

Like Buttonware before it, PKWare was a shareware company. Its business model was slightly different from the one that Knopf and Flugelman devised, and is the direct ancestor of the models used successfully today by Linux distributions like Red Hat and Mandrake. Users who wished to register their copy of PKZip (the next generation of PKArc) paid a $47 fee, and received a printed manual and upgrades in exchange.

When System Enhancement sued Katz in 1988 for copyright and trademark infringement, he was finally forced to settle, and to change his product's name to PKZip. This would, however, turn out to be an early instance of the many times that a software giant has been hoist by its own petard. Backlash circulating through the Bulletin Board Services (BBS) community caused more users to migrate to Katz's product. PKWare finally sealed Arc's tomb by creating a version with better compression algorithms (i.e., it made smaller files than the competition)—and no backwards compatibility, so people couldn't use files made with older versions and were forced to migrate to Katz's new software (this is an underhanded but time-honored trick in the software industry).

Katz's personal problems grew proportionately with his success. After firing his own mother via a hostile buyout in 1995, he had a series of alcohol-related run-ins with the law. He spent less and less time at the office and more and more at strip clubs and fleabag motels. Chastity Fischer, a stripper and close friend of Katz, says that by the end of his life he was drinking a liter of liqueur and two bottles of rum a day. He was dead before his 37th birthday.[11]

But despite his disastrous personal life, Phil Katz created a revolutionary program and helped to pioneer a distribution method that changed our notion of how software should be sold. Along with Jim Knopf and Andrew Flugelman, he paved the beginnings of the road to the copyleft.

Copyleft

'Copyleft.' Say the word out loud. Roll it around in your mouth a little, whether you like the taste of it or not. Even if the word is entirely new to you, you'll probably get the gist of it right away. *Copyleft: some kind of twist on the notion of copyright ... clever wordplay with legal implications ... sounds like something that some kind of anarcho-leftist libertarian longhair would dream up.* Which is exactly right.

The brainchild of Richard M. Stallman, copyleft is the legal principle that makes the Free Software revolution viable. The copyleft (actually a special form of copyright rather than its opposite) ensures that any piece of creative work (from software to spreadsheets) protected by it can circulate freely—and can even be modified and extended—without being subsumed into someone's private intellectual property. Further, the copyleft stipulates that all modifications that anyone makes to the original work must also be copylefted.

Exactly why copyleft is interesting and/or useful will become evident after we spend a little time exploring some of the other options for protecting one's creations in a networked environment.

Why not patent it?

In relation to software in general and the Internet in particular, patent law is a big, ugly mess that shows no signs of rectifying itself any time soon.

Patents apply to specific techniques that are used to construct larger assemblies of software and to specific features of completed software systems. If a patent has been filed on a particular technique or feature, anyone wishing to implement that technique or feature in another context requires the permission of the patent holder (which usually means that money must change hands). Because contemporary software is so complex, and any given package has many features and presents a wide array of techniques to accomplish a given task, it's entirely possible for any piece of software to infringe on several patents at once.

For many people, the notion of multiple patent infringements translates into visions of dancing dollar signs. The patent offices of the world have been deluged with patents for software, and, because the 'prior art' (examples of existing inventions that would invalidate an application for a new patent that duplicates any of those inventions) for software is largely unknown to many patent officers, a number of patents have been granted on obvious and ubiquitous software technologies. Two of the most infamous examples are Amazon.com's claim to have a patent on the 'one-click' sale of a product on a Web site and BT (British Telecommunications)'s claim that it has a patent on the hyperlink itself.

Copyleft is the legal principle that makes the Free Software revolution viable.

Patenting software doesn't really fit with the ultimate aim of either free or commercial software developers.

Many prominent Web theorists and software developers have argued for years that a great number of software patents are not only 'land grabs'—attempts to capitalize on the overworked patent office—but are contrary to the nature of the gift economy that underlies the Web. On the subject of the Amazon one-click patent, publisher Tim O'Reilly writes,

It is a slap in the face of Tim Berners-Lee [inventor of the Web] and all of the other pioneers who created the opportunity that Amazon has done such a good job of exploiting. Amazon wouldn't have existed without the generosity of people like Tim, who made legitimate, far-reaching inventions, and put them out into the public domain for all to build upon ... The gift was given to all of us, and anyone who tries to make it their own is stealing our patrimony.[12]

More and more people are coming around to O'Reilly's point of view. Patenting software, moreover, doesn't really fit with the ultimate aim of either free or commercial software developers.

A company or individual making free or open-source software has no need for a patent, because their stated goal is to disseminate the software as widely as possible, as long as it stays free.

If a commercial company decides to patent a piece of software, they're faced with an immediate contradiction. The patenting process itself requires that the company applying for the patent fully disclose the quickest and most logical way to produce their invention. Though US patent law then protects that invention from infringement for a period of 20 years (longer than the life span of almost all programs written so far), that's often not enough reassurance for corporations staking their existence on particularly precious pieces of code. There are other factors to consider as well. It costs a lot of money to be constantly seeking out and prosecuting patent infringers, and, if you can get through the trial without your patent being declared invalid (which is always a risk), you may not receive much more than the royalty you would have received if the thief had simply licensed your patent in the first place. So in many cases software companies find that it's often simpler to ignore the issue of patents and proceed straight to licensing.

... Which is not to say that software licenses aren't fraught with difficulties of their own.

Do you own your software?

Depends who you ask.

If the license agreements that you have to click on before you install almost all software these days are legally valid, then you don't own anything except the right to use the software according to the terms of the license. Unlike a straight sale, a non-exclusive license for use allows the manufacturer to retain a much greater degree of control over what the licensee can do with the software. What's gained by the consumer in trade for the freedoms she gives up (which can include things such as the right to use a piece of software on more than one machine, or to use it in ways or for purposes that are physically possible, but not in the software manufacturer's best interests, such as using it to duplicate other pieces of software or copyrighted documents, or even to make printouts of content viewable inside the software) when she licenses a piece of software is a savings in cost, at least in particular markets.

Say you run the campus bookstore at a university or community college, and you have an opportunity to sell copies of Adobe Photoshop at an educational discount price. If software were sold like other commodities—say, the books in your store—rather than licensed, and you had the right to resell that software to corporate clients at a profit, that special pricing scheme wouldn't be around for long. The intent of a license is to prevent exactly this kind of abuse, and ensure that special markets like students retain the privilege of paying less for their software than a corporate client would. At least, that's the theory, but there are plenty of people out there who'll argue that most software companies use draconian licensing schemes to hobble their customers while gouging them financially—and it's still not even clear that mass-market licenses are enforceable.

According to Daniel B. Ravicher, a lawyer whose practice focuses on intellectual property and information technology, there are also more than a few judges who have ignored software licenses and ruled that software transactions actually are sales. In a paper titled 'Facilitating Collaborative Software Development: The Enforceability of Mass-Market Public Software Licenses,' Ravicher writes that until 1996, every US court decision on the issue and the vast majority of legal scholarship staunchly opposed enforceability of license agreements in the mass distribution of software.[13]

It is only since a case titled *ProCD v. Zeidenberg* that the majority of courts ruling on the enforceability of mass-market licenses have held them enforceable as long as the software consumer is given three things by the license:

- proper notice of the license before purchase
- adequate time to review and decide whether to assent to the license's terms
- the opportunity to return the software for a full refund if the license is unacceptable

Nonetheless, Ravicher notes that since many courts haven't ruled on mass-market software licenses at all yet, their future is still highly uncertain.

Perhaps the most interesting kind of mass-market license—and one that's definitely surrounded by uncertainty and controversy—is the one that concerns us directly: the public license, or copyleft.

Copyleft: Copyright with a twist

If you want to give away something for nothing, the simplest and most direct thing to do would be to place it in the public domain, with all copyrights waived. But what if someone less altruistic than yourself came along, scooped up your free widget, copyrighted it, then released it under their own name as a commercial product?

This is the last thing that Richard Stallman and the other members of the GNU project/Free Software Foundation wanted to happen. So, guided by what Stallman calls 'pragmatic idealism,' they made some rules to protect their freedoms, and called them the copyleft.

Copyleft is a simple but revolutionary combination of a copyright plus a special set of distribution terms. Those terms dictate that anyone has the right to use, modify and redistribute the code of a copylefted program— or any program derived from it—*but only under the condition that the distribution terms remain unchanged.* The copyleft method for designating a program as free (as in 'speech') thus guarantees that anyone who redistributes that program, with or without modifying it in any way, must pass along the same degree of freedom, i.e., they cannot modify it to make it less accessible for subsequent users. They must distribute the source code for all their modifications so that subsequent users can also modify their work. In Stallman's words, 'the code and the freedoms become legally inseparable.'[14]

(Though Stallman popularized the term copyleft by providing it with its most widely used definition, he didn't originate it. 'In 1984 or 1985, Don Hopkins [a very imaginative fellow] mailed me a letter,' Stallman writes. 'On the envelope he had written several amusing sayings, including this one: "Copyleft—all rights reversed."[15] In all likelihood, Hopkins was a Discordian—a parodic, chaos-worshipping 'anti-cult' that has had a surprising amount of influence on science fiction and geek culture—or knew someone who was, because this phrase appears frequently in the chief Discordian text, *Principia Discordia, OR How I Found Goddess And What I Did To Her When I Found Her.*[16])

The main purposes of the copyleft are:

• to guarantee that every user has the freedom to redistribute and improve GNU software

• to provide an incentive for other programmers to add to the existing free software base (examples include the GNU C++ Compiler and OpenOffice)

• to convince cash-strapped institutions that they should use free software, and allow their programmers to donate their work[17]

Don't make the mistake of assuming that a copylefted program isn't copyrighted, because it is. Copyleft is a modification of the traditional notion of copyright, not its antithesis. All copylefted works contain a copyright statement that identifies the author and asserts that they own the work in question.

What distinguishes copyleft from other copyright methods is its distribution terms, which ensure that a powerful legal bond exists between the code and the philosophical ideals that are so important to GNU and the FSF (see 'GNU as Philosophy,' page 79). These distribution terms are detailed in the General Public License, or GPL. (The complete text of the GPL, as well as that of a number of other Free Software licenses and a document comparing their features, is included in the Appendix.)

General Public License (GPL)

As Ravicher notes, 'compared to typical software licenses, the GPL is relatively short, fairly straightforward and extremely user friendly.'[18] Its structure is simple. The preamble outlines the philosophical beliefs behind Free Software and explains what the GPL is actually supposed to do. The terms and conditions follow, along with detailed instructions for applying the GPL to your software.

The GPL abrogates some of the restrictions normally associated with copyright. Not only are you free to redistribute a copylefted work, you are

While copyright
usually places
restrictions on how
a work *can't* be
copied, the GPL
goes in the other
direction, dictating
when a work *has*
to be copied.

also free to change it. This doesn't mean that you can claim to have written the work you've adapted, nor does it mean that you can disown the changes that you make to the work. You must place all derivative works under the GPL as well, and you can't include your derivative work in a commercial program, unless you've licensed it under the Lesser General Public License (see the Appendix for the LGPL). Further, while copyright usually places restrictions on how a work *can't* be copied, the GPL goes in the other direction, dictating when a work *has* to be copied—in effect, bringing the gift economy into play. It's also unclear whether once a work has been GPLed there's any turning back. When a person places a work in the public domain, it cannot be made private again ... but the FSF says repeatedly that the GPL isn't the same as the public domain.

While Ravicher admits that such restrictions are unusual in a license, and may appear to be unfair, a proper analysis concludes that they are not substantively unconscionable:

In essence, each of the provisions, whether the publication of source code requirement or the license of modified works restrictions, only limits what the licensee can do with respect to the original licensed code. The rights of the licensee in intellectual property derived entirely independent of the licensed software are not encumbered in any way.[19]

Still, Ravicher's opinion is one among many. The sorts of contradictions that arise out of making 'freedom' mandatory have raised a number of serious questions about whether or not the GPL is suffering from an identity crisis.

Is the GPL enforceable?

Since the GPL has yet to be tested in court, legal opinion about its enforceability is split.

On the one hand, Professor Robert P. Merges of the Berkeley Law School presents the opinion that the GPL's terms for the handling of software and other works is probably not legally enforceable. In 'The End of Friction? Property Rights and Contract in the "'Newtonian" World of On-Line Commerce' he writes, 'What is most significant about the agreement is that it purports to restrict subsequent transferees who receive software from a licensee, presumably even if the licensee fails to attach a copy of the agreement. As this new transferee is not in privity with the original copyleft licensor, the stipulation seems unenforceable.'[20] In other

FREE

words, it's not usually possible to use a contract to place obligations on parties who didn't agree to the original transaction—the people who come across the code somewhere down the line.

Bracketing the question of enforceability, Merges raises the question of how to determine damages if the license has been found to have been broken. Damages are usually determined in terms of what sort of profit has been lost. But what do you do in the event that the licensor expects its work to make no money, and someone uses it to generate profit? On some level this may be sophistry—even nonprofit organizations like the FSF need an operating budget, and damages from a GPL violation would probably go to such a cause—but it's difficult to know what a judge might think.[21]

There are also problems of jurisdiction to consider. In the US, copyright is a federal law bolstered by international copyright conventions like the Paris Berne Convention and WIPO. Contract law, meanwhile, falls under the jurisdiction of the individual states. So, if something goes wrong, who enforces the license, and how?

On the other side of the legal fence—the free side—is Eben Moglen, articulate and prolix champion of all things free and open. He uses the analogy of bookselling to explain why he doesn't agree with Professor Merges's opinion about the GPL and privity.

A person who buys a book can give it away to anyone she likes, but the person that the original purchaser gives the book to isn't allowed to copy it or distribute those copies. If he does, copyright law will allow copyright to be enforced against him, even though he wasn't privy to the original sales contract. Moglen reasons that with works under the GPL, the difference is that contractual obligation doesn't begin until the work has been given away, whether modified or unmodified. 'Because copying and redistribution, or the making of derivatives, are never authorized in the absence of a license, undertaking to redistribute is clear acceptance of our terms for redistribution. There's nothing unorthodox about that, and no barrier to enforcement.'[22]

Ravicher's opinion splits the difference between arguing exclusively for either an open or closed development model. He believes that a multiplicity of licensing choices is the best possible scenario for both producers and consumers of software, because in such an environment it will be possible to craft a customized license to accommodate a wide variety of situations.[23] Want an open development stream but a parallel proprietary stream? Fine. Want to go one way or the other? That's fine too. What's important is the ability to choose.

As for the 'no privity' argument about the GPL, Ravicher dismisses it, stating flatly that 'there exist no valid arguments to hold mass-market public software licenses procedurally unenforceable.' In fact, Ravicher believes that there's little to be gained by declaring the GPL and other such licenses as unenforceable. All that would happen is that software users would lose the rights that the licenses had granted in the first place. In his opinion, the societal benefits gained from facilitating an open model of software development (such as actually having a competitive software marketplace instead of a monopoly) are substantial.

What about the cost? There isn't one. Public licenses don't compromise anyone's rights, or their ability to benefit from copyright of any form. Further, they offer an alternative to closed development models that do little but gum up the speed of software innovation and inflate everyone's R&D costs. And (big surprise) the people who end up getting hurt the most by closed licenses are the consumers, because those inflated costs are reflected in the price of commercial software.

Despite his belief in the validity of open licensing models, Ravicher does offer a note of caution relating to the untested nature of such licenses in court. Because there are still almost no precedents for the legal defensibility of Free Software licenses, a company that chooses to use an open development model for its software had better have a war chest for court costs in case it has to defend a user's license.

But you can tell that Ravicher is cheering for the open model. Why? Because he compares the societal benefit of open development to the societal benefit of having lawyers.

In the legal profession issues are settled through the market place of ideas created by the publishing and dissemination of intellectual thought in court opinions and articles of scholarship. Such is also the case for computer program development, in that society can benefit from experts in the field openly sharing their analysis and conclusions to common software problems.[24]

(You may now begin converting your lawyer jokes to hacker jokes.)

The BSD License: More 'free' than Free Software?

The GPL and its variants aren't the only form of Free Software license that exists (though, after doing some research on the subject, one gets the distinct feeling that Richard Stallman and his associates wish it were otherwise). The FSF provides a long, annotated list of these licenses on its Web site <www.gnu.org/licenses/license-list.html#Introduction>; they are of varying degrees of interest and usefulness. The most controversial of these other licenses—and therefore the most interesting—is the BSD License.

BSD is an acronym for 'Berkeley Software Distribution,' and refers to the flavor of Unix that was developed at the computer science department at UC Berkeley. BSD Unix was a hybrid from the outset—a combination of free and proprietary software that resulted from hackers at Berkeley extending AT&T's proprietary Unix version. The free parts of BSD Unix circulated as free software usually does. But AT&T used stratospheric licensing costs to maintain an iron grip on the proprietary portions of the system, with an eye to selling BSD as a commercial product in order to make back the millions it had poured into the system's development. In his book *Free for All*, Peter Wayner reports that the AT&T Unix license was initially over $250,000 per unit—in 80s dollars.[25]

In an environment filled with hackers, it's not hard to imagine what happened next—people started to scheme up ways to liberate small chunks of BSD code, with the eventual goal of creating an entirely free version of the operating system. The first pieces of GNU software were starting to make the rounds, which added fuel to the fire.

The transition from commercial to free software was particularly interesting because it was explicitly linked to the question of licenses. In June 1989 the Berkeley Computer Systems Research Group released a piece of the BSD code called 'Network Release 1'; it was, in essence, the core of the TCP/IP protocol that is still essential to the process of connecting computers across the Internet. It had been written by Berkeley hackers without the help of any of the AT&T people, so no one was too worried about being sued.

The operating premise behind the GNU General Public License is that guaranteeing true freedom actually requires some restrictions in order to work. The BSD License, on the other hand, places virtually no restrictions on its users. Initially, it contained what the FSF has always disparagingly

The operating premise behind the GNU General Public License is that guaranteeing true freedom actually requires some restrictions in order to work. The BSD License, on the other hand, places virtually no restrictions on its users.

The BSD daemon, a history of which can be found at <www.mckusick.com/beastie/>.

referred to as 'the Obnoxious BSD advertising clause,'[26] which stipulated that all advertising materials mentioning features or use of BSD software had to acknowledge UC Berkeley. The advertising was more of an annoyance than anything else; subsequent developers added their own names to the necessary credits, until by 1997, some versions of BSD had over 75 different credit sentences attached. Eventually, the advertising clause was dropped entirely from the BSD License ... which meant that software under this license placed almost no restrictions on its users whatsoever. The first thing that happened with Network Release 1, for example—which was exactly what its creators had intended—was that people placed the code they had purchased on the Internet, freely available for download. After all, there was nothing in the license that stopped them from doing so. There were two major repercussions: first, hundreds of companies paid the licensing fee, demonstrating that software could be simultaneously available for free and generate revenue, and second, the BSD TCP/IP became the *de facto* standard for the Internet.[27]

The Berkeley Computer Systems Research Group had been hard at work gathering all the free bits of BSD Unix and rewriting the proprietary ones. In the summer of 1991 they produced 'Network Release 2,' which, with the addition of six commercial files, produced a complete Unix operating system. And it was all licensed under the BSD License, so several free (as in beer) versions of BSD Unix (notably, NetBSD and FreeBSD) began to circulate on the Internet. But it wasn't until someone—a company called Berkeley Software Design Incorporated—tried to make money off of it that AT&T sat up and took notice. A long, messy lawsuit ensued with AT&T suing BSDI and UC Berkeley. AT&T's case grew smaller and smaller as BSDI used the BSD License to demonstrate that yes, it had paid for the BSD files, and it could do what it damn well pleased with them. After arguing for more than three years over the status of the handful of files that weren't part of Network Release 2, the case was finally settled in 1994. The details of the settlement remain sealed, but the existence of several BSD Unices is testament to the triumph of the free over the proprietary. (Unbeknownst to all of them, while the lawsuit was grinding on, Linus Torvalds was putting the finishing touches on his eponymous kernel.)

The BSD code base is an important part of the development of Linux, and BSD distributions continue to be popular (the new Mac OS X is essentially a tarted-up version of BSD Unix). But even for non-BSD systems, the BSD License is becoming an increasingly popular choice among software manufacturers. While BSD developers have usually followed hacker tradition and donated their modifications to the BSD code base back to the software community that made them possible, unlike the GPL, there's nothing in the BSD License that requires them to do so. This means, among other things, that if a company wants to keep the source code of part of what they write under wraps as a moneymaker, but still participate in the Free Software community, the BSD License can be a more compelling choice than the GPL.

As I write this, a debate is raging on this very subject between Tim O'Reilly, on the 'more free than Free' side of BSD, and Richard Stallman and Bradley Kuhn of the FSF, holding the party line. The debate started in O'Reilly's personal weblog when he took Stallman at his word in the 'Free Software Definition' <www.gnu.org/philosophy/free-sw.html> over 'Freedom Zero,' 'The freedom to run the program, for any purpose.' From O'Reilly's perspective, 'Freedom Zero ... is to offer the fruit of your work on the terms that work for you.'[28] He wants to see competition in the marketplace: 'Let people use whatever license they choose and if their customers don't like it they will have other choices.' From such a perspective, the major problem with Microsoft's business practices is not that they make commercial software, but that they use anticompetitive tactics to take away the right to use competitors' software by the creation of deliberate incompatibilities between their products and those of others.

Stallman and Kuhn reject O'Reilly's argument on the grounds that he's confusing freedom of choice with power, because when a company has the 'freedom' to choose any license it wants for its software, it ends up making a decision for millions of users about the sort of access that they then have to that software.

Discussions of rights and rules for software use have usually concentrated too much on the interests of programmers alone. Few people in the world program regularly, and fewer still are owners of proprietary software businesses. But the entire developed world now needs and uses software, so decisions about software determine what kind of world we have. Software developers now control the way the world lives, does business, communicates, and is entertained. The ethical and political issues cannot be avoided under the slogan of 'freedom of choice (for developers only).'[29]

Kuhn and Stallman argue that if it's truly inevitable for programmers to escape making decisions for others, the only ethical route is to choose an option that guarantees the freedom for each user: the GPL. From their

If a company wants to keep the source code of part of what they write under wraps as a moneymaker, but still participate in the Free Software community, the BSD License can be a more compelling choice than the GPL.

Software licensing
will probably
never again be an
either/or,
commercial/free
proposition.

perspective, the 'freedom' of the BSD License is immediate and selfish; the argument that if users don't like the choices they have they can go elsewhere depends on the existence of multiple options in the first place. If everyone opts for closed licenses, that choice is rendered moot.

O'Reilly rebuts that, first of all, Stallman and Kuhn must recognize that the GPL, like a commercial license, exercises a certain amount of power over its users (the argument becomes almost Foucauldian here: 'power over' is also always 'power to'). He also states that he believes

free software and open source are really a "better mousetrap" for all the practical reasons that Bradley states ... We need forceful licenses like the GPL because everyone doesn't realize that yet, and so it's a defensive move against proprietary vendors who treat harm to their users as 'collateral damage' in wars against their competitors.

O'Reilly's position is attractive because he believes in a multiplicity of choices. That vision fits with the way the world seems to be developing; software licensing will probably never again be an either/or, commercial/free proposition. O'Reilly plays the pragmatist to Kuhn and Stallman's idealism; his argument is couched in terms of freedom, but the subtext is all about the business of making Free Software safe for business (more on this later). Ultimately, the two positions probably need each other to keep Free Software from calcifying into commercial software on the one hand or being reduced to an energetic but unusable chaos on the other. A vibrant range of licenses and strategies is very likely what will make Free Software an attractive option for business solutions.

Microsoft, however, apparently remains unconvinced.

Why Microsoft is attacking the GPL

For most of the past year, Microsoft's spin doctors have been ramping up to a full-out verbal assault on all things GNU/Linux. The aspect of Free Software that seems to upset them most is the GPL itself. Why?

Bryan Pfaffenberger, an associate professor of Technology, Culture and Communication at the University of Virginia, has some ideas. Here they are, in convenient point form:

• Microsoft's core business model relies on an at-all-costs defense of its overwhelming market dominance in end-user operating systems, because this dominance is the lever by which the company hopes to achieve all of its myriad other ambitions, including its ambitions in the server market.

- To defend its overwhelming market dominance in end-user operating systems, Microsoft must discourage or prevent the formation of a critical-mass pool of non-Microsoft end-user applications. People don't switch to a different end-user operating system until there's a sufficiently large pool of applications from which to draw.

- To prevent pools of non-Microsoft applications from forming, Microsoft likes to appropriate what it calls 'commodity protocols' (off-the-shelf, public protocols such as HTML, JavaScript, CSS and many more), and add proprietary extensions that prevent the formation of competing application pools.[30]

Much of Microsoft's distaste for Free Software dates back to the Microsoft/Netscape war for control of the browser software market. When it came to the Web, Microsoft was initially caught asleep at the switch. No one at Redmond seemed to think that the free Web would ever amount to much, so they spent virtually no energy developing browser software, which allowed Netscape's browsers to initially achieve market dominance. When Microsoft stopped snoozing and finally came to the realization that there was a significant corner of the software world that someone else controlled and started devoting some serious development time to building its own browser, their Explorer browser quickly became a force to reckon with.

Faced with sudden direct competition from Microsoft—a non-Netscape browser would now be shipped with every new copy of Windows—Netscape had to do something to try to maintain their ubiquity. As a solution, they developed a Free Software license for their browser (see page 82 for more on this). Pfaffenberger believes that Netscape's original reason for being interested in the open source model was to move their product away from simply being a browser to become an applications platform—a direct competitor to Windows. People were already starting to imagine a world where it didn't matter which computer you were using if all your files and even all your software were stored remotely and were accessible through a sophisticated piece of browser software. If Netscape could create a browser that was open enough and extensible enough to support all sorts of such expansions, they could actually take the fight back to Redmond.

Of course, Netscape failed miserably. They not only got their asses kicked by Microsoft, who eventually produced a better browser than Netscape Navigator—they were also swallowed whole by the AOL leviathan in a move that many people believe was the beginning of the end for the golden age of the Internet startup sector.

Perhaps the only factor that kept Microsoft from triumphing sooner is the crucial difference between the Netscape Public License and a license like BSD. The FSF has nothing good to say about the NPL, claiming that it's 'not a strong copyleft, and incompatible with the GNU GPL' and explicitly urging people not to use it.[31] Their chief complaint is a clause in the license that permits Netscape to use code that's been added to NPLed software even in their proprietary versions of the program, without giving users permission to use their own code in an analogous way. Still, if Netscape had gone with a BSD-style license, Microsoft could have paid for the code initially like any other user and then duplicated it at will without having to contribute back to the code base or even having to explain themselves in any way.

Microsoft is infamous for a business strategy they call 'embrace and extend,' which basically means taking someone else's ideas and technologies and altering them to the point where they'll function only in a Microsoft-centric universe. (This behavior is what has led to the multiplicity of comparisons between Microsoft and *Star Trek*'s all-assimilating, technology-hungry Borg.) Now that Microsoft has gotten used to the idea that Free Software (and its descendant, the open source movement) exists, they're actually trying to take credit for its very existence. In fall 2001 Bill Gates actually had the temerity to say, 'The reason that you see open source ... at all is because we came in and said there should be a platform that's identical with millions and millions of machines, and the BIOS of that should be open to everybody to use, and all the extensibility should be there.' Doing what they do best, the writers at The Register added a reality check: 'Historians will note that this is absolutely not what Microsoft came in and said, if it can be deemed to have come in and said anything at all of significance, back in the early days.'[32]

In any event, Microsoft has been working like mad to embrace, extend and neutralize the ideology of Free Software, if not the software itself. The official Microsoft version—neutered and altered almost beyond recognition, but still vaguely recognizable under all the spin rhetoric—is something called 'Shared Source.'

Shared Source: Meet the new boss ...

While Microsoft's behavior around how they handle their source code hasn't changed at all, they have a fancy new name for it: Shared Source.

The Shared Source conference made its public debut at the New York University Stern School of Business on March 3, 2001, during Microsoft Senior VP Craig Mundie's infamous speech titled 'The Commercial Software Model.'[33]

The preamble to Mundie's speech is a lengthy and none-too-subtle suggestion that the Free Software phenomenon is merely a side effect of the late 90s Internet boom, and that, like the endless stream of dot-com corpses, it too has had its day.

Mundie proposed that early Internet business models based on advertising-based revenue, or on the assumption that achieving the highest profile in a given niche would result in revenue, need to evolve into a third phase: 'Free now, pay later.' That may sound good to some people, but it also sounds a lot like the stereotypical pusher's come-on: the first one is free.

Barring that small moment of cynicism, let's return to Shared Source. According to the Microsoft Shared Source FAQ, the principles of the Shared Source philosophy are full of admirable sentiments such as enabling the successes of customers and partners, fostering software development communities, being more responsive to the needs of both customers and developers, increasing access for students and so on.[34]

These are all admirable goals, but they're benevolently generic enough that they could be the aims of almost any business, including an open software development company. Even the last of their stated goals, 'protecting software intellectual property,' could also be said to be true of the GPL's aims. While each side is hell-bent on 'protecting' intellectual property from the other, the way they go about it is very different.

So where are the concrete examples of Shared Source at work? In his speech Mundie cited the following initiatives as being already in effect: licensing of sections of Windows source code to academic institutions and enterprise customers all over the world, for little or no cost; licensing source code to ISVs (Independent Software Developers) and OEMs (Original Equipment Manufacturers); providing 'sample code' to developers free of charge; and submitting the standards for the .Net Web services platform to international standards bodies. Nothing revolutionary going on here—it's certainly not a free exchange of Microsoft's source code, because nobody's getting all of it, and when they do get something, you can bet there's a license involved that's far more complex and restrictive than any public software license yet written. In addition, there's usually a price tag attached somewhere along the line.

Following Mundie's list of initiatives comes the attack on open source: its code base contains 'a strong possibility of unhealthy "forking"' (i.e., splitting into multiple, independent and competing versions; to a certain extent, this happens all the time, and is often good and necessary, but forking means choice, which is always a bad word to monopoly-holders); it has 'inherent security risks'; and last but not least, the 'viral aspect of the GPL poses a threat to the intellectual property of any organization making use of it.' Mundie is using 'viral' here in its pejorative sense—he's explicitly comparing it to computer viruses (note the close proximity of the word 'threat'). While 'viral' is not always used negatively in contemporary writing about technology—there are many cheap and effective methods of propagating ideas or 'memes' that use strategies analogous to the way that biological viruses spread, some even utilized by Microsoft themselves—Mundie is clearly aiming to spread the fear that if you use Free Software, one day you may wake up to discover that your intellectual property is no longer your own ... Mundie went on to say that open source software 'mirrors the .com business models that proved the least successful during the past year. They ask software developers to give away for free the very thing they create that is of greatest value in the hope that somehow they'll make money selling something else.'

The interesting thing about the speech is its invocation of the notion of an 'intellectual commons' at its conclusion. 'As we think about technology, IP [intellectual property] rights, and the public sector of knowledge, we need an intellectual model that encourages interaction, not a model that drives them apart,' said Mundie. Both Microsoft and the GNU/Linux movement claim to believe in the same thing—the encouragement of interaction between the people who develop technology and the people who use it. The question is: which side's *actual practices* live up to the hype?

Reactions: Same as the old boss

Andrew Orlowsi of The Register was unimpressed with Mundie's list of Shared Source projects, observing that Microsoft offered no changes to their educational licensing programs; that Windows CE source is already available in a limited way to IHVs; and that the rest of these initiatives range from being stale to, in the case of Microsoft's .Net Web services platform (think of an even larger version of AOL), paying lip service to the concept of openness, since submitting it to the ECMA doesn't entail opening source code.[35]

There was also a collective response from other community leaders in the Free Software movement, which follows in its entirety.

FREE SOFTWARE LEADERS STAND TOGETHER

The Craig Mundie speech is old news by now, so hopefully this is the last word. A number of the free software evangelists, in informal discussion, felt that the proper response to Microsoft would be to stand together. Mundie's speech shows that Microsoft's strategy is to keep us divided and attack us one at a time, until all are gone. Thus, their emphasis on the GPL this time. While we didn't try to represent every group and project, many major voices of Open Source and Free Software have signed this message. We took a while, because we're not used to this, but we'll be better next time. So, please note the signatures at the bottom of this message—we will stand together, and defend each other.

Bruce Perens

We note a new triumph for Open Source and Free Software: we have become so serious a competitor to Microsoft that their executives publicly announce their fear. However, the only threat that we present to Microsoft is the end of monopoly practices. Microsoft is welcome to participate as an equal partner, a role held today by entities ranging from individuals to transnational corporations like IBM and HP. Equality, however, isn't what Microsoft is looking for. Thus, they have announced Shared Source, a system that could be summarized as Look but don't touch—and we control everything.

Microsoft deceptively compares Open Source to failed dot-com business models. Perhaps they misunderstand the term Free Software. Remember that Free refers to liberty, not price. The dot-coms gave away goods and services as loss-leaders, in unsuccessful efforts to build their market share. In contrast, the business model of Open Source is to reduce the cost of software development and maintenance by distributing it among many collaborators.

The success of the Open Source model arises from copyright holders relaxing their control in exchange for more and better collaboration. Developers allow their software to be freely redistributed and modified, asking only for the same privileges in return.

There is much software that is essential to a business, but which does not differentiate that business from its competitors. Even companies that have not fully embraced the Open Source model can justify collaboration on Free Software projects for this non-differentiating software, because of the money they will save. And such collaborations are often overwhelmingly successful: for example, the project that produces the market-leading Apache web server was started by a group of users who agreed to share the work of maintaining a piece of software that each of their businesses depended on.

The efficiency of this cooperation is in the best interests of the user. But Free Software is also directly in the user's interest, because it means that the users control the software they use. When they do business with Open Source vendors, the vendors do not dominate them.

With very little funding, the GNU/Linux system has become a significant player in many major markets, from Internet servers to embedded devices. Our GUI desktop projects have astounded the software industry by going from zero to being comparable with or superior to others in only four years. Workstation manufacturers like Sun and HP have selected our desktops to replace their own consortium projects, because our work was better. An entire industry has been built around Free Software, and is growing rapidly despite an unfavorable market. The success of software companies like Red Hat, and the benefits to vendors such as Dell and IBM, demonstrate that Free Software is not at all incompatible with business.

The Free Software license singled out for abuse by Microsoft is the GNU General Public License, or GNU GPL. This license is the computer equivalent of share and share alike. But this does not mean, as Microsoft claims, that a company using these programs is legally obliged to make all its software and data free. We make all GPL software available in source form for incorporation as a building block in new programs. This is the secret of how we have been able to create so much good software, so quickly.

If you do choose to incorporate GPL code into a program, you will be required to make the entire program Free Software. This is a fair exchange of our code for yours, and one that will continue as you reap the benefit of improvements contributed by the community. However, the legal requirements of the GPL apply only to programs which incorporate some of the GPL-covered code—not to other programs on the same system, and not to the data files that the programs operate upon.

Although Microsoft raises the issue of GPL violations, that is a classic red herring. Many more people find themselves in violation of Microsoft licenses, because Microsoft doesn't allow copying, modification, and redistribution as the GPL does. Microsoft license violations have resulted in civil suits and imprisonment. Accidental GPL violations are easily remedied, and rarely get to court.

It's the share and share alike feature of the GPL that intimidates Microsoft, because it defeats their Embrace and Extend strategy. Microsoft tries to retain control of the market by taking the result of open projects and standards, and adding incompatible Microsoft-only features in closed-source. Adding an incompatible feature to a server, for example, then requires a similarly-incompatible client, which forces users to 'upgrade.' Microsoft uses this deliberate-incompatibility strategy to force its way through the marketplace. But if Microsoft were to attempt to 'embrace and extend' GPL software, they would be required to make each incompatible 'enhancement' public and available to its competitors. Thus, the GPL threatens the strategy that Microsoft uses to maintain its monopoly.

Microsoft claims that Free Software fosters incompatible 'code forking,' but Microsoft is the real motor of incompatibility: they deliberately make new versions incompatible with old ones, to force users to purchase each upgrade. How many times have users had to upgrade Office because the Word file format changed? Microsoft claims that our software is insecure, but security experts say you shouldn't trust anything but Free Software for critical security functions. It is Microsoft's programs that are known for snooping on users, vulnerability to viruses, and the possibility of hidden 'back doors.'

Microsoft's Shared Source program recognizes that there are many benefits to the openness, community involvement, and innovation of the Open Source model. But the most important component of that model, the one that makes all of the others work, is freedom. By attacking the one license that is specifically designed to fend off their customer and developer lock-in strategy, they hope to get the benefits of Free Software without sharing those benefits with those who participate in creating them.

We urge Microsoft to go the rest of the way in embracing the Open Source software development paradigm. Stop asking for one-way sharing, and accept the responsibility to share and share alike that comes with the benefits of Open Source. Acknowledge that it is compatible with business.

Free Software is a great way to build a common foundation of software that encourages innovation and fair competition. Microsoft, it's time for you to join us.

Bruce Perens, Primary Author: The Open Source Definition
co-signers:
Richard Stallman, Free Software Foundation.
Eric Raymond, Open Source Initiative.
Linus Torvalds, Creator of the Linux Kernel.
Miguel de Icaza, GNOME GUI Desktop Project.
Larry Wall, Creator of the Perl Language.
Guido van Rossum, Creator of the Python Language.
Tim O'Reilly, Publisher.
Bob Young, Co-Founder, Red Hat.
Larry Augustin, CEO, VA Linux Systems.

A master copy of this document can be found at <http://perens.com/Articles/StandTogether.html>. You may copy and reproduce this document with the

Shared Source is a very misleading name. Sharing is a two-way process.

formatting changes and translation necessary for your publication, but please don't change what we say. See perens.com for press contact information. Thanks to Dave Edwards for his work on putting this document together.

The private response of Alan Cox, one of the key programmers on the Linux kernel, was more damning in some respects, but less partisan in others.

Cox's first observation is that the Internet and the Web were not the products of one corporation, nor of a closed development model. The .Net initiative, he believes, 'is an attempt to build a proprietary service network on top of an open Internet' in order to lock customers into using Microsoft products.[36] As MS rolls out .Net's advanced features, he believes, the openness will disappear, and companies will be forced to migrate to Microsoft clients, Microsoft operating systems and Microsoft servers. For Cox, Shared Source is a smokescreen of words that's all about maintaining control and owning code. 'Shared Source,' he writes, 'is a very misleading name. Sharing is a two-way process.'

Cox's defenses of Free Software are extremely pragmatic, focusing on the viability of open software as a business model. Free Software, he argues, 'is about generating revenue from doing work the customer wants and will pay for.' He cites Cygnus and Red Hat as examples of successful companies working with an open model. And forking, he argues, happens everywhere (look at all the flavors of Windows, for example)—but when it happens in Linux, it's because someone wants to pay for a specialized development, such as adapting the Linux kernel to run as the embedded OS in one of the many Internet-enabled devices that Mundie himself suggested would be connecting to a .Netted universe.

As for Mundie's criticism of the GPL, Cox notes that the GPL requires licensees to provide the source code of their products only to their customers, not to the world at large, and further, that it requires that source code be provided at the cost of the labor that it took to produce it, not for nothing. Open software companies operate on a service model—as customers spread their software further, they generate further business opportunities (such as providing 24-hour tech support, printing manuals, providing proprietary applications that work with the free parts, etc.) without requiring any action from the parent company.

And Cox actually agrees with Mundie on some points, especially the contention that the GPL may not be the best license for releasing some kinds of works, such as those that have been created using a for-profit corporation's research dollars. In such cases, the BSD license would allow both a for-profit and a not-for-profit stream of the same code to exist simultaneously. Cox does note that the GPL is not totally without options for making money; for example, under some conditions 'it allows a research institution to sell that work to people who do not wish to contribute back to the common good—thus generating funding for further investment.'

As for security concerns, Cox has only scorn for Mundie's claims that Microsoft's products are superior to Linux:

I pity his timing for the comments about security risks and forking. To say the things he did on the same day as hackers issue 'time to die' messages to millions of sites requiring immediate IIS [Windows NT] security fixes and the same day the Linux Standard Base publishes the road-map and timetable for the 1.0 release internally must be a PR manager's nightmare.

The subsequent ravages of the Code Red and Nimda worms and the SirCam virus, coupled with several significant Hotmail cracks and the revelation of massive security holes in PowerPoint and Excel,[37] only splattered more egg on Microsoft's face.

Cox's conclusion is that 'proprietary software with all its overheads is in fact not a sustainable business for commodity products.'

Them's fightin' words. But the Free Software community has been preparing for the battle for almost 30 years, as we'll see in the coming chapters.

Share and enjoy

The major paradox of online freedom is that maintaining it requires some rules—but not too many. In the process of trying to make sure that everyone has adequate access to resources, it's all too easy to give away the farm by failing to provide adequate safeguards for those resources. During the short history of the Internet, it's happened time and again—people have made the assumption that the altruistic values of their local gift economies will persist when and if their products and services become wildly popular, only to find that they have been victimized by digital carpetbaggers.

Thus the need for public software licenses, which ensure that the largesse continues for a little bit longer than it might otherwise. From the early days of the shareware boom to the current Linux groundswell, it's been the licensing schemes that have created a buffer zone between the cutthroat business world and various freewheeling digital potlatches. In many respects, the invention of the copyleft is itself as least as important as GNU/Linux, if not more so, because it's what's made it possible for the technology to take hold of its current broad user base. Without the copyleft, the GNU/Linux operating system would just be another Unix clone.

It's also worth considering that copyleft holds the potential to foster gift economies focused on the exchange of many things other than software. After a certain point, using computers to talk solely about computers becomes *really, really, boring*; it's time to extend the revolution out into the realm of actual content. Anything that can be digitized and copyrighted can also be potentially copylefted: music, film, video, visual art of all varieties, literature and so on. There are already a few concentrated knots of people experimenting with such notions, such as the musicians and artists at Detritus <www.detritus.net>. Maybe there will never be more than a handful of such gift-based communities percolating away at the edges of commercial culture, but from our current vantage point, two things are very clear. First, in the digital milieu, gift economies have reasserted their power and efficacy with a vengeance. And second, their very existence is proving to be extremely irritating to those who hold the purse strings of the new economy.

PART 2

...as in speech

Cooperation is more important than copyright.[1]

—RICHARD M. STALLMAN

All your base are belong to us

3

In A.D. 2101
War was beginning.

Captain: What happen?
Mechanic: Somebody set up us the bomb.
Operator: We get signal.
Captain: What!
Operator: Main screen turn on.
Captain: It's You!!
Cats: How are you gentlemen!!
Cats: All your base are belong to us.
Cats: You are on the way to destruction.
Captain: What you say!!
Cats: You have no chance to survive make your time.
Cats: HA HA HA HA ...
Captain: Take off every 'zig'!!
Captain: You know what you doing.
Captain: Move 'zig.'
Captain: For great justice.[1]

In AD 2001, war was beginning. And, oddly enough, the perfect metaphor
to describe that war arrived in the form of a poorly translated dialogue
from the opening of an obscure Japanese video game.

Zero Wing is an old-school sideways-scrolling spaceship shoot 'em
up arcade game dating from the days when video games only came in
black cigarette-burned cabinets the size of refrigerators. Originally

developed by a company called Toaplan, and released by Taito in 1989, Zero Wing was ported to the SEGA Genesis system circa late 1991. In 1995 Toaplan went bankrupt, and the game vanished from the concerns of all but one of the more exotic subspecies of computer nerds: 'abandonware' aficionados. (For more on abandonware, see Chapter 2.)

As video games go, Zero Wing itself is unremarkable; there's a cheesy digital soundtrack, plenty of dramatic explosions, thousands of implausibly shaped but cool-looking spaceships, and so on. But the introductory text from the Sega version—as quoted above—has an odd sort of poetry about it.

In early 1998, this introduction, accompanied by screen grabs from the game, began to circulate in the forums of gaming-fan sites as an animated .gif file. By the turn of the millennium, a blizzard of Photoshop-altered images drawn from all aspects of pop culture began to choke the forums of those same sites, all of them containing, in some form, the slogan 'ALL YOUR BASE ARE BELONG TO US' (AYB for short). The first was ostensibly a skeleton from the cult classic film *Army of Darkness* with a speech balloon beside it <hubert.retrogames.com/images/armydark.jpg>, but this was only the thin edge of the wedge.

Before long, AYB was everywhere: under O.J. Simpson's mug shot. On a pixelboard in Times Square. On the Blue Screen of Death that appears during a Microsoft Windows crash. On the hoarding at a soccer game, painted on the nude body of a streaker, wrapped around the nubile forms of the Budweiser bikini models, on the side of a pack of Marlboros, painted on roads, engraved on plaques, being slowly revealed on Wheel of Fortune by Vanna White, hidden inside fortune cookies, in monolithic white letters on the side of the Hollywood hills, on the lips of Alf, George W. Bush and Al Gore, on the cover of *Time*. Everywhere.

The 'All Your Base' sites started linking the images together. JRR, a musician with a collective known as The Laziest Men on Mars, wrote a soundtrack called 'Invasion of the Gabber Robots' ('gabber' being a type of extremely fast, relentless techno music). It was the most popular track on MP3.com for several weeks running, and has made the artists over $17,000 to date. In early 2001, another hacker-artist, Bad_CRC, stitched together the animated Zero Wing introduction, a handful of the Photoshopped images and the 'Gabber Robots' soundtrack into a Shockwave Flash video.

A full-blown meme (i.e., a highly transmissible chunk of information that spreads through culture the way a virus spreads through a body)

The image that started it all.

began to sweep the Internet ... and the physical world beyond it. Stories ran in both online and print media, including *Wired, The Register, The San Francisco Chronicle, Time, The Guardian, The Daily Mirror* and elsewhere. Leaflets, posters and graffiti spread across university campuses. Comic strips worked AYB into the background. Five students at Bowling Green State University projected AYB against a dormitory wall using 125mW lasers. After Russell Crowe won his Oscar, he showed up on the campus set of his next film to discover, written in a courtyard in 10-foot-high letters, ALL YOUR OSCAR ARE BELONG TO US.[2]

For its metaphorical 15 minutes, All Your Base was big and truly annoying, in a Britney Spears kind of way.

But what did it *mean*?

The new paranoia

The war has been lost, long live the new world order: proprietary devices, proprietary interfaces, copy protection, limited functionality, and prepare your credit card accounts for all those monthly rental and service charges you will be paying for every 'computer controller consumer electronics device' you use.[3]

—HALE LANDIS

'All Your Base Are Belong to Us' is important because it touches a nerve that's close to the deepest insecurities of contemporary culture. In essence, it's a revisiting of the kind of mass paranoia about hostile alien invasion that was first created by the Orson Welles radio broadcast of *The War of the Worlds*. The major difference is that AYB wears its irony on its sleeve.

By extension, AYB has become the online community's metaphor of choice for hostile corporate attempts at assimilation of any kind, especially those that lead to a reduction of choice. And make no mistake: events that are transpiring online right now could well lead to the replacement of the open standards on which the Internet was built.

Sound alarmist? A summer 2001 report from Jupiter Media Metrix found that four Web sites controlled half of all surfing time: America Online, Yahoo!, Microsoft and the original-flavor Napster.[4] Two years earlier, the top 50% of our online attention was split between 11 sites. The consolidation of cyberspace is no fiction.

What's more interesting—and either worrisome or encouraging, depending on which side of the fence you're on—is that people don't just visit these megasites and then leave (sort of the digital equivalent of the Hotel California: 'You can check out any time you like ...'). These four companies, and others like them, are building their own networks of Web sites, with their own proprietary services and features. While there's nothing wrong in principle with adding greater functionality to any network, the end effect is the creation of a two-tier system, composed of haves and have-nots.

When people at organizations like the Free Software Foundation and the Electronic Frontier Foundation <www.eff.org> talk about preserving and increasing online freedoms (that's 'free as in speech,' remember?) questions regarding this ongoing 'balkanization' of the Internet are at the root of many of the issues that concern them most. In order to better understand what motivates their passionate rhetoric, it's worth taking some time to explore some of the forces creating the problems, such as the growth of online gated communities (and the corresponding asymmetry in services); the pressures that the entertainment industry is putting on the Net to develop it into a vehicle for shilling their wares; the proliferation of Net-connected devices; and the .Net-related business practices of Microsoft corporation.

While there are definitely people who would categorically label some of these forces (particularly Microsoft) as unequivocally evil or destructive, most of them are the result of the logical growth of what the Internet does—and so the problems they present are, to a degree, inevitable. What's not inevitable is the manner in which we as a society decide to deal with these problems. And, as we'll see, there are strong reasons for maintaining that all your base are still belong to you.

There are strong reasons for maintaining that all your base are still belong to you.

There goes the neighborhood: The coming of the virtual suburbs

In its ideal form, the Internet is all about symmetry of connection at the cultural level. The fact that any machine on the Internet can potentially function as either a client or a server (i.e., a sender or a receiver) has created a culture that encourages everyone to think of themselves as a publisher or a collaborator. No one is forced to remain a passive viewer ... though that's always an option.

Once upon a time, or so the story goes, all computers on the Internet were technologically equal as well. Each machine had a stable, fixed IP address (Internet Protocol—the equivalent of a street number for a networked machine), was accorded the same abilities to function as both client and server, and could connect to every other machine. This was at a time when the demands on the system were much lower than they are today—no large graphics, no e-commerce, no peer-to-peer file-sharing, no massively multiplayer games, no Web appliances. The degree of technological equality was, to a large extent, a function of the Net's simplicity.

But with the mid-90s rush online, simplicity was no longer an option. What was needed was first a means of connecting millions of computers to the Net in a rapid, efficient fashion, and then a method of providing security for those computers. The solution to the problem, as computer book publisher and online pundit Tim O'Reilly relates in the introduction to *Peer-to-Peer: Harnessing the Power of Disruptive Technologies*, was a combination of dynamic addressing systems like NAT (Network Address Translation) and firewalling.[5] As home users connected to their local Internet Service Providers (ISPs) they were assigned a temporary IP address, and when those users disconnected, the IP number they had been using could circulate to someone else or lie dormant for a time. Many users with such temporary addresses could share one connection to the Internet through a NAT box with an old-fashioned 'static' IP address. This not only allowed the ISPs to add a huge number of clients to their service without doing a lot of messy networking, but also provided a degree of protection for those clients, because NAT boxes act as firewalls, protecting the users behind them from the probings of crackers and script kiddies elsewhere on the Net.

The tradeoff for the convenience was the introduction of asymmetry. Now there were computers that could function only as clients, or couldn't connect directly to others because of firewalls, or couldn't be located in searches because they had no static address. In essence, the Internet had developed its own class system, with upscale, well-serviced neighborhoods where traffic zipped along and dodgier areas where connections were unreliable and the services were poor.

Another phenomenon contributing to mass asymmetry is neighborhood caching. As more and more people get access to broadband Internet connections (high-speed cable or DSL) it's becoming difficult for the current Internet backbone to support all the traffic. To address this problem, some DSL and cable Internet providers are setting up mass caches—storage bins for large, commonly used files (anything from images to text, though caching also looks to be a key strategy for making 'video on demand' possible)—and alternative backbones of high-speed fiber to serve their local networks of subscribers. At first, these seem like innocuous and maybe even brilliant technical hacks. They mean that popular files are available faster (since they're housed on the local network) and bandwidth to the outside world is reserved for more unusual traffic. But while such technologies may create business opportunities for network providers (i.e., the ability to offer increased efficiency to the corporate Web sites they host), they do so at the expense of the average Net surfer—and the existing free Internet infrastructure. If caches and dedicated backbones provide better performance, especially for high-bandwidth multimedia files, why not charge the end users for the privilege of using them? Those who can afford to pay will receive good performance; those who don't had better have a good book handy whenever they want to download some serious high-bandwidth content. Imagine having to choose between seeing Disney films in full-screen, HDTV-quality video and *The Blair Witch Project* in a QuickTime window the size of a postage stamp.

As this last scenario suggests, the ISPs are only part of the picture. A good chunk of the reason for the burgeoning online asymmetry is the entertainment industry's desire for hardware and software that will play content only in proprietary, digital rights management (DRM) formats. Aiding and abetting this process, Microsoft recently announced a new version of its Windows Media video compression/decompression (codec) technology, which, they claim, will allow users with broadband connections to receive streaming full-length movies smoothly and quickly.[6] Moreover, the next generation of DVD players will ostensibly support Windows Media playback, simultaneously giving Microsoft a huge market lead on the right to stream Hollywood content to the home, and requiring consumers to upgrade their brand-new DVD players yet again. One also imagines that a new generation of DVD players would have some manner of encryption scheme stronger than the current one, perhaps requiring that the media itself be replaced (see Part 3 for more details on the current failings of the DVD encryption system and the battles that are being fought around it).

The problem is that there's more at stake here than making money. The decisions that lawmakers allow in the entertainment arena will have a huge impact on the survival of the Internet as a bazaar of ideas. As things stand right now, those with the money will get the rights to pipe prime content at high speed, and will therefore win the eyeballs of the world.

The growing use of firewalls and dynamic addressing systems, caching and closed alternative high-speed networks are the major technical factors in the growth of 'gated neighborhoods' like AOL and MSN. To the extent that they're attractive at all (and there's a large segment of the Internet-using population that finds them very attractive), it's because they herald the dawning era of 'Web services' (fast and simple online banking, ticket reservation, e-commerce, Webmail, access to music and text, etc.) and the attendant feeling of security that these services offer.

But these are the 'hows' of what is happening; to find the 'why' we have to look at the world of commerce. Frustrated businesses that have been unable to make a profit on an open network with abundant resources had a sudden revelation: *All they had to do was close off the network, and they could create artificial scarcity.* And as soon as something is scarce, you can charge for it.

The decisions that lawmakers allow in the entertainment arena will have a huge impact on the survival of the Internet as a bazaar of ideas.

Pay as you go

Software licensing practices are changing to reflect this ideology, particularly at Microsoft. We are rapidly moving from a world where the software you buy as commodity is yours to do with what you will (barring the right to use or adapt source code, as you can with Free Software) to a metered world, where commercial software is delivered like a utility, and as long as you keep using it, you'll pay for the privilege of doing so.

Under the existing Microsoft licensing scheme, companies purchase three-year 'enterprise agreements'; over those three years, customers pay annually for each of their users. After the three years, the software is theirs to use for as long as they choose ... provided they don't violate the terms of the agreement.

Under a metered model, at the end of the negotiated term, companies would either have to begin another set of payments to Microsoft or stop using the software entirely. In a recent C|Net article, Gartner Group analyst Neil MacDonald commented, 'What people don't realize is you're going to pay Microsoft a monthly bill, the same way you do electricity or water.'[7]

Why is this shift taking place? Because of abundance. Most PC users already have all the Microsoft products they need, so if Microsoft wants to keep selling things to those users, they have to create some scarcity.

Currently, the sale of Microsoft products is tied closely to the sale of actual hardware, particularly in the case of businesses and other institutions. But something is happening in the market. A July 2001 report from Gartner Dataquest says that for the first time in 15 years, computer sales worldwide have slumped.[8] Just about everyone who wants a PC has one, and the people who used to upgrade their machines every two years are discovering that their current PCs do pretty much what they want them to do, and they don't really need any more processing power. And in the PC world, almost every lost sale of a computer equals a lost sale of the Windows operating system that is inevitably bundled with it.

But it's not just the Windows operating system that's suffering. Microsoft's market for applications is suffering as well. Take Office as an example. More than 50% of Microsoft's income is derived directly from sales of Office, the world's most popular productivity package. *But as many as 60% of the people and companies that use MS Office are content with versions older than Office 2000.*[9] Accordingly, Microsoft's spanking-new Office XP is going to be a hard sell, as this 'news release' from SatireWire suggests:

Less than a week after kicking off what it called its 'most important' software launch this year, Microsoft today conceded Office XP contains a major bug that causes potential customers to find no reason to actually buy the software.[10]

It's all too easy to see how the satire could become reality. When you factor in the Business Software Alliance and the Software & Information Industry Association's estimate that about 63% of business software used worldwide is pirated, the reason that Microsoft needs a new business model becomes all too clear.[11] Hale Landis, proprietor of the <ata-atapi.com> Web site, concurs:

Microsoft thinks we should all be 'renting' our software. I'm not surprised since the only business model that many companies seem to be trying these days is one that collects money every month from every household. No one wants to 'sell' a product, they only want to 'rent' something or provide a 'service.' These products and services are usually proprietary and have carefully crafted and limited functionality.[12]

Live fast, die young

Even the people who lay the very wires that the Net is built on are suffering crippling setbacks. In 'The Future Will Be Fast But Not Free,' a cover story for *Wired* magazine, SF writer Charles Platt contends that the vast changes the Internet has undergone over the last five years due to increased consumer use—and consumer expectation—mean that the current ethos of 'mostly free' content is about to give way to a pay-as-you-go environment.[13]

The most important reason for the coming change, according to Platt, isn't the profits-really-do-matter epiphany that flattened the dot-coms into not-coms over the past year. Nor is it the recent victories of the recording industry over Napster in the ongoing debate about copyright's future, or the slew of free Web services that went belly-up (or stopped being free) soon after. No, the immediate reason centers on the wires and cables on which the Internet runs.

Platt's argument is that the current network, which still consists mostly of twisted-pair wiring, places an arbitrary speed limit on the great bulk of Net transactions. Because it just wasn't possible to cram huge amounts of high-quality bandwidth-pigging content (like full-screen streaming video) through such a network, it was plausible to bill for network use on a flat-rate basis. No one used more than their share because no one *could* use more than their share. But when some users with ultra-fast connections and high-end computers start using thousands of times more bandwidth than others, and slowing down traffic incrementally as a result, a variable payment system has to emerge.

Replacing wires and transistors with fiber isn't cheap. Not only does the main fiber have to be laid and maintained, but there's also the old but persistent problem of bridging the last mile to reach tens of millions of consumers. Even in instances when companies discover that existing fiber lines can carry more data than they expected, they often find themselves saddled with contracts stating that they still have to lay miles and miles of cable that they don't particularly need at the moment.

The upgrading of the existing twisted-pair network to fiber-optic isn't going be completed any time soon, either. The Canadian government is already hedging on its $4 billion new 'national dream' to provide broadband access to all Canadians by 2004,[14] and the US lags far behind Canada in broadband adoption.[15]

As for bandwidth, its cost shows no sign of diminishing as the fiber networks grow larger. On the contrary, higher bandwidth has meant higher monthly fees for users everywhere. That trend shows every sign of continuing, especially with so many high-speed service providers struggling for their very survival. Companies like Akamai, which are busily constructing 'edge networks' of high-speed fiber-optic for those willing to pay the price for ultra-fast pipes, are taking a pummeling in the markets (Platt writes that Akamai stock lost close to 97% of its value by mid-March 2001, with its competitors doing even worse). In late September 2001, Excite@home, the leading broadband Internet access provider, filed for Chapter 11 bankruptcy protection and announced that it will be selling its network to AT&T for $307 million.[16]

Free Net service, then, is going to be out of the question, argues Platt. The best that we can hope for in his new, 'million-movie universe' is that the cost of content becomes tolerable as a result of the abundance of choice. Steve Lerner of Speedera (a company specializing in optimizing content delivery through techniques such as caching and the use of high-speed 'edge networks') presents the following analogy: 'When you toast a bagel, it costs money, but not enough for you to think about. That's the model the Internet has to evolve to.'[17]

Cooler but dumber

Online, it seems, two steps forward technologically always involves taking one step back freedom-wise. It's not the technological imperatives themselves that are the culprit, but rather the fact that making it easier to sell information seems to require the restriction of consumer autonomy and control.

The championing of a metered/service-based model by the software industry, along with the entertainment industry's demand for broadband access to the consumer market and their desire for hardware and software that will play only proprietary, digital rights management formats, comes at a high price. Some industry insiders believe that these changes will bring with them the death of the autonomous 'personal computer.' In the place of the current ugly but versatile multi-purpose devices, easily configured to do a variety of tasks, we'll have a variety of sleek, dedicated 'Internet appliances' that run on proprietary standards.

Hale Landis is one of those insiders. He's been building and advocating the open standards that have made the hard drive industry run for a quarter of a century. Here's his dim prognosis:

In my opinion if you are someone, like myself, that needs and uses low cost general purpose computers then you should start praying that there will be some hardware vendor left selling such a computer and that you will be able to run some general-purpose OS and adequate applications software. And I would say it will be unlikely that such a computer will have an Intel processor or that any of that application software will come from Microsoft. This possible future must be driving product planners at Intel and Microsoft crazy.[18]

The future of computers, then, is cooler but dumber, prioritizing novel consumer widgets with focused but limited capabilities at the expense of versatile machines like our current desktop computers. On a technological level, we are in the process of trading The Beatles for The Backstreet Boys (or, if you prefer, Public Enemy for P. Diddy) … and if we do that without protest or reflection, we'll get exactly the technoculture we deserve.

All your base are belong to Microsoft

Failure is not an option. It comes bundled with your Microsoft product.

—FERENC MANTFELD

If it's a hobby for us and a job for you, then why are you doing such a shoddy job?[19]

—LINUS TORVALDS TO MICROSOFT

The future of computers is cooler but dumber, prioritizing novel consumer widgets with focused but limited capabilities at the expense of versatile machines like our current desktop computers.

... Which is why it's necessary to take a long, hard look at Microsoft's actions over the last few years.

It's inevitable: Microsoft is SO big that many of the initiatives that threaten the openness of current online culture originate from them. The geek community knows it, too, which explains the frequency with which (if you've been paying attention) the phrase 'All Your Base Are Belong to Microsoft' appears on the Net.

AYB meshes neatly with many of the other parodies that surround the giant corporation like a cloud of gnats, including Microsoft as Borg (on Slashdot and in the comic strip *User Friendly*) and the infamous 'Microsoft Purchases Evil from Satan' story on the BBSpot Web site:

Microsoft already had 15% of the evil market; now that number is closer to 100%. The Department of Justice has voiced concerns over one corporation controlling so much evil, and has begun investigations into the deal.

'We feel that there are real opportunities with evil, and that when evil is integrated into our next generation of Windows products consumers will appreciate evil on their desktop,' said Microsoft Chairman Bill Gates. 'Businesses haven't been able to fully realize their evil potential. With evil integrated into Office 2001, corporations big and small will begin to see enhanced evil productivity.'[20]

Jokes aside, though, Microsoft's unprecedented growth and the subsequent antitrust lawsuit that, even after the supposed settlement of the case, continues to lurch its way through the US court system, do raise some difficult questions for computer users of all stripes.

KMFMS

KMFMS is a German acronym for *Kein Mitleid Für Microsoft*, meaning 'no pity for Microsoft.' (There's also another, nastier English interpretation of the acronym, but I'll leave you to figure that one out for yourselves.)

KMFMS is also a Web site <www.kmfms.com>; both its name and visual style are *hommages* to the German industrial band KMFDM. The first thing that visitors to the site see is a cartoon by graphic artist 'Brute!' <www.bruteprop.com> depicting a giant penguin (Tux, the Linux mascot) with a baseball bat, laying the smackdown on a figure that looks remarkably like Bill Gates, only much the worse for wear.

So what do the site's operators have against Microsoft? Plenty. They have complaints from a software user's perspective (bloat, backwards incompatibility, predatory business practices, buggy software, security issues, etc.), from a technical perspective (closed standards and 'mutilation' of existing standards), and from the perspective of 'everybody else' (attempts to dominate markets and earn the public's trust through 'deception').

Many of KMFMS.com's grievances are not new, but Microsoft's reputation as an Evil Empire hasn't been helped by a series of recent scandals related to the implementation of their new .Net networking service. Now that the US government isn't seeking the breakup of Microsoft, the prospect that such behavior could proceed unchecked is worrisome.

No pity for Microsoft <www.kmfms.com> as Tux the Linux mascot lays the smackdown on corporate greed.

.Net: May I see your ID?

Microsoft is currently in the process of rolling out an incredibly ambitious and complex initiative called .Net. In a nutshell, .Net is an attempt to add an entirely new layer of commercial services to the existing Web, such as

> .Net is an attempt to add an entirely new layer of commercial services to the existing Web, such as content and rights management, quick and effortless e-commerce, on-demand entertainment content and consumer services.

content and rights management, quick and effortless e-commerce, on-demand entertainment content and consumer services. All this is laudable, but it will require substantial changes to the existing Internet protocols. The issue is whether those changes will produce another set of open protocols, or a new set of proprietary protocols that are expensive and difficult to use on anything other than a Microsoft platform.

The linchpin of the .Net initiative is Microsoft's HailStorm. The inaugural version of HailStorm will consist of a universal password and a service that delivers e-mail and instant messages to computers and other Internet-enabled devices (e.g., PDFs and cell phones). HailStorm will also coordinate calendars and assist in the storage and management of files. Over time, the plan is to integrate HailStorm into all the annoying details of daily planning: time management, filing, shopping and so on.

To do this sort of work effectively, however, will mean that users will have to trust Microsoft with virtually all the sensitive personal information they carry around in their wallets and purses, such as credit card numbers, addresses, drivers' licenses and other identifiers. This is substantially different from the present situation, where a variety of businesses and services have *some* of our personal data, but virtually none of them have *all* of it. The radicalness of this step hasn't escaped Microsoft senior VP Craig Mundie, who says 'We're talking about changing society's infrastructure.'[21]

While Microsoft believes that the majority of people will trust HailStorm to handle such information within the next decade, online privacy advocates like Marc Rotenberg, director of the Electronic Privacy Information Center, a nonprofit policy group in Washington, D.C., have their doubts. Rotenberg believes that one of the major methods that people use to protect their privacy is to selectively disclose some but not all of their personal information (credit card numbers, social insurance numbers and other personal data) to a wide range of organizations. In his eyes, the consolidation of all of an individual's personal information at one organization poses potentially large privacy risks. [22]

Microsoft's ability to protect that data is also in question. Richard Stiennon, security-research director for the Gartner Group, says '[Microsoft is] the No. 1 target for hackers ... For Microsoft to take the step of having a centralized repository of information, a login or whatever it is, is something that Gartner clients won't be advised to do.'[23] ZDNet reports that, according to statistics posted at Attrition.org, a Web site that records hackers' exploits, from August 1999 to November 2000, 56% of all the successful, documented hack attacks occurred on systems using Microsoft server software.[24]

The threat of external compromise of a centralized ID database is only part of the problem. First, there have to be some assurances that any company that wants to run such a database won't (a) give away the data themselves, or (b) decide that they want more information from their customers than they're willing to give.

All your e-mail, etc.

Early 2001 was a bad time for anyone concerned about their intellectual property to be using Microsoft's Hotmail and MSN Messenger. Why? Because, from Microsoft's point of view, anything that users communicated through these services, which are powered by their Passport document management system, was pretty much theirs to do with as they pleased.

Every online service has, somewhere on its site, a document that specifies its 'Terms of Use'—the rules to which consumers must assent if they wish to make use of the service in the first place. An article by Bob Trott on ITworld detailed the absolute nature of the original Passport Terms of Use:

The terms of use ... gave Microsoft control of whatever users transmitted 'by posting messages, uploading files, inputting data, submitting any feedback or suggestions, or engaging in any other form of communication with or through the Passport Web site.'

Under the old guidelines, Microsoft could 'use, modify, copy, distribute, transmit, publicly display, publicly perform, reproduce, publish, sublicense, create derivative works from, transfer, or sell any such communication.' The company also had assumed the right to sublicense such content to third parties, and publish user names in connection with any of the data.[25]

As The Register (the news site that broke the story, and prompted a sizable exodus from Hotmail) noted, the original Passport Terms of Use claimed that these rights included 'the right to exploit any proprietary rights in such communication, including but not limited to rights under copyright, trademark, service mark or patent laws under any relevant jurisdiction,' and that 'no compensation will be paid with respect to Microsoft's use of the materials contained within such communication.'[26]

In the same article, The Reg quotes Microsoft spokesperson Tom Pilla trying to lessen the PR carnage by observing that Microsoft had never actually exercised these terms, and that 'they should have been updated, and we unfortunately were way behind in catching them up to Passport's stated privacy statement.'

So what do the new terms look like? The revised terms state clearly that Microsoft has the right to use customer communications only when said customers are communicating with Microsoft, and that the terms are 'inapplicable to any documents, information, or other data that you upload, transmit, or otherwise submit to or through any Passport-Enabled Properties.'[27] But not everyone is satisfied.

For one, Andrew Orlowski of The Register continues to have doubts, because, at the time of this writing, 'Microsoft's revision of its Passport Terms of Use applies only to American users. Or users Microsoft thinks are in North America.'[28] Orlowski notes that any Windows computer with its Regional Options set to locations outside of North America still receives the old notice.

Moral of the story: ALWAYS read the fine print.

What you *really* meant to say was ...

The magic pixie dust of XML (eXtensible Markup Language) promises to fix many of the problems associated with the current data structures that identify documents both online and on more localized networks (such as HTML 'meta' tags, which provide only a rudimentary idea of the sort of information a document contains). But, as with the implementation of any new technology, there's plenty of room for abuse.

Microsoft's Smart Tags feature, originally announced at the end of March 2001 as part of the Office XP launch, uses XML to provide context-sensitive help for keywords (such as names) inside documents. Clicking on a Smart Tag could lead to contact information for a person or corporation, or it could lead to a Web site for an online service associated with a particular tag. John Wilcox, a Microsoft employee, enthused about the benefits of Smart Tags in The Scripting News: 'Smart tags I argue actually make an author's work better, more effective if for no other reason than it makes it possible for every reader to extract the maximum amount of "learning" from each thing they read in the most productive manner.'[29]

Sounds great, until you realize that Smart Tags not only appear in the places where they've been programmed to appear, but also in other documents being viewed by people using Smart-Tag-enabled software. For example, viewing a Web site—*any* Web site—through a Smart Tag-enabled browser could potentially pepper that page with Smart Tags, even if the original programmer didn't want them there. There have been other attempts to retag the Web in the past, such as Third Voice <www.thirdvoice.com>, but none has had much impact because such companies lack the market penetration of Microsoft.

Walter S. Mossberg described the likely results of Smart Tagging in *The Wall Street Journal*, noting that while there will inevitably be smart tag systems that try to compete with Microsoft's, unless they're actually bundled with future versions of Windows they're unlikely to catch on. Further, Smart Tags will probably spur something like a hostile graffiti war between rival corporations: 'Ford would be able to impose its own links on Chevrolet's site, and Republicans could insert links on Democrats' sites. Once the hate groups, the spammers and the junk marketers on the Web get their hands on these Smart Tags, they'll be plastering their links on everything.'[30]

In such a scenario, who wins? In all cases, Microsoft, because they would control an entirely new layer of proprietary hyperlinks sitting on top of the existing free system. Smart Tags, warns Mossberg, are dangerous: 'Microsoft has a perfect right to sell services. But by using its dominant software to do so, it will be tilting the playing field and threatening editorial integrity.'

And integrity may be what the whole argument of Web annotation such as the Smart Tag system hinges on, at least according to Internet columnist and provocateur Dave Winer. In Winer's view, annotation is fine as long as a reader can decide if annotations should be allowed at all, and can clearly discern who has done the annotation as well as what their specific biases and inclinations might be.

It should be possible to take a Web document, specified through its URL, add comments, creating a new Web document identified by its own URL, and then publish that URL, probably on a weblog, clearly marked as Juan's annotations of Alice's document. Juan should not be allowed to mark up the document pointed to by the original URL because that would cloud the authorship of the document, and this would destroy its integrity.

If it's unclear who said what, then there is no integrity.[31]

In other words, annotation is not a software feature; *it's a form of content*. Imagine a future where it's possible for someone to pay for all instances of the word 'dinosaur' in digital text to point to a Barney site, or a Jurassic Park site, or a Flintstones site or any other branding franchise, even on an educational or archaeological site. It's frighteningly easy, isn't it?

Imagine a future where it's possible for someone to pay for all instances of the word 'dinosaur' in digital text to point to a Barney site, or a Jurassic Park site, or a Flintstones site.

Due to massive public protest, Smart Tags have been removed from Windows XP—for now. However, there are apparently no plans to remove Smart Tags from Office XP. According to CINet, 'external feedback' was one of the factors that led Microsoft to remove the feature, although a company spokesperson implied that Smart Tags could well reappear in future releases of Windows.[32]

The hardened cynics at The Register note that it's naive to believe that Smart Tags have simply gone away. Surprisingly, they even see some good coming out of the delay of their implementation, in the form of a more rational long-term deployment of the technology:

Microsoft will now use services to drive them into the market, rather than spamming the world with tags whose underlying services are at best dubious. It can and will implement specific and attractive smart tag support in its own web sites and communications, and it will encourage third party development and deployment in businesses. So start with stuff users will find useful and attractive, and people will naturally buy into the technology.[33]

By beefing up the performance of Office with Smart Tags, and making them available in Internet Explorer 6 on an opt-in basis, Microsoft will likely manage to convince the great bulk of users that they need and want Smart Tags.

There will undoubtedly be Free Software contestation of this technology—UseTheSource.com has already released its own version of GPLed smart tags <www.usethesource.com/cgi-bin/article.pl?sid=01/06/25/1544249& mode=thread>—but unless GNU/Linux remains a clear competitor to Microsoft, and other large firms broadly implement a competing annotation standard, the odds of victory in this particular battle are low.

School bullies

One of the most lucrative income sources for any software company is group licensing. The license agreements of most software companies specify that in environments where there are multiple computers, each computer must have a purchased license to use a particular piece of software. Depending on the size of the organization and the number of computers, group licenses can usually be purchased for less than the cost of an equivalent number of individual user copies, but the cost is still considerable.

Many public schools, particularly those in poorer urban and rural areas, are hard-pressed to comply with the cost of group licenses. But that hasn't stopped organizations like the Business Software Alliance (BSA)— which represents Adobe, Intel, IBM and Macromedia—and Microsoft itself from auditing poor school districts and fining them heavily for license violations.

In 'Microsoft to Schools: Give Us Your Lunch Money!' Salon magazine reporter Damien Cave cites occurrences of several such instances in Philadelphia and Los Angeles school districts. Jenny Blank, the BSA's director of enforcement, says "'What is it we're trying to teach these children anyway? Are we teaching them that it's OK to steal? The message we need to get to them is that intellectual property deserves to be respected'"— a rather Old Testament point of view, considering that the license violations were perpetrated by school staff, not students.[34]

To be fair, Microsoft is not the only bad guy here. In 1999 they even pledged to donate $25 million over a five-year period to schools and nonprofit organizations. And for its part, the BSA puts all of its profits back into its enforcement efforts. But they haven't stopped simultaneously enforcing their licenses in the schools, which is a lot like robbing Peter to pay Paul.

Cave notes, moreover, that quite apart from the issue of liberal calls for corporate philanthropy in the education system, by conducting software audits in the schools, Microsoft and the BSA are (a) losing a public relations battle and (b) driving the schools to adopt widespread implementation of Free Software solutions. He quotes David Bucknell, cofounder of Opensourceschools.org <members.iteachnet.com/opensourceschools/>, a resource for teachers tired of fighting an uphill battle against commercial software vendors: "'A project [like the open-source software movement] that is people-oriented, open to scrutiny and altruistic by design—successive generations are guaranteed the rights of their forebears—is right for education.'"

Educators in Australia agree. A charity named PCs for Kids has been waging public war with Microsoft for the right to install its now-obsolete (and no longer for sale) Windows 95 operating system on refurbished PCs, which they then give to disadvantaged children in locations like East Timor. With Microsoft refusing to cooperate, Sun Microsystems and Red Hat have parachuted in to save the day, helping with the installation of

By conducting software audits in the schools, Microsoft and the BSA are (a) losing a public relations battle and (b) driving the schools to adopt widespread implementation of Free Software solutions.

StarOffice and Red Hat Linux 6.2 in the stead of Microsoft products. Sun's marketing manager, Denis Fairweather, said

On one hand I understand Microsoft's need to protect its copyright, but on the other hand it is reasonably generous to other charities, so why are they being tough on this particular one? ... Especially when the software they have been using is discontinued—it's not as if they're losing out on a potential sale.[35]

Maybe all our base don't belong to them after all. Not yet, anyway. Which appears to be making some people at Redmond very anxious.

Rat out a customer! Win valuable prizes!

As I mentioned earlier, a big chunk of Microsoft's income derives from the sale of 'plain-vanilla' computers with Windows included under an OEM (Original Equipment Manufacturer) license. Evidently, Microsoft is worried enough about losing such sales that they're willing to spy on their customers and dangle wampum in front of their dealers to determine who would be mad enough to buy a PC without Windows.

For a brief period in 2001, the Microsoft OEM Western Region Pilot Program offered contest-style prizes to anyone who sent in copies of any RFQs (Requests For Quote) they received that didn't include Windows on each box. Prizes were as follows: five Microsoft games for an RFQ on 250 boxes; that plus a Fossil Big Tic watch for 500 boxes; and those plus a Fast Cook and Grill Combo and Travel Chair for 1,000 or more.[36]

The byzantine Microsoft site licenses for operating systems specify that while customers can upgrade the operating systems on boxes that they've purchased with the OS pre-installed, customers aren't allowed to install (or transfer) their purchased operating system onto any new machines. This is always a tempting option, because plain-vanilla clones are much cheaper than name-brand systems with operating systems already in place.[37]

As in the Passport Terms of Use affair, Microsoft begged off with the excuse that even if they gathered some data, they didn't *do* anything with it. In an article in the *Seattle Post-Intelligencer Reporter*, Microsoft spokesperson Matt Pilla said the program was 'a super-brief pilot program that was admittedly stupid but absolutely didn't share information' with law enforcers. 'It was just an opportunity to contact customers to explain the limits of their site licenses.'[38] An opportunity that it's hard to imagine any customer relishing.

Security and the whole can of worms

What's more secure, Free Software/open source or proprietary/closed source software?

Steve Lipner, manager of Microsoft's security response team, argued at the 2001 RSA Security Conference (the largest cryptography and data security conference in the world) that a closed source development paradigm is inherently more secure than open source, on the contention that 'the often-voluntary nature of creating works like the GNU/Linux operating system make it less disciplined, and less secure. "The open source model tends to emphasize design and development" [said Lipner]. "Testing is boring and expensive."' Lipner asserted that, in contrast, Microsoft's patches take so long to appear because Microsoft extensively tests every product they produce, including every patch.[39]

Who believes Microsoft's claims? Not the insurance companies, for starters.

ZDNet reports that J.S. Wurzler Underwriting Managers, one of the first insurance firms to offer insurance against cracker attacks, charges their clients 5 to 15% more if they use Microsoft's Windows NT software rather than open source in their Internet operations.

In the 400+ security assessments that Wurzler made over the past three years, they found that system administrators working on open source systems tend to be better trained and to stay with their employers longer than those at firms using Windows software, where turnover can exceed 33%. Turnover contributes to shoddy maintenance; sysadmins have a hard time tracking what their predecessors did; and implementation of NT security patches is particularly poor.[40]

And the results of not keeping up with the latest patches can be dire, as the Code Red and Nimda worm outbreaks of fall 2001 demonstrated all too clearly. Insult was added to injury on August 8, when Code Red took down some of Microsoft's own Hotmail servers.[41] After spending months warning others of the security hole in NT, and urging the sysadmins of the world to download the appropriate patch, one would think Microsoft would have patched their own machines. There are also persistent rumors that Microsoft's internal corporate network fell victim to Code Red via an employee's infected laptop.[42] One user at Slashdot suggested slyly that Microsoft might be using a beta version of the new NT server software that came with the Code Red worm pre-bundled.[43]

In the 400+ security assessments that Wurzler made over the past three years, they found that system administrators working on open source systems tend to be better trained and to stay with their employers longer than those at firms using Windows software.

An offer you can't refuse

With substantial doubt in the marketplace as to the value of upgrading to the XP generation of Microsoft products, the corporation has resorted to what many observers see as strong-arm tactics.

Andy Brown of The Tech Report goes into considerable detail about Microsoft's recent attempts to 'convince' (in what he refers to as 'the Tony Soprano sense of the word') companies to upgrade earlier generations of Windows products.[44] And ClNet reports that any business users who didn't upgrade any Microsoft product to the new XP version before October 1, 2001, will have to pay anywhere from 33% to 107% more to do so in the future. In effect, this ultimatum forced a good 80% of Microsoft's corporate clients to consider upgrading two or three years before they normally would, throwing final quarter budgets into chaos in a time when many companies are trying to trim expenses rather than take on more.[45]

Many companies—and many pundits—were righteously pissed. Rupert Goodwins of ZDNet almost blew an artery in his description of Microsoft's misdeeds. His metaphor is aquatic, but it might as well be AYB again:

Microsoft's relationship to its users is that of the blue whale to krill. Our only purpose is to breed, feed and get squeezed against its giant tongue until every last drop of money is released. There was a slight diminution in the aggressive, monopolistic feeding frenzy last year when, let us not forget, the company was found guilty of abusing its position. Now that Bush is in power, Microsoft is right back in those fertile Antarctic waters.

When he calms down, Goodwins presents a sober, well-considered alternative to despair or disobedience: the assembly of a consortium whose mandate is to fund the development of a unified Linux product that would be a true competitor for Microsoft's Windows and Office. Goodwins believes that the difficulties involved in migrating entire companies from one operating system to another would be diminished because the companies would be able to specify which features they wanted to foreground in this new ultra-slick GNU/Linux distribution.[46]

Such a scenario is entirely possible, but before such an occurrence, there's a lot of FUD to dispel.

FUD and loathing in cyberspace

FUD /fuhd/ n.
Defined by Gene Amdahl after he left IBM to found his own

company: 'FUD is the fear, uncertainty, and doubt that IBM sales people instill in the minds of potential customers who might be considering [Amdahl] products.' The idea, of course, was to persuade them to go with safe IBM gear rather than with competitors' equipment. This implicit coercion was traditionally accomplished by promising that Good Things would happen to people who stuck with IBM, but Dark Shadows loomed over the future of competitors' equipment or software. See _IBM_. After 1990 the term FUD was associated increasingly frequently with _Microsoft_, and has become generalized to refer to any kind of disinformation used as a competitive weapon.[47]

—THE JARGON FILE

The history of FUD is inextricably entwined with the history of the marketing of computers and operating systems.

You're a large company. A competitor debuts a product that not only works better than yours—it costs less. It might even be free. What do you do?

Sometimes, you spread FUD.

Your biggest fan

As Roger Irwin's Linux FUD FAQ details, the history of FUD is inextricably entwined with the history of the marketing of computers and operating systems. It's still around because it's a surprisingly effective tool, as Irwin's favorite FUD anecdote demonstrates.

In the early 80s, the UK computer company AMSTRAD introduced a line of attractive, efficient home computers. (As it happens, my own first PC was an AMSTRAD.) Unlike today's PCs, the AMSTRAD's power requirements were relatively low—both the monitor and the computer ran off the same low-wattage power supply. The box itself was nearly empty; since heat dissipation was minor there was no need for today's monster arrays of multiple fans and Cadillac-fin heat sinks.

AMSTRAD did very well, expanding into the office machine market, where its machines typically cost about half of what its competitors were charging. They even made inroads into North America.

This is when the FUD kicked in.

Rumors began to circulate that because AMSTRAD PCs had no cooling fan, they would melt a hard disk if you added one to the case. Of course, this wasn't true, but it scared enough customers that AMSTRAD was forced to build fans into their boxes, in the back corner where the power supply would usually be.

But remember, there was no power supply—the fan was a placebo. Irwin writes that 'Rational people in the know simply cut the wires to the fan (and never had any problems), but the majority of users just accepted the constant whine of the fan as necessary.'[48]

Ultimately, AMSTRAD was reduced by FUD to the status of a curiosity, just as technological innovations like the Tucker car, the Avro Arrow and the Dvorak typewriter keyboard had been before it.

The question that remains to be answered is whether Microsoft can force such a compromise on GNU/Linux.

Microsoft vs. Linux: From the Halloween Documents to cancer

Until the last two or three years, GNU/Linux operated under the radar. Few but the people actually inside the community knew or cared much about it.

All that has changed, and changed rapidly, because Microsoft spent most of 2001 ramping up to an aggressive GNU/Linux FUD campaign. But it's not like GNU/Linux caught Microsoft off-guard; the corporation began to realize that they had some serious competition as early as 1998.

Halloween I

> *Here ... we start to see the actual outlines of a Microsoft strategy emerge from the fog of corporatese. And it ain't pretty; in fact, it's ugly enough to make it appropriate that it's pushing midnight on Halloween as I write.*[49]
>
> —ERIC S. RAYMOND, NOTES TO THE HALLOWEEN DOCUMENT I

In late October 1998, someone anonymously leaked an internal Microsoft memorandum to Eric S. Raymond, hacker, open source guru and author of 'The Cathedral and the Bazaar' <www.tuxedo.org/~esr/writings/cathedral-bazaar/>, one of the open source movement's seminal documents.

The long and detailed memo, authored by then-Microsoft engineer Vinod Valloppillil, with comments and contributions by a host of highly placed Microsoft executives (including Jim Allchin), warned that the quality of open source software (OSS) was already high enough to compete with Windows and other Microsoft products:

OSS poses a direct, short-term revenue and platform threat to Microsoft, particularly in server space. Additionally, the intrinsic parallelism and free idea exchange in OSS has benefits that are not replicable with our current licensing model and therefore present a long term developer mindshare threat.[50]

The subject of FUD raised its head explicitly and immediately. As *The New York Times* reported,

In addition to acknowledging that free programs can compete with commercial software in terms of quality, the memorandum calls the free software movement a 'long-term credible' threat and warns that employing a traditional Microsoft marketing strategy known as 'FUD,' an acronym for 'fear, uncertainty and doubt,' will not succeed against the developers of free software.[51]

Evidently, either no one at Microsoft read the memo, or they read it and simply didn't care, because by early 2001 the FUD was flying thick and fast.

Red penguins

The year began innocently enough, with Microsoft CEO Steve Ballmer identifying 'the Linux phenomenon' as 'threat no.1' to its business.[52] Nothing unusual here; just a competent CEO demonstrating that he's aware that his company is not the only fish in the sea. But Ballmer's tone began to change, rapidly and melodramatically.

During the 2001 annual Microsoft financial analysts' meeting in Seattle, Ballmer resorted to a tactic straight out of the J. Edgar Hoover playbook: the red scare.

Linux is a tough competitor. There's no company called Linux, there's barely a Linux road map. Yet Linux sort of springs organically from the earth. And it had, you know, the characteristics of communism that people love so very, very much about it. That is, it's free.[53]

Jim Allchin, another Microsoft VP, waded in with his two cents, labeling GNU/Linux un-American. "'I'm an American, I believe in the American Way," he said. "I worry if the government encourages open source, and I don't think we've done enough education of policy makers to understand the threat.'"[54]

According to Microsoft's spin doctors, while Allchin wasn't 'misquoted,' he was 'misunderstood.' What really worried him was not GNU/Linux in general, but paragraph 2B of the General Public License in particular: 'You must cause any work that you distribute or publish, that in whole or in part contains or is derived from the Program or any part thereof, to be

> During the 2001 annual Microsoft financial analysts' meeting in Seattle, Ballmer resorted to a tactic straight out of the J. Edgar Hoover playbook: the red scare.

If Microsoft was worried about open source software being un-American, then maybe the steelworkers and the construction industry should be worried about the subversive nature of Amish barn-raisings.

licensed as a whole at no charge to all third parties under the terms of this License.'[55] (For more on the GPL, see Chapter 4.)

The response of the GNU/Linux community was more amused than angered. One user on Slashdot ('Sandlund') dryly noted that if Microsoft was worried about open source software being un-American, then maybe the steelworkers and the construction industry should be worried about the subversive nature of Amish barn-raisings.[56]

However, it appears that the specter of incipient communism just isn't scary enough in a post-Soviet world.

Red penguins with diseases

In an interview with the *Chicago Sun-Times* published June 1, 2001, Ballmer ratcheted the rhetoric up another notch:

Open source is not available to commercial companies. The way the license is written, if you use any open-source software, you have to make the rest of your software open source. If the government wants to put something in the public domain, it should. Linux is not in the public domain. Linux is a cancer that attaches itself in an intellectual property sense to everything it touches. That's the way that the license works.[57]

Again, the GNU/Linux response was as tempered with amusement as anger. In Iliad's pro-GNU/Linux comic strip *User Friendly*, news broadcasters announced:

The medical researchers at Beaker-Bunsen took up the challenge to carefully dissect Ballmer's statement. They discovered that there was indeed medical precedent for calling Linux a cancer. We asked them what the medical equivalent would be for Windows. 'Tourette syndrome, of course' they replied.[58]

When Bill Gates himself finally voiced his opinion on the subject, it was oddly bathetic. The General Public License, he said, is like Pac-Man.[59] Pac-Man?

... Which leaves one wondering what manner of devastating rhetorical comparison could possibly follow. Maybe Linus Torvalds is more evil than Darth Vader.

Rhetorical gambits like FUD are easy to implement and cost almost nothing in terms of physical resources. And if they don't work, you can always try something else.

Embrace and extend

Let's return to the Halloween Documents. For Eric Raymond, FUD is a secondary concern. The more troubling tactic recommended in the Halloween memo is the potential 'decommoditization' of protocols:

OSS projects have been able to gain a foothold in many server applications because of the wide utility of highly commoditized, simple protocols. By extending these protocols and developing new protocols, we can deny OSS projects entry into the market.

David Stutz makes a very good point: in competing with Microsoft's level of desktop integration, *'commodity protocols actually become the means of integration'* for OSS projects.[60]

In non-engineerese, what this means is that as long as Microsoft uses or creates software programs that function as *open products* (commodities) rather than *closed services*, it is creating opportunities for its competitors, such as various open source initiatives, to be able to design products to work with those same protocols.

Turning products into services is one way to shut out competition, but it's not the only one, nor even the principal one in Microsoft's toolbox. The alternative is a strategy known as 'embrace and extend.' Briefly, embrace and extend involves taking an open standard and, under the guise of improving it, adding proprietary features that effectively force people to use the new proprietary version if they want to continue to view data 'correctly.' If the company doing the embracing and extending can distribute its product widely, it not only eliminates the ability of those using open standards to compete, but also locks a large sector of the potential user base into a reliance on its products. Microsoft's monkeying with Netscape's DHTML (Dynamic HTML) and Sun's Java language are two classic examples of embrace and extend at work.

There are two schools of thought on embrace and extend. Net pundit Dave Winer presents the more charitable of the two interpretations, where embrace and extend represents a mature, sum-sum sequel to FUD. If FUD represents straightforward bullying based on violence and threats, embrace and extend is more of a process of seduction, where there's room for both resistance and recognition of the underdog's accomplishments.[61] In Winer's view, embrace and extend is about magnanimity. Everyone wins, and the game becomes more interesting because of the increased number of participants.

The other take is that embrace and extend really means 'All your base are belong to us,' or, to quote the Borg collective, 'Resistance is futile. You will be assimilated.' This is Eric Raymond's argument—that embracing and extending really means corrupting the open protocols that drive the Internet by modifying them just enough that the original, non-Microsoft versions won't work in an all-MS environment:

What the author is driving at is nothing less than trying to subvert the entire 'commodity network and server' infrastructure (featuring TCP/IP, SMTP, HTTP, POP3, IMAP, NFS, and other open standards) into using protocols which, though they might have the same names, have actually been subverted into customer- and market-control devices for Microsoft (this is what the author really means when he exhorts Microserfs to 'raise the bar & change the rules of the game').[62]

In this case, changing the rules involves either subtly changing open protocols and extensions or introducing entirely new ones that appear to be open standards ... as long as they're not scrutinized too closely. These new standards and protocols then become the object of an extensive and aggressive marketing campaign whose goal is to make corporate clients feel that they're absolutely necessary and to prevent the easy creation of legitimately open protocols that will work with future and existing Microsoft software. While many observers worry that Microsoft's .Net initiative is about accomplishing exactly this sort of maneuver, 'embrace and extend' is a game that two can play.

But before we get into detail about *that* (in 'Embracing and extending back,' page 86) it's probably time to take a closer look at exactly what all of Microsoft's fussing is about.

The need for alternatives

It's fair to conclude from all of the above that having *some* viable alternatives to Microsoft products is a desirable end, even if only a portion of the online community opts to use them. Do such alternatives even exist, and if so, what do they look like? Increasingly, it looks like the answer is the digital potlatch—a gift economy fueled by bits.

4

'A stark moral choice': Free software and open source

We have confused the free with the free and easy.

—ADLAI STEVENSON, *PUTTING THINGS FIRST*

The digital potlatch has many names: the Free Software movement; *software libre*; open source; GNU, Linux ... and sometimes GNU/Linux. They all have slightly different connotations, and under some circumstances, exactly which label is correct can be hotly contested, but they all share a common history, so let's begin with that. Sherman, set the Wayback Machine for 1971.

Two ways of thinking

The roots of the Free Software and open source movements stretch back to that fateful year, when Richard Stallman began working at the MIT Artificial Intelligence lab. The environment in computer labs at the time was very different from what it is now (or was, until the advent of GNU/Linux)—sharing code was not only a routine practice; it was expected. 'Harvard's computer lab used to have the policy that no program could be installed on the system if its sources were not on public display, and upheld it by actually refusing to install certain programs,' wrote Stallman in 1984. 'I was very much inspired by this.'[1]

And, for most of the decade to come, that was how the labs continued to work. Someone wrote some code, they posted it, then everyone discussed it and tried it out. Suggestions were made and improvements to the original code followed. It may not have been a perfect system, and it's not worth mythologizing as a lost golden era, but two observations are inescapable: (1) the 'free' MIT system produced code that worked just fine, and (2) no one had to pay anything in order to use it.

But in the early 1980s, with the home computer revolution just beginning to build up steam, there were plenty of other young geeks hunched over their keyboards, some of them with very different ideas about how software authoring and distribution should work. Like Bill Gates, for example. His 'An Open Letter to Hobbyists,' written in 1976, shortly after his co-invention of the BASIC programming language, positions him as the anti-Stallman out of the gate. After opening with the observation that most of the people who used his Altair BASIC language did not pay for it, the future Chairman Bill goes straight for the jugular:

Most of you steal your software. Hardware must be paid for, but software is something to share. Who cares if the people who worked on it get paid?

Is this fair? ... One thing you do do is prevent good software from being written. Who can afford to do professional work for nothing? What hobbyist can put three man-years into programming, finding all bugs, documenting his product and distribute for free? The fact is, no one besides us has invested a lot of money in hobby software. ... Most directly, the thing you do is theft.[2]

For better or worse, this is the mindset that eventually came to define the software market.

What's GNU?

While Gates was assembling the beginnings of his home software empire in the early 80s, 'big-iron' computer labs like MIT were also moving toward a commercial software paradigm.

At MIT's AI Lab, a change in hardware—the purchase of a new PDP-10 computer—brought with it a change in software. During the free software-sharing 70s, the lab's computers used a timesharing operating system called ITS (Incompatible Timesharing System), designed and written by the lab staff. When the lab's main computer was replaced in the early 80s, the administration opted instead to use a proprietary operating system written by Digital. Shortly before, many of the AI Lab hackers had left to work at a spin-off company called Symbolics, so there was no one to replenish the original shared code base. The implications of this turn of events would be huge.[3]

AT&T's Unix operating system project, which began as an experiment, started to look like it might be useful for actual programming.

Welcome to the GNU age—the Free Software mascot (as rendered by the Nevrax Design Team) is a big improvement on the original Free Software <www.gnu.org> logo.

Elsewhere, AT&T's Unix operating system project, which began as an experiment, started to look like it might be useful for actual programming. When Bell was forced to break up, AT&T began to wonder how they could cash in on their work on the nascent operating system. They had been letting programmers at universities play with it for free, but that was all about to change. AT&T began asking campus programmers working with Unix to sign agreements to not share the code with anyone else. Other contemporary computer systems, such as the VAX, followed suit.

Stallman summarizes the change in computer culture succinctly:

This meant that the first step in using a computer was to promise not to help your neighbor. A cooperating community was forbidden. The rule made by the owners of proprietary software was, 'If you share with your neighbor, you are a pirate. If you want any changes, beg us to make them.'⁴

... as in speech   **77**

Faced with the 'stark moral choice' between a desire for code that could be traded freely and the emergence of the closed commercial system, Stallman left MIT to begin the GNU Project, whose goal was a completely free (as in 'speech'—Stallman is the originator of this phrase) operating system.

'GNU' is a recursive acronym for 'GNU's Not Unix.' (A recursive acronym is one that refers to itself, usually by incorporating the acronym as the first word in the expanded phrase. Geeks love recursive acronyms; they smack of infinity and fractals and other unspeakably cool things.) From the beginning, the goal of the GNU Project was to produce an operating system that was 100% compatible with Unix, yet completely free of the restrictive licensing structures that Stallman found so distasteful.

An operating system is a complex, loose baggy monster, consisting of hundreds (if not thousands) of programs. The GNU system is no exception, and may even be the extreme example. All the programs in the GNU system are free, but most of them are not GNU software, i.e., they were not written by Stallman or other members of the GNU Project itself. (This fact has always been a source of some contention—and insane amounts of territorial pissing, which we'll explore in some detail later.)

Stallman quit his job in 1984 and began writing what would become the core GNU software, the GNU C Compiler and the GNU Emacs editor, GDB and GNU Make. Members of the newly minted Free Software Foundation (founded by Stallman in 1985) supplied other key components. By 1990 the GNU system was almost complete, save for one crucial element—the kernel.

The kernel is the part of the operating system that loads first and remains in a computer's main memory. It manages processes, tasks, memory, disks and so on. No kernel, no show. Stallman was (and is) working on a kernel for his system called the GNU Hurd. But in 1991, Linus Torvalds famously shortened the distance to a completely free operating system by developing a Unix-compatible kernel called Linux, and combined it with the not-quite-complete GNU system to create the system Stallman refers to as GNU/Linux, and just about everyone else calls Linux.

Of the two men, one might generalize that Linus Torvalds is the pragmatist, the project management guru, the settler of disputes. Richard Stallman is a philosopher, or better yet, a prophet in the John the Baptist mold. It was Stallman's vision that led to the GNU Project, the Free Software

Foundation and the General Public License, but it may not be Stallman's vision that makes GNU/Linux work in the long term.

GNU as philosophy

I consider that the golden rule requires that if I like a program I must share it with other people who like it. Software sellers want to divide the users and conquer them, making each user agree not to share with others. I refuse to break solidarity with other users in this way.[5]

—RICHARD M. STALLMAN, *THE GNU MANIFESTO*

Stallman is the first to admit that the existence of free software leads to some complex situations. Releasing software directly into the public domain doesn't necessarily guarantee that it will stay free, because anyone who wants to can hoover it up and copyright it themselves. This is exactly what happened to the X Window System (which provides the environment for most modern GNU/Linux applications) when it was first released. X was developed at MIT, and released as free software under a license with very few strictures. A number of companies quickly added X to their proprietary Unix systems, in binary form only, and slapped their own nondisclosure agreements over them, effectively walling off what was for all intents and purposes a free program.

As I outlined in the discussion of Copyleft, instances such as this led directly to the development of the General Public License, the Free Software Foundation's main tool for, well, keeping software free.

Pay attention—this next part is important.

When Richard Stallman says software should be 'free,' he has a very specific usage of the word in mind. He is referring to the freedom—the liberty—of the user to do certain things with software that's been designated as 'free' by its license, namely:

- You have the freedom to run the program, for any purpose.

- You have the freedom to modify the program to suit your needs. (To make this freedom effective in practice, you must have access to the source code, since making changes in a program without having the source code is exceedingly difficult.)

- You have the freedom to redistribute copies, either gratis or for a fee.

- You have the freedom to distribute modified versions of the program, so that the community can benefit from your improvements.

Since 'free' refers to freedom, not to price, there is no contradiction between selling copies and free software. In fact, the freedom to sell copies is crucial: collections of free software sold on CD-ROMs are important for the community, and selling them is an important way to raise funds for free software development. Therefore, a program which people are not free to include on these collections is not free software.[6]

Free Software is free as in 'freedom of speech.' It asserts, by its very existence, a belief that software and other types of intellectual property should circulate among users without placing any limits on how that software is to be used or modified. The only proviso is that any changes made to the code base of that software must be placed back into circulation under the same licensing scheme, in order to ensure that the code remains available to other users.

In a recent interview, Stallman summarized Free Software as 'a political philosophy (or a social movement).'[7] If this seems like belaboring the point, there is, nevertheless, a reason for doing so.

What's in a name?

As Stallman explains in detail in several documents on the GNU Web site, the name of his operating system is GNU/Linux. Semantics are important to him: 'If you call our operating system "Linux," that conveys a mistaken idea of the system's origin, history, and purpose. If you call it GNU/Linux, that conveys (though not in detail) an accurate idea,' he writes.[8]

Stallman argues that the name 'Linux' is tainted with commercialism: 'Ever since it was first coined [it has been associated] with a philosophy that does not make a commitment to the freedom to cooperate. As the name becomes used increasingly by business, we will have even more trouble making it connect with community spirit.'[9]

Stallman is by nature a no-compromise kind of guy. In most cases, he'd far rather ensure the purity of his vision than widen the popularity base of his software by mixing it with commercial products.

Most of the various commercial Linux distributions, on the other hand, have no such compunctions. Many companies add some proprietary or commercial software packages (especially drivers) to their version of GNU/Linux in the name of convenience and power. Because of the low-end nature of the distribution model, there's rarely any clear or obvious documentation describing which software packages are free and which ones aren't. As Stallman writes,

When the non-free 'add-on' is a library or programming tool, it can become a trap for free software developers. If our community keeps moving in this direction, it could redirect the future of GNU/Linux into a mosaic of free and non-free components. Five years from now, we will surely still have plenty of free software; but if we are not careful, it will hardly be usable without the non-free software that users expect to find with it.[10]

Because there is a political element to Stallman's crusade as well as a technological one—there are legal struggles as well as technical decisions to be made in both the present and future of Free Software—he's justified to an extent in arguing for fine distinctions in nomenclature. Nevertheless, almost everyone else in the software community—even those who understand the issue—persists in using 'Linux' instead of 'GNU/Linux' for the sake of convenience. As I'm writing this, it is August 24, 2001—the 10th birthday of Linux. The BBC article that details the story, linked to the front page of Slashdot, contains no mention of Richard Stallman or the FSF.[11]

This is a turn of events that seems to annoy Stallman intensely. You don't have to look too hard online to find stories of Stallman chastising those who mistakenly use 'Linux' instead of 'GNU/Linux,' some of them extremely off-putting. The only time Stallman uses 'Linux' is when he's talking about the kernel to the exclusion of all else. Brian Proffitt of LinuxPlanet calls this Universal Law No. 312: 'If you ... automatically equate GPL'd software with "open source," you *will* get a corrective statement from the FSF or Richard Stallman. It's like smoke and fire, can't have one without the other.'[12]

In the eyes of many programmers and users, the inclusion in virtually every Linux distribution of crucial elements such as the Linux kernel itself and the X Windows system—elements not produced by anyone at GNU or the FSF—is enough reason to use 'Linux' instead of 'GNU/Linux' if you so choose. (Observant readers will have noticed by now that I've used 'GNU/Linux' throughout this book. This is not because I'm an ardent supporter of the FSF over the open source people—see below—but just a gesture toward avoiding what GNU/Linux users call 'holy wars'—stupid and counterproductive arguments over which version of Unix/GNU/Linux/BSD etc. is superior.) And frankly, there are a large number of people who choose to do so, for many good reasons. Collectively, they're known as the open source movement.

There is a political element to Stallman's crusade as well as a technological one.

Open source: The spin doctors

On January 22, 1998, something big happened—something unprecedented in the history of commercial software. Netscape, at that time still independent of the all-consuming AOL-Time Warner empire and one of the cornerstones of the dot-com revolution, 'announced bold plans to make the source code for the next generation of its highly popular Netscape Communicator client software available for free licensing on the Internet.' Simultaneously, the already-available Netscape Navigator and Netscape Communicator 4 were released free for all users. The inspiration for this remarkable course of action was Richard Stallman's General Public License. Netscape's press release specified that the company would be 'building on the heritage' of the GPL by releasing their own source code (albeit under a license of their own, with significantly different terms from those of the GPL), and that the company's express interest was in capturing the imagination and loyalty of the burgeoning free software community.[13]

This momentous decision wasn't made in the dark. Netscape had invited free software guru Eric Raymond to help them plan the release and its aftermath. On February 3, 1998, in Palo Alto, California, a gathering of hacker luminaries including Todd Anderson, Chris Peterson, John 'maddog' Hall, Larry Augustin, Sam Ockman and Raymond met to discuss this turn of events. Raymond writes,

We realized that the Netscape announcement had created a precious window of time within which we might finally be able to get the corporate world to listen to what we have to teach about the superiority of an open development process ...

We realized it was time to dump the confrontational attitude that has been associated with 'free software' in the past and sell the idea strictly on the same pragmatic, business-case grounds that motivated Netscape.'[14]

The label 'open source,' coined by Chris Peterson in the subsequent brainstorming session, was part of the result.

At the first Open Source Summit in April 1998, a larger group considered the neologism carefully, weighing it against various other options. But the label itself is not as important as the underlying reason for it, which Raymond states plainly: 'We intend to convince the corporate world to adopt our way for economic, self-interested, non-ideological reasons.'[15]

So the 'open source' label stuck. The important players seemed to like it; apparently even Richard Stallman considered adopting it at one point. As mentioned above, he has since taken an oppositional stance toward the term, due in large part to Raymond et al.'s explicitly 'non-ideological' mission to sell open source to the corporate world as a development model.

The coining of the term 'open source' sparked something of a spin-doctoring renaissance in the software world. Tim O'Reilly's article 'Remaking the Peer-to-Peer Meme,' in *Peer to Peer: Harnessing the Power of Disruptive Technologies*, is perhaps the best indication of how explicit that process of doctoring was. The article begins with the premise that free software has 'image problems' that need to be addressed before the software can achieve the 'synergy' that will lead to wider acceptance.[16]

In his article O'Reilly uses a type of organizational chart he calls a 'meme map' to explain the spin that the Open Source Summit has been (more or less successfully) trying to place on free software.[17] What follows is a simplied version of the information on one of his meme maps. The transformations are subtle but telling—check out the shift in strategic positioning, user positioning and core competencies that O'Reilly identifies:

Free Software	Open Source
strategic positioning	
GNU's not UNIX. We're building a complete replacement for the Unix operating system.	'Network-enabled collaboration makes for better software.'
user positioning	
Free software is a moral issue.	You control your own destiny.
core competencies	
We have the best hackers.	Understanding Internet-era software development methodologies.
Information wants to be free.	Organizing and managing developer communities.
	Using free code distribution to gain marketshare.
	Commoditizing markets to undercut dominant players.
	Brand building, marketing and distribution.
other key messages	
	The Internet infrastructure depends on open source.
	You can make money even when you give away the software.

The coining of the term 'open source' sparked something of a spin-doctoring renaissance in the software world.

In O'Reilly's opinion, the appellation 'open source' has the following distinct advantages over 'Free Software':

- the strategic positioning of open source is much clearer for non-technically minded audiences

- the benefits to the user are much less heavy and more immediately appealing (the user positioning of open source was suggested by Bob Young, CEO of Red Hat)

- the core competencies are more focused, providing clear goals and obvious strategies to achieve them[18]

The transition from free software to open source involves other changes as well. The projects that open source emphasizes as being key to their efforts (Bind, Sendmail, Linux, GNU, Apache, Mozilla and Perl) are different from those that the FSF touts (GCC, Gnome, GNU Emacs, the GIMP, Linux, GhostScript and the GPL)—the list is less Stallman-centric, if you will, and the GPL is notable in its absence. The OSI also set out to create explicit positive messages to counter the negative charges usually leveled at free software, providing examples of successful companies using free software and testimonials to its ease of use and reliability.

O'Reilly contextualizes his vision of open source using bestselling business-theory books. He cites such works as Christopher Locke, Rick Levine, Doc Searls and David Weinburger's *The Cluetrain Manifesto* (which presents the very open source message that markets are conversations and businesses need to participate in them in frank and straightforward ways) and Clayton M. Christensen's *The Innovator's Dilemma* (which describes how disruptive technologies can and do emerge from the fringes of the market to usurp their high-end competitors) as arguments that help make sense of open source in the current business management environment.[19]

Ideologically, open source is a long way from Free Software, even if the two share a common background and many of the same components. But it's possible to move even further away from Stallman's vision and still be part of the same spectrum.

'Free? That word doesn't work'

Believe it or not, there are people in the Linux community who actually *agreed* with Microsoft's Craig Mundie that, while open source might be a great development model, its merits as a business model remain to be seen. (See pages 37–43 for a discussion of Mundie's infamous speech.)

Ransom Love (no, not the protagonist of a paperback bodice-ripper, but the dashingly named CEO of Caldera Systems) sees Mundie's speech as a backhanded compliment to the Linux community. 'Read between the lines of what they [Microsoft] are saying. They are saying that open source is a winning development model. It's forcing a change in Microsoft's business model. Why? Because customers are demanding it.'[20]

Despite Love's support for the GPL as a license for development models, he broke ranks with the bulk of Linux supporters in summer 2001 by stating openly that he also questions whether it's possible to build a commercial enterprise around GPLed software:

We need to use GPL when it is appropriate, when we need to create a standard … to make something ubiquitous … But we need to use it where it is suited. To drive more commercial development, to provide the financial freedom to developers, it's OK to be honest. The GPL does not provide the protection needed to make a commercial model. That's a fair statement.

Love sees no problem with maintaining parallel software streams for different purposes—Caldera will continue to produce GPLed software products (and recently began to open-source significant pieces of the original Unix code base itself), but it will also have products marketed under the BSD License, or something similar. He sees having a variety of licenses available as the key to success in this situation, and notes that Microsoft's FUD campaign is focused on identifying all open source software with the GPL. (This line of argument actually makes sense of Stallman's vigilance about free software nomenclature—it's not really in anyone's interest to sow confusion, except Microsoft's.)

Love also emphasizes that more rigid standards need to evolve if Linux is going to hold the attention of independent software developers (ISVs) and system integrators. Linux, in his view, has to grow up—and develop schedules, structure and the other hallmarks of accountability if it's going to continue to evolve. His argument for the necessity of what amounts to a set of rules for the Linux community is based on the existence of the US Constitution itself—a set of rules and standards that creates freedom instead of restricting it.

Like most of the other major Linux distributions, Caldera supports the Linux Standard Base <www.linuxbase.org>, a set of standards for

The development
of a GNU/Linux
method of talking
to .Net could be as
or even more
important for the
long-term survival
of the operating
system than the
development of
Linux on the
desktop.

developers, but Love goes a step further, claiming that the LSB, not the kernel itself, is now the essence of the Linux system.

The kind of hybridization that Caldera is touting is also happening in other quarters of the Linux community. VA Linux Systems, owners of key Linux sites Slashdot <www.slashdot.org> and Freshmeat <www.freshmeat. net> and maintainers of the SourceForge development environment, announced in August 2001 that they will be marketing closed-source enhancements to SourceForge for the corporate market. CEO Larry Augustin's remarks echo Love's: 'The mixture of open and proprietary software "is a model we saw a lot of people going to," Augustin said. With VA still backing an open-source core to SourceForge, "We felt we could still be true to the open-source roots and at the same time go to a business model that was proven."'[21]

It is this combination of proven business models and open source development strategies that will likely make the biggest impact on the software industry as a whole. It may even be the ticket to ensuring that the Internet remains open and useful in a .Netted world.

Embracing and extending back

Despite their ongoing legal woes, Microsoft has remained determined to launch its .Net initiative and accompanying XP generation of software without delay. Many pundits consider this turn of events a mixed blessing at best: while .Net will usher in a new era of online services (sometimes called 'Web services'), it may also provide Microsoft with more control over the Internet than ever before, due to the technology's use of closed protocols and patented software.

But the open source world hasn't taken .Net lightly. Eric Raymond, Bruce Perens and Miguel de Icaza have all been writing about Project Mono <www.go-mono.net>, an open source initiative to embrace and extend .Net.[22] Icaza, the project leader, is well known in the open source community for his Ximian Gnome desktop, an extremely usable and well-designed graphic user interface for GNU/Linux. He became interested in .Net 'initially because C# was a cute little language, and then because there were some really promising concepts in there.'[23]

The development of a GNU/Linux method of talking to .Net could be as or even more important for the long-term survival of the operating system than the development of Linux on the desktop. The goal of the Mono project is to provide all the tools necessary to build applications and services for .Net that are capable of running on Windows, GNU/Linux or Unix. The Mono project leaders expect to produce their first results within a year.

Like .Net itself, Mono components will include a C# compiler (the language on which .Net is built; C# is very similar to Java), a Common Language Runtime (CLR) compiler for languages including Java (which is significant, because Microsoft is no longer directly including Java support in its programs, the result of a longtime feud with Sun) and a full set of class libraries (collections of frequently used files) based on the specifications Microsoft submitted to the ECMA standards body.

And Mono isn't alone. Where there's an open source project, there's usually an FSF project running in tandem. Enter DotGNU <www.dotgnu.org/>, a project focused specifically on providing an alternative to .Net's linchpin, the Microsoft HailStorm authentication service. Rather than being a GNU/Linux hook into .Net, DotGNU aims to replace it entirely. The project's intention is to correct two fundamental problems it sees with .Net: the lack of security and overcentralization. A DotGNU system would allow no one company to totally control authentication, and would use encryption wherever possible to ensure data integrity.[24] While the chances of DotGNU successfully replacing .Net are not high, the project does, like all good GNU initiatives, represent ideals for which to strive.

Even more recent was an announcement from Sun Microsystems of its own alternative to the Passport component of .Net, the Liberty Alliance Project <www.projectliberty.org>. Like Passport, the Alliance project is focused on the creation of a single ubiquitous user sign-on and authentication system for Web services that can be used by any device connected to the Internet (cell phones, TVs, cars, credit cards and point-of-sale terminals are all likely candidates). Unlike Passport, the Alliance system will be based on open standards. Further, it will ensure that no one company controls and stores all user data for the system, but that various components will be able to share that data effortlessly.

Initial supporters of the Liberty Alliance include Nokia, General Motors, NTT DoCoMo, Koninklijke Philips Electronics and Bank of America. Although they don't appear on the initial press release, Philips, Telstra, Visa USA, SAP and Eastman Kodak are included on a list of other potential Alliance partners obtained by the IDG News Service.[25]

Officially, Microsoft is being very polite about Mono, DotGNU and other such projects. Gavin King, Microsoft's developer product manager, says 'We regard Mono as a very positive endorsement of the dot-Net product and strategy ... The fact that Ximian is looking to implement standards under ECMA bears testimony to the reason why we submitted elements of dot-Net in the first place.' The caveat is that Microsoft has a hole card: it didn't submit anything to the ECMA standards body concerning HailStorm or its libraries for graphic user interfaces, which means that there could be hidden patents there, lurking to trap unwary and overzealous Free Software developers. And rest assured that Microsoft will be watching carefully for any such violations.[26]

All the controversy seems to be having the desired effect. One week before the announcement of the Liberty Alliance Project, Microsoft announced that it was considering turning over the management of Passport to a federated group consisting of its rivals and corporate partners. The corporation also said it would open Passport to work with similar competing services.[27]

There's plenty of time for Mono, Sun and the others to work out the kinks, because despite the rhetoric, .Net is still firmly in the vaporware category. After Windows XP, the next Windows release, dubbed Longhorn, isn't scheduled until 2003 (and who knows if Microsoft can meet that schedule). Longhorn will increase the functionality of .Net, but it won't be until 2005 that the first pure .Net operating system, codenamed Blackcomb, will see the light of day.

Penguin realpolitik

If the Free Software Foundation represents the moral center of the Free Software Movement by serving as the most ardent defenders of the motion of 'free as in speech,' then the open source movement is closer to *realpolitik*—a politics based on material needs and expediency.

From the start, the open source leaders have been candid about their aims. They want the business world to use Linux software for a variety of reasons: compared with commercial software, it's often more stable, more powerful, more flexible, cheaper, and so on ... but the question of freedoms isn't central to the endeavor, except in the context of freedom from a Microsoft-dominated world. Open source advocates want a world where software development is rapid, efficient and unencumbered by complex commercial restrictions, but they want it because they believe it will make everyone's daily life better here and now, not because they wish to use their code to champion an abstract moral principle.

The emergence of open source is a totally understandable development. As a naturalization of a more unruly form of gift economy, it occupies a space somewhat analogous to New Orleans during Mardi Gras—liberty turned to the purposes of profit. If this makes open source cynical, it is certainly less cynical than the commercial software world that surrounds it. The open source movement is still different enough that it has managed to inflame the imagination, and occasionally the enmity, of the business world at large. But if it's to maintain that energy, it needs to ensure that its links to its origins in Free Software remain healthy.

Free Software and open source aren't yet two different movements; rather they're still two facets of a single community. In the majority of cases, their membership overlaps—they share software and personnel as a matter of course. As long as that remains the case, wild new ideas will continue to drift in from the 'free' fringe, *and* the business world will get a rapid and efficient open source development model that it can live with and profit from. Moreover, there'll be a fighting chance of establishing a true alternative to the Microsoft monopoly—not just a separate company or companies, but an entirely different way of doing business.

PART 3

...and beer

*Fact is, no one wants to replace Napster. We just want our f***ing free music.*

—ZEROPAID <WWW.ZEROPAID.COM>

5

Bait and switch

Where does one not find that bland degeneration which beer produces in the spirit!

—FRIEDRICH NIETZSCHE, *TWILIGHT OF THE IDOLS*

The flipside of 'free as in speech' is 'free as in beer.' The concept is intuitive: someone is offering you something that you'd normally have to pay for, something cool and fun and possibly slightly illicit ... for nothing.

Or *are* they?

Inherent in the notion of 'free beer' is the possibility of a bait-and-switch. Free beer is simply too good to be true; there *has* to be a catch. In music circles there's an old joke that the best possible band name would be 'Free Beer,' because every venue would be forced to put 'Free Beer Tonight!' on their marquee, with predictable results. Free beer may taste good and give you a slight buzz, but in most cases, all that you'll be left with in the end is a headache and a bad taste in your mouth.

It's possible for something to be free as in speech *and* beer, but the combination is rare, except in the world of GNU/Linux. A substantial amount of GNU/Linux software happens to belong to both categories: it's GPLed, and its creators usually don't charge for it as long as the user bothers to download (and sometimes compile) it themselves. When people or companies do ask for a little bit of money to cover distribution of their software on CD-ROM, the printing of manuals, and so on, very few GNU/Linux users will complain. The price is almost always far less than what you'd pay for comparable commercial software, and anyone who wanted to bother to take the time could still get the software for free off the Net, in most cases. It's nice to maintain the notion of 'free as in speech and beer' as a utopian possibility to strive for, but even if present reality came a little closer to it than it is currently, we'd be a happier species.

As long as the Internet has existed, there's been a lot of digital free beer kicking about. Shareware and abandonware (discussed in Chapter 2) have a strong free beer element to them. While such software can often be used for free, there's still the expectation that someone involved in its creation will, at some point, see some money from you.

And then there's always the strong possibility that if you're getting something for free, you might actually be stealing it. (People steal Free Software all the time. The FSF's lawyer, Eben Moglen, spends a good chunk of his year enforcing the General Public License in order to ensure that copyleft is upheld.[1])

People have always copied and distributed files illegally (i.e., without the express permission of their creators). All kinds of files: software, pornography, fonts, full-length Hollywood films, digital art, e-books and music. Just about anything that can be digitized is being swapped.

Before the advent of fast modems, people swapped floppies. In the pre-Internet days of BBSes, they stored their files in special 'elite' directories out of the reach of the hoi-polloi. When people other than scientists and academics first started using the Net, these files migrated to anonymous FTP sites (and some of them are still there); for a while, you could find them openly on the World Wide Web, but such occurrences are diminishing ... because file swappers have found a more efficient venue. *Much* more efficient.

With the advent of peer-to-peer (P2P) networking software and high-bandwidth connections, the quantity of files being swapped, and the speed with which it's possible to do so, have increased dramatically. People from many sectors of life feel no guilt after downloading dozens of MP3s of their favorite music, or installing bootleg software on their computers (or their mothers' computers. I have to wonder how many moms out there are using software whose registration screen says something like 'Hax0r3d by Phr0z3n Kr3w' ... and why they haven't noticed).

The type of material in circulation, however, is still predominantly limited to the kinds of things that look very good to adolescents, but can be much more easily obtained by adults with even tiny amounts of disposable income.

Want some porn? You can spend 10 minutes downloading a two-minute-long file that will pig up about 10 megs of your hard drive, play back in a business-card-sized window, have no sound or poor-quality sound, and probably end abruptly because the last guy who downloaded it had his connection dropped suddenly due to the vagaries of the network. Or, you can walk down to the corner store, lay out 10 to 20 bucks and get yourself a pristine three-hour full-screen video.

Want some music? You can spend three hours or more trying to find and download all the cuts from that new Metallica album on the various online networks while negotiating bad connections, firewalls, mislabeled files and a host of other nagging difficulties. Once you actually have all the files on your hard drive, you still have to worry about testing them for corruption, then sorting and burning them onto a blank disc. Or you can get on your bike, go down to the mall, lay out 15 bucks and get the whole damn thing immediately. Most people's time is worth at least 15 dollars an hour, despite what their employer might think. You do the math.

So why do so many people download? And why are more of them doing so all the time?

Alien nation

If people feel entitled to swipe software, music, movies and other forms of digitized content, it's because they feel alienated. There's a huge disparity between the ease with which digital data can be reproduced and the price tag that's attached to it.

Let's take music as an example (we've been discussing why people are pissed off about the cost of software for most of this book so far, and will return to that topic all too soon). The most common medium on which people receive digital content is the compact disc, and the most common form of digital content on those discs is music. Everyone has at least a few of them; some of us have far too many for our own good. And, I would argue, CDs are a big part of the source of our collective feeling of alienation about the cost of digital property.

When compact discs were introduced in the early 80s, they cost about $24 each. The technology was new and flashy and scarce and difficult to make, so compared with the $12 for a vinyl LP, it seemed justifiable. So did the decision to continue paying artists the same royalty they had always received for having their work released on vinyl.

By 1989, record company execs were becoming impatient with the amount of time it was taking to replace LPs with CDs. So the major labels played their trump card, canceling the returnability of vinyl, deleting nearly their entire back catalogs, and issuing new titles on CD only. Record stores had no option but compliance; the risk of carrying a huge

There's a huge disparity between the ease with which digital data can be reproduced and the price tag that's attached to it.

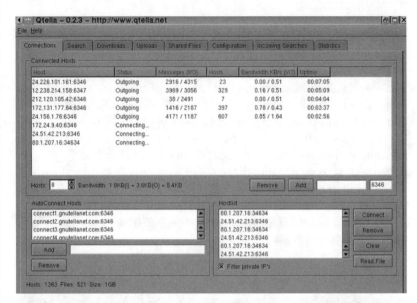

Free beer software running on free speech software: Qtella, a Gnutella client for GNU/Linux, doing what it does best.

Why we feel alienated

nonreturnable inventory was too great. Within a year, vinyl was gone from all but the specialty shops and a few dump bins in the dusty back corners of mall stores (I should know; I was managing a mall store for a very large music chain at the time).

When CDs became the industry standard, production methods improved and manufacturing costs dropped substantially ... *but the retail price didn't*. It now costs less to make a CD and its packaging than it did to make an LP—somewhere between 80 cents and $2.50 per unit, depending on the size of the run—and the price of CDs has remained at 150% to 200% of what it used to cost to buy vinyl.[2] Even accounting for inflation, that's an outrageous profit margin, and most of it is absorbed by the industry before it ever gets back to the artist. No wonder consumers are annoyed. And what do you think the odds are that the cost of buying music will drop when the physical CD itself is removed from the equation? Don't bet the farm on it.

But this is only the consumer-side perspective. The artists and creators have legitimate concerns of their own.

Authors fight back: I have no attorney and I must scream

Faced with the current rate of information exchange on the Internet, many of the people who create 'content' are asking the following question: how many copies of their work can/will be sold if it's possible to cheaply and easily circulate digital copies of that work? Their nightmare is that the answer is one.[3]

While there are many figures leading the charge on their behalf, few do so as colorfully as the renowned science fiction writer Harlan Ellison, winner of the most prestigious awards in his field many times over and author of (among many other things) some of the most popular episodes of the original *Star Trek* series.

That Ellison should be at the vanguard of digital rights advocates isn't surprising; he's championed the cause of writers' rights many times in the past (*and* is a notorious control freak to boot). On February 22, 2001, Ellison dispatched a press release detailing a suit that had been filed because bootleg digital copies of several of his books were appearing in a Usenet newsgroup.

Ellison's section of the document is written in his trademark polemic style, with the added *gaucherie* of full capitalization. (Either no one ever told him that full caps online is the equivalent of yelling, or, more likely, that's exactly the effect he's trying to achieve.) A partial excerpt follows, detailing his contention that the notion of 'fair use' and the slogan 'Information wants to be free' (which he uncharacteristically misquotes as 'Information must be free') are, in essence, havens for the worst sort of thieves:

A WRITER'S WORK IS NOT INFORMATION: IT IS OUR CREATIVE PROPERTY, OUR LIVELIHOOD AND OUR FAMILIES' ANNUITY. WHY SHOULD ANY ARTIST, OF ANY KIND, CONTINUE CREATING NEW WORK, EKING OUT AN EXISTENCE IN PURSUIT OF A CAREER, FOLLOWING THE MUSE, WHEN LITTLE INTERNET THIEVES, RODENTS WITHOUT ETHICS OR UNDERSTANDING, STEAL AND STEAL AND STEAL, CONVENIENCING THEMSELVES AND 'SCREW THE AUTHOR'? WHAT WE'RE LOOKING AT IS THE DEATH OF THE PROFESSIONAL WRITER![4]

When you're done wiping the virtual spittle off your face, consider this. The lawsuit was filed not only against one Stephen Robertson, the individual who had been posting plain-text versions of Ellison's texts to the Usenet newsgroup <alt.binaries.e-book>, but also against RemarQ Communities and its parent company Critical Path (which runs servers that

> Many of the people who create 'content' are asking the following question: how many copies of their work can/will be sold if it's possible to cheaply and easily circulate digital copies of that work?

carry the newsgroup, and/or provide access for their subscribers to it) and America Online. Robertson, the perpetrator of the bootleg postings, settled out of court 'almost immediately,'[5] but the suit against the companies persists.

Amazingly, AOL is named in the suit because the Gnutella protocol (another popular venue for trading bootleg e-books) was developed in their Nullsoft lab. Ellison has reason for complaint about Gnutella; a quick search while I'm writing this shows that at least five of his better-known stories (including 'The Deathbird,' 'Pretty Maggie Moneyeyes,' 'Count the Clock That Tells the Time,' 'Love Ain't Nothing But Sex Misspelled' and '"Repent, Harlequin!" Said the Ticktockman') were circulating in several different versions. But whether or not AOL is responsible for the pirated descendant of an unauthorized project that they themselves tried to kill (see page 155 for more on this) is another matter.

Ellison's suit has already created a significant amount of controversy (once again, this should surprise no one familiar with Ellison's history) in the writing community, the SF fan community and elsewhere. In an open letter to Ellison's lawyer, writers Timothy A. Cooper and Marissa K. Lingen challenge Ellison's claim to speak for all writers, or even all science fiction writers:

It has become clear to us that Mr. Ellison has gone beyond being motivated by the appreciation of his work, and even beyond pure greed. It seems to us that he is now motivated solely by a desire to start a witch-hunt against a few miscreants for all of the wrongs done to all authors in all time.[6]

Ironminds <www.ironminds.com>, an online arts and culture magazine, penned a particularly funny parody titled 'I Have No Attorney and I Must Scream' (after Ellison's award-winning story 'I Have No Mouth and I Must Scream'):

In a collection of his latest works, the nine-time Hugo Award winner covers new territory, creates perhaps a whole new literary genre, with the brilliant *I'll Sue Every One Of You Dumb Bastards* (HarperCollins, $95).

This collection groups nine of Ellison's short stories revolving around one unifying theme: Ellison is tired of creating fiction; he'd rather just sue people.[7]

Parts of Ellison's suit have undeniable merit. Even though many people are choosing to take a page from the Free Software book by simultaneously releasing new creative work in paper editions with price tags and in freely available or cheaper online editions, authors and other artists deserve to have their contracts and their traditional copyrights honored online and off, if they choose to utilize them in the first place. Because the General Public License depends on copyright for copyleft to work at all, it's logically impossible to defend the Free Software cause *and* champion piracy on the same grounds. But the prevailing social attitude still seems to be that if it's available online, it's free. Even through the mountain of press about file-sharing in general and Napster in particular, there's been very little popular recognition that there might be a problem.

One tiny exception to this also came from the science fiction community. A recent episode of Matt Groening's cartoon series *Futurama* featured a storyline about characters downloading the personalities of 20th-century entertainers onto blank robots via the 'Nappster' network. When confronted, a Nappster employee protested, 'You can't shut us down. The Internet is about the free exchange of other people's ideas!' (Back in the realm of realpolitik, though, there may be other things to say in defense of file-sharing ... more on that later.)

Wrong as it may seem, however, Ellison is evidently more than somewhat hampered in his quest by his reputation. In any event, he seems unwilling to engage in the possibilities that online publishing has to offer. The writer who has done so with the most fanfare is none other than Stephen King.

The process of weeding out

King's online serialization of *The Plant* is probably the most publicized e-book launched to date. Originally a serial, annual Christmas letter to family and friends, *The Plant* was a low-risk method for King to test the waters of online publishing.

In the summer of 2000, King launched the first episode of *The Plant* into cyberspace. Approximately 120,000 people downloaded the first installment in PDF (Adobe Acrobat) and/or Palm Pilot-readable versions. By the fifth installment, that number had dropped to 40,000 people, and the price had doubled to two dollars (King stated that the price for the entire work was not to exceed $13). The payment system was structured on the shareware model—readers were supposed to pay to ensure the story's continued appearance, but fewer and fewer people bothered.[8]

King had stated that as long as 75% of the readership paid for their downloads the installments of the story would continue to appear. When the tally hit 46% for installment 5, King killed *The Plant*, at least for the short term, but claims he will finish the project at some point.

Because the General Public License depends on copyright for copyleft to work at all, it's logically impossible to defend the Free Software cause and champion piracy on the same grounds.

Only in the realms of the most successful popular authors could this experiment be labeled a failure. Journalist and new media theorist Jon Katz writes that 'according to the *Times*, publishers say typical e-books sell far fewer than 10,000 copies. One publishing analyst says the actual number is closer to 3,000.'[9] By King's own estimation, '*The Plant* will end up grossing at least $600,000, and may end up over a million'—and it cost virtually nothing to produce.

King draws three conclusions about Net users from this experiment: they are extremely fickle; they believe that anything they find online is free for the taking; and they don't see e-books as being 'real' books. None of these conclusions seems to faze him, because, as usual for King, everything is coming up greenbacks.

I don't believe the on-line publication of *The Plant* has done more than graze whatever potential it might have as a book. The two markets aren't quite apples and oranges, but there is still only a small overlap. In other words, we seem to have discovered an entirely new dimension to the sort of publishing which used to be called 'first serial rights.' Only instead of generating ten or twenty or perhaps even fifty thousand dollars for pre-publication print rights (in a traditional magazine like *Cosmopolitan* or *Rolling Stone*, let us say), we're talking about much bigger numbers.[10]

While he dismisses the project in the end as a lark, let's face it: King could publish his laundry list and people would buy it; as perhaps the most popular writer in human history, King might as well just stop printing books and print money. Whether or not a book in electronic form is capable of making money appears to be, at least for the moment, a function of the author's celebrity.

The electronic publishing adventure

But that doesn't make the experiment unworkable or without merit on a smaller scale. As one of the editors of Coach House Books <www.chbooks.com>, the only literary press in the world with its entire frontlist online in unexpurgated form (60 titles and counting), I'm speaking from experience.

In 1997, at the time of its resurrection from bankruptcy, Canadian literary institution Coach House Books decided to try something different. Instead of focusing exclusively on short-run finely printed editions of literature and poetry, why not simultaneously produce full-length online editions of the same work? The rationale was that the online versions of

Coach House titles would allow readers all over the globe to access work that would normally be found only in a few specialized Canadian bookstores, and would double as a sales platform for the print editions (while the online versions are all interesting and occasionally innovative enough to win awards, few people still have the patience for reading through an entire text online, and will usually order the print version if interested at all).

Of course, ventures as novel as this online publishing program inevitably raise questions, the two largest of which concern the financial viability of electronic publishing as a whole and the management of authors' intellectual property rights.

Coach House recognized from the outset that, if small-press literary poetry, fiction and drama is already a niche market, digital versions of those texts would appeal to a group perhaps only slightly larger. While the scope of the potential audience would be worldwide, it would also consist mostly of those 'early adopters' who were interested in both online literature and the small press—an admittedly small constituency, so no one was expecting to get rich. And no one was expecting to be pirated, really, partly because of low demand (though a pirated poetry book would be the PR coup of the decade) and partly because Coach House electronic books aren't PDFs or other downloadable formats—they're essentially mini-Web sites that make full use of animation, sound, plugins such as Flash, Javascript programs and so on. If the Web was all about making information ubiquitous, we reasoned, and if connections were getting faster all the time, why would anyone want to download an electronic book in the first place?

Over the last five years, Coach House has explored several different models for author payment. We still use a shareware-style payment system for funneling reader payments directly to the authors (the press makes no money off the proceeds of the Web site, considering it an exercise in the production of culture, not cultural industry). Since online publication is entirely voluntary, none of our authors feel pressured into putting their work in electronic form (no one on the frontlist has yet chosen to opt out, either, which is a testament to the perceived benefit on the part of the writers). The press sees its electronic editions as an investment in posterity: should a ubiquitous e-book format with full digital rights management built in ever arise, it will be a relatively simple manner to port the existing electronic titles to that system.

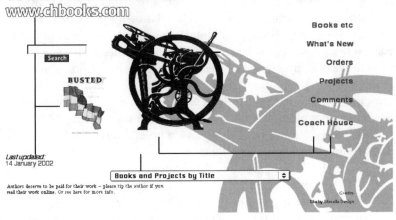

Coach House Books
www.chbooks.com

Search

BUSTED

Last updated:
14 January 2002

Authors deserve to be paid for their work – please tip the author if you read their work online. Or see here for more info.

Books etc

What's New

Orders

Projects

Comments

Coach House

Books and Projects by Title

Credits
Site by Bhavalla Design

Coach House Books <www.chbooks.com>, an ongoing experiment in simultaneous online and print publication.

One of the problems with electronic publishing now is that anyone interested in engaging in it also has to be willing to engage in the construction of the infrastructure to support it. Coach House has put an enormous amount of energy into writing about electronic publication for trade magazines, speaking at conferences, working with industry associations and lobbying at the national level for rights management and royalty systems for online publishing. While we've made some inroads, the glacial rate of bureaucratic movement, combined with the current slump in interest in e-books and online publishing, means that Coach House will likely remain an anomaly for the foreseeable future.

In the meantime, the Coach House Web site has functioned as an extremely efficient advertising system for the press. Not only has it yielded sales from all over the globe, its uniqueness has resulted in an enormous amount of media coverage for a small literary press.

While there are definite benefits of electronic publishing, they may not always or immediately translate into direct sales. Unfortunately, this may well keep all but the smallest and the least risk-averse of companies from publishing electronically. In November 2001, Random House, the largest publisher of trade books in the United States, shut down AtRandom, its e-book imprint. Though they're continuing to digitize their backlist, they have no plans to market electronic editions any time soon.[11]

Jon Katz argues convincingly that the failure of the entire first wave of e-book publishing was a result of the misrecognition of publishers of some of the fundamental rules of digital media: 'More information at less cost, and the information system that meets the information needs of humans will always prevail. The most successful information vendors aren't those that create information, but those that connect people with the information they want and need.'[12] These sites—'open media vendors' such as the first incarnation of Napster, neo-situationist publisher textz.com and ubu.com, writer Kenneth Goldsmith's archive of concrete, visual and sound poetry—operate in a manner that's closer to the zeitgeist of the Net than any commercial online publishing ventures have managed to date. 'Invariably,' Katz writes, such sites 'share a common utility with their consumers—free music, open source, archived materials—and they give their readers and browsers work to do and a role to play: contributing, moderating, commenting and arguing, reviewing, sharing information, linking.'

Under contemporary conditions, then, the idea of a *salable* popular fiction 'e-book' may be a contradiction in terms. As Katz notes, free online textbooks, scientific publications and works of art seem to be thriving. People will pay for paper, but they won't pay for bits ... and the only bits that people online want are the ones that speak to them directly, through their own communities. A viral marketing campaign (relying on word-of-mouth and direct swapping of files between aficionados), such as setting segments of *The Plant* loose on Gnutella, might well have been a more successful precursor to a print edition than a straight attempt to hawk a digital version. (For more on the possible merits of distributing free-beer content over peer-to-peer networks like Gnutella, see the 'Pro-P2P' section on page 151.)

Other writers, particularly journalists, have made real strides in protecting their rights to their own work online, and in getting paid for it, albeit on a much humbler scale than King's.

Pyrrhic victory

On June 25, 2001, in a 7–2 ruling, the US Supreme Court decided that newspapers and magazines cannot place articles written for print media by freelance authors in Lexis-Nexis or other electronic databases, or on storage media such as CD-ROMs. The ruling brought to an end a case that has been a long legal rollercoaster ride: a District Court ruled in favor of the

> People will pay for paper, but they won't pay for bits ... and the only bits that people online want are the ones that speak to them directly, through their own communities.

publishers in August 1997, and the 2nd U.S. Circuit Court of Appeals reversed the decision in September 1999.

The New York Times, Newsday, Time, Lexis-Nexis and University Microfilms (the defendants) had been arguing under the 1976 Copyright Act that reproducing print articles in databases was essentially a 'revision' of the original work, and therefore permissible (this is the provision that allows newspapers to reprint articles in late editions without compensating the authors). The court, however, would have none of it, stating instead that 'the massive database no more constitutes a "revision" of each constituent edition than a 400-page novel quoting a sonnet in passing would constitute a revision of that poem,' and that databasing a work disconnected it from its original context by making it searchable (an observation that may have serious consequences for other cases, as we'll see later).[13]

From the perspective of freelance writers looking to get paid, this decision is a victory, but from the position of posterity, there is a definite Pyrrhic quality to the triumph. Rather than pay writers for the articles that are already in their various databases, most of the news companies have opted to delete the articles, thus creating large gaps in the digital historical record. In addition, the Special Libraries Association has argued that this ruling will create a chill on the willingness of newspapers to use articles by freelancers in the future.[14]

The question of digital copyright is a complex one, and there are at least two sides to the issue.

Digital copyright: The nerfing of cyberspace

John Gilmore is the cofounder (along with Mitchell Kapor and John Perry Barlow) of the Electronic Frontier Foundation <www.eff.org>—the Internet's equivalent of the Lone Ranger, a white-hat hacker fighting against stiff odds on behalf of the rights of Internet users everywhere, whether they realize it or not—and the founder of Cygnus Solutions (now a part of Red Hat). In essays such as 'What's Wrong with Copy Protection' <www.toad.com/gnu/whatswrong.html> he's written passionately and at length about the major irony of the ongoing copyright protection wars. In Gilmore's view, 'What is wrong is that we have invented the technology to eliminate scarcity, but we are deliberately throwing it away to benefit those who profit from scarcity.'[15]

In other words, we're taking technology that works perfectly well and making it work a little *less* well, because of pressures that have more to do with current economic conditions than with planning for the future. In geekspeak, this sort of technological compromise is called *nerfing*, because it's about taking something that's perceived as dangerous and rendering it inoffensive to the point of uselessness, like Nerf balls (the Nerf projectile weapons beloved of cubicle warriors everywhere are another matter).

It's a given that it's now possible to replicate digital objects with no appreciable costs. Gilmore sees this as the tip of a very large and revolutionary iceberg that extends beyond the bounds of cyberspace and into the physical world. In industrial manufacturing, three-dimensional prototyping systems (approximately, photocopiers that make objects instead of images) are quickly becoming capable of reproducing physical copies in much the same manner as digital ones. Stratasys, a Minneapolis-based manufacturer of prototyping systems, recently handled the first instance of 'replicating' an actual replacement part for working production equipment when they manufactured a polymer replacement for a metal part from CAD (Computer-Assisted Design) drawings in a couple of hours.[16] Some people believe that nanotechnology (the science of making very tiny machines, popularized in the 80s by Eric Drexler's book *Engines of Creation*) will extend the possibility of instant real-world replication even further, because it will be possible to use nanomachines to build many kinds of complex objects from the atoms up.

Nanotechnology has a long way to go to make the transition from science fiction to reality, but regardless of whether or not it succeeds, Gilmore sensibly believes that we need to prepare ourselves for the present era of digital plenty, which means creating new business models that will function in such an environment. To this end, his company, Cygnus, invests more than $10 million annually in the writing and distributing of Free Software.

Gilmore provides an extensive list of the factors that he sees as detrimental to the development of an economy based on plenitude. Most of these focus on the negative effects of letting companies—especially large corporations—gain rights over their content that compromise the public's rights of free speech and publication.

The concrete examples he presents include the following:

- A company called Streambox created a program that allows streaming video channeled through RealPlayer software to be saved as a file. Under the Supreme Court's Betamax decision whereby technology that has 'substantial noninfringing uses' can't be outlawed, this should be legal. However, Streambox was sued by Real under the Digital Millennium Copyright Act (DMCA), and subsequently took their product off the market.

- The DVD-R drives on new Apple computers are incapable of recording the key-blocks needed to copy-protect your recordings, or of copying a DVD-General disk. While this means that the drive can't be used to duplicate copyrighted material, it also means that you can't copy-protect your own disks, or create your own mixed video disks.

- Sony mini-disc recorders only come with digital input jacks. They can record media, but can't be used to output digitized material to other media, digital or otherwise.

- Microsoft Windows 2000 features DNS protocols that Gilmore claims are 'deliberately incompatible' with those used on Unix machines. When Microsoft released a specification for those protocols, it did so under an encrypted file format that required that readers agree not to use the information to compete with Microsoft's products—a digital Catch-22. Inevitably, someone decrypted the encryption without agreeing to the terms, and Microsoft threatened to use the DMCA to sue Slashdot when they published the results, though they later backed down.

- Manufacturers of DVD media and players have instituted a system of 'region coding' that prevents DVDs bought in one region from being played on players bought in another region, even if both were purchased legally. While this is ostensibly to prevent the pirating of films not released in particular countries, it has the effect of exempting DVDs from the usual free trade of consumer goods. The manufacturers of hardware and software that would allow consumers to use DVDs bought in another region (such as the infamous DeCSS program; see page 128) have been rigorously pursued under the DMCA by the motion picture industry.

While 'copyright doesn't grant the right to prevent competition, or to restrict global trade,' Gilmore writes, 'the legislation that was enacted to protect copyrights is being used to do just those things.' (For more on this subject, see the section on the Digital Millennium Copyright Act in the next chapter.)

And this is one of the major complexities of dealing with free-beer issues. In their zeal to stamp out the frequently-but-not-always-illegal trading of digital files of all kinds, the powers that be (the Recording Industry Association of America, Microsoft and other large corporations, governments) have all too often begun to erode free speech rights as well.

For an example of the chill created by the battle to protect copyright, we need look no further than the case of Professor Edward Felten.

Blinded by science

On September 6, 2000, the Secure Digital Music Initiative (SDMI), a group whose mandate is to 'protect the playing, storing, and distributing of digital music' <www.sdmi.org>, issued a public challenge to break four 'digital watermarking' schemes that were being developed for use with CDs and other digital music formats.[17] A *digital watermark* is an imperceptibly tiny bit of information that has been embedded in a digital file (such as an MP3, a photograph, or anything else that someone wants to protect). The SDMI's scheme was designed to watermark an audio file so that it could be recognized by specially equipped hardware (CD players, disc drives, whatever) as copyrighted. If that watermark was absent or damaged, in theory, the hardware would refuse to play or record the clip.

Though some portions of the hacker community boycotted the challenge, arguing that successful results would only play into the hands of those who wish to restrict the right of the average citizen to publish.[18] Princeton University professor Edward Felten <www.cs.princeton.edu/~felten/> and his team not only accepted the challenge but defeated the encryption and maintained the high quality of the audio file. They reasoned that they were helping neither the recording industry to impose restrictions nor pirates to bootleg music, because the restrictive technology didn't work and pirates would have no use for their findings if the technology was never deployed.

But when Felten's team proceeded to prepare to discuss their findings at the Fourth International Information Hiding Workshop (held in Pittsburgh in April 2001), and later to publish them in the conference proceedings, they were threatened by the SDMI, the Verance Corporation and the Recording Industry Association of America (RIAA) with prosecution under the Digital Millennium Copyright Act (DMCA).

Rather than face prosecution, Felten and his team read a prepared statement at the conference.[19] While the RIAA backpedaled almost

In their zeal to stamp out the frequently-but-not-always-illegal trading of digital files of all kinds, the powers that be (the Recording Industry Association of America, Microsoft and other large corporations, governments) have all too often begun to erode free speech rights as well.

immediately, claiming they never intended to bring any legal action against Felten,[20] he and his team nevertheless felt sufficiently threatened by a letter from the RIAA[21] that they filed a suit asking a federal court to allow them to legally publish their paper. At this point the Electronic Frontier Foundation (EFF) joined the fray, asking the court to overturn the anti-distribution provisions of the DMCA 'as unconstitutional restraints on the freedom of expression.'[22] Princeton and Rice universities were openly supportive of Felten, and even contributed some funds to the suit, but the EFF funded the majority of the case.

On August 15, 2001, the paper was published at the Usenix Security Conference with the permission of the RIAA, SDMI and Verance (its full text is available as a PDF on Felten's site). The RIAA et al. haven't dropped the lawsuit, however, because they continue to insist on veto power over Felten's work and future publications.

Science fights back

This case has made Felten something of a *cause célèbre* in online free speech circles. On August 17, 2001, 17 prominent scientists (a mixture of academics, cryptographers and software programmers) testified in federal court about their belief that the DMCA stifles not only freedom of expression, but the process of scientific research.[23]

But the Felten case isn't the only area where scientists have been criticizing the negative effects of overzealous attempts to protect intellectual property. The Public Library of Science <www.publiclibraryofscience.org> has launched an energetic campaign to ensure that scientific and medical literature remain freely accessible to scientists and the general public worldwide. At the time of this writing, over 27,000 scientists from 171 countries have signed the following open letter:

We support the establishment of an online public library that would provide the full contents of the published record of research and scholarly discourse in medicine and the life sciences in a freely accessible, fully searchable, interlinked form. Establishment of this public library would vastly increase the accessibility and utility of the scientific literature, enhance scientific productivity, and catalyze integration of the disparate communities of knowledge and ideas in biomedical sciences.

We recognize that the publishers of our scientific journals have a legitimate right to a fair financial return for their role in scientific communication. We believe, however, that the permanent, archival record of scientific research and ideas should neither be owned nor controlled by publishers, but should belong to the public, and should be freely available through an international online public library.

To encourage the publishers of our journals to support this endeavor, we pledge that, beginning in September, 2001, we will publish in, edit or review for, and personally subscribe to, only those scholarly and scientific journals that have agreed to grant unrestricted free distribution rights to any and all original research reports that they have published, through PubMed Central and similar online public resources, within 6 months of their initial publication date.[24]

While the PLoS acknowledges that many journals allow for the free reading of articles from back issues under controlled circumstances (such as reading on the journal's own site), they argue strongly (and convincingly) for the value of centralized online repositories of related materials. The comparative ease with which centralized collections can be searched makes them considerably more useful than individual documents posted on publishers' Web sites scattered all over the Internet. Public scientific databases, they argue, represent a 'greater good' because they place the interests of the public and of posterity over the urges of individual authors and publishers to control their productions.[25]

It's interesting that the PLoS seems to be advancing an argument that runs against the Supreme Court's decision in the case of *The New York Times* et al. freelancers. The PLoS argues that value derives directly from the act of placing articles into a comprehensive database, while the Supreme Court says that it's exactly this sort of recontextualization that requires that authors be paid for a separate usage of their work. While there isn't exactly a direct contradiction here, it does indicate possible rough waters ahead—proponents of creators' rights want one thing, and those interested in efficiency and posterity want another. And there are definite merits to both arguments.

The PLoS is not ruling out the idea of publishing for profit, though. They suggest a model where a journal gains a six-month 'lease' of exclusive print and electronic rights over the period immediately following the publication of an article. Libraries and other subscribers to all forms of the journal would gain the information immediately, and, since the text doesn't disappear from the original print or electronic editions after that period, there's no decrease in the journal's value as a storage medium after that period if the article reappears elsewhere. In the same way that a midwife doesn't have to keep the babies she delivers in order to make money, they reason, a journal shouldn't have to maintain control of the

Public scientific databases, it is argued, represent a 'greater good' because they place the interests of the public and of posterity over the urges of individual authors and publishers to control their productions.

articles that it publishes to make the same amount of money. In the near future, the PLoS plans to establish 'a financially sustainable model for non-profit publication of scientific research articles without ever charging for or restricting access or use of the published work,' details of which will presumably be available on their site.

It is at this point that the ethics of journal publication rears its head. Most people who contribute to academic journals do so for free, or for minuscule honoraria at best. Many journals are funded largely by government grants. Under such circumstances, why should journals be allowed to maintain exclusive control of the record of scientific research?

On the Internet, as it exists today at any rate, the notion of 'exclusive control' seems risible. In the long run, the kinds of texts that work best online might have more in common with projects like the online encyclopedias Wikipedia and Everything$_2$ than they do with either journalism or popular fiction.

Online encyclopedias: Edit this page

Encyclopedia Britannica has been around in print for 232 years, and during the height of the dot-com boom, it looked as though it might well extend that existence into the far future by migrating online. In 1999, Britannica created a free Web site to accompany the subscription-based online version of its famed encyclopedia that had actually been available since 1994.

At the dawn of the millennium, things looked good for the venerable publication. In September 2000, Britannica.com was the 98th most visited site on the Web, but not long after, its fortunes began to flag. By February 2001 it had slipped to the 159th spot ... and no one was paying for any of it. Less than a month later Britannica.com canned about 16% of its employees, and announced that it would be switching to a subscription-based for public users model and placing more emphasis on selling enhanced services to elementary and secondary schools.[26] By June 2001, Britannica had declared that it would resume producing its print encyclopedia, which it had stopped producing in 1998.[27]

Spokesman Tom Panelas said 'The economics of the all-free model has changed,' and cited fall-offs in advertising revenue as Britannica's chief reason for its retreat from the Web. By early 2001, it was clear to everyone that banner advertising alone wasn't going to be enough to support the expense of putting large amounts of content online for unmetered use.

But perhaps the economics of the all-free model hasn't changed at all. Perhaps companies are finally starting to realize that there are some kinds of free that can't be commoditized. As if to support this thesis, competition is already appearing for the online encyclopedias—competition that's free of both advertising and subscription fees. Larry Sanger explains why in a recent article on Kuro5hin: because of the ease of posting material to the Net, it will always be easy to find good content. As long as there are even a small number of altruistic souls who are also good writers and researchers, there will always be a free alternative to commercial content (cf. the entire Free Software movement, used by millions, but authored by a comparative few). And the number of good writers and researchers who do post their work to the Net for free is growing all the time. [28]

In a sense, Sanger's argument about free encyclopedias brings us back to the argument that the scientific community is presenting: online content—especially content of a scholarly nature—needs to be aggregated in one place to be truly useful (i.e., searchable).

Concentrating data requires intense effort, and one of the primary business models for dealing with free content is that those who do the aggregation should be able to charge for their efforts (e.g., Red Hat or the other commercial Linux distributions). Conventional wisdom says that large-scale processes of aggregation don't happen for nothing ... but the examples of the free online encyclopedias show that sometimes they do just that.

By using the same 'open content' model as free software itself, within a few years online encyclopedias such as Wikipedia and Nupedia could conceivably fill the space that Britannica has abandoned. The two projects are run by the same people, and work in a complementary fashion.

Nupedia <www.nupedia.com> is the highbrow version—it's rigorously edited, has a professional peer review system, solicits material from experts in the field and has extensive and well-formulated policies. And, since Nupedia uses the GNU Free Documentation License, it has the explicit GNU stamp of approval to boot <www.gnu.org/copyleft/fdl.html> to manage its content (Stallman and company were apparently in the process of beginning a free encyclopedia at the precise moment that the Nupedia came along, so they simply endorsed it and moved on).

The problem is, accumulating content this way—the old-fashioned way—is painfully slow. What was needed was a kind of scoop to gather as much information as possible, as quickly as possible, for use as raw

As long as there are even a small number of altruistic souls who are also good writers and researchers, there will always be a free alternative to commercial content.

material. That meant getting more people involved, which is one of the things that the Internet has always done extremely well. Enter Wikipedia.

Wikipedia is Nupedia's kid brother, powered by the kind of technology that works best online: quick-and-dirty. WikiWiki, the software on which WikiPedia is based <www.c2.com/cgi/wiki?WikiWikiWeb>, consists of a set of Web pages that are stored in a database and managed using Perl CGI scripts. The base version of this code and its many clones and offshoots are kicking around if you want to build your own Wiki site. Many people have. WikiWiki pages are completely open—*anyone* can edit them as they wish, though the site's administrators may override or delete those edits.

The original idea was for Wikipedia articles to serve as the first draft of articles for the Nupedia, and in some cases, to be ported over directly if the writing and research meet the Nupedia editors' criteria. But the overall success of Wikipedia was enough to inspire a hybrid middle stage, in the form of the Nupedia Chalkboard. The Chalkboard is a Wiki area managed by Nupedia's editors and peer reviewers. The best of the Wikipedia texts move to the Chalkboard for touchups by Nupedia editors and experts. Finally they enter the Nupedia system itself.

Wikipedia grew at an amazing rate—over 6,000 articles appeared in its first six months of existence and about 1,000 per month are being added; the total at the time of this writing sits at over 10,000 entries. It's entirely reasonable to expect this rate of growth to continue; as Sanger points out, the wilder, woolier, unvetted Everything$_2$ <www.everything2.com> recently added its millionth node (article). And as search engines such as Google and the C|Net encyclopedia metasearch engine begin to direct more and more traffic to Wikipedia and Nupedia, interest in the project will grow along with its recognition factor, and more people will add to the database.

Everything$_2$, a collaboratively filtered database whose contents are created, like those of other free online encyclopedias, by a small army of volunteer users, is more a recreational enterprise than a scholarly one. As the FAQ says, 'When you make an account here you join not only a team of dedicated writers but an entire micro-society and community with its own pop culture, politics, beauty and blunders. It's not perfect. In fact, it can be pretty messy. It's cool as hell, though ... So that helps.'[29] This doesn't make Everything$_2$ a purely recreational endeavor—Slashdot <www.slashdot. org> for one uses it as an online glossary—but it does mean that you probably don't want to take everything on the site at face value.

In cyberspace, tools matter. A lot. This is true because the kind of tools that an organization uses to accomplish its goals determine how the people involved in their project relate to each other. Experience has shown that tools that empower their users to act collectively succeed online to a far greater extent than tools that relegate the participants to the status of passive audience members. People who are part of the online community not only like to participate, they expect to. Few tools have met those expectations like the kind of systems we have come to call peer-to-peer (P2P) ... and few have caused as much trouble.

6

Introducing P2P

P2P is not a technology; it is a mindset.[1]

—JOHN ORWANT

What is peer-to-peer?

Good question. Here's what we know about it:

- It's a phrase that came into currency about the same time that a little program called Napster was changing everything about the way people commonly assumed the Internet works.

- It describes a kind of network system architecture where each node on the network has more or less equivalent processing power and privileges for the purpose of sharing files. Its opposite is a form of architecture called *client-server*, where large, powerful computers called *servers* manage resources such as network traffic, file management and storage and printers for a series of smaller, much less powerful computers or terminals called *clients*. In the early days of its existence the Internet functioned as a network of peers, but it has gradually become more client-server focused due to massive increases in traffic, the introduction of gated systems and so on. (More on this in a moment.) Today's peer-to-peer systems basically ignore the powerful, server-based centers of the Net in favor of establishing small, unstable networks of connected users with minimal resources, in order to accomplish specific short-lived tasks.

- P2P doesn't care who you are or which computer you are using. All it cares about is that you want a file, and someone else has it, or vice versa. It's quick and dirty. And it works.

Why bother? Well, since the explosion in public Internet use that followed the invention of the graphical Web browser (ca. 1994), the mode of connecting users to the Internet has changed dramatically. As I discussed in Chapter 3, the influx of new users meant that the old system of one static IP address per computer had to change, because there simply weren't enough IP addresses to go around. When home Internet use started to explode, around 1995, Internet service providers began assigning IP addresses dynamically to their users when they connected, which the users conceded when they disconnected. While this solved the traffic problem, it created the current client-server incarnation of the Net, with dialup users unable to consistently and reliably serve files or applications to the Net because of their unstable identity. For example, it would be very difficult and almost pointless to host a Web site on your home computer if you connected it to the Internet for only four hours every day, and your ISP assigned the site a different address every time you came online. The hassle involved in locating the site would be far too great for most readers to bother.

As the dialup user base grew, so did the untapped computer processing power they were using. Home computers were increasing in power and capability, and most people never use anywhere near their full potential (like their brains, for that matter). Peer-to-peer guru Clay Shirky <www.shirky.com> writes, 'At a conservative estimate, the world's Net-connected PCs presently host an aggregate ten billion Mhz of processing power and ten thousand terabytes of storage, assuming only 100 million PCs among the Net's 300 million users, and only a 100 Mhz chip and 100 Mb drive on the average PC.'[2] People started wondering about how to tap into all of that power. And inevitably, they found it.

The answer lay in the creation of an entirely new class of machine addresses, dependent on specific software programs. Perhaps the first software to use such a system was ICQ <web.icq.com>, the first instant messenger program; others, including Napster, soon followed suit. As new file-sharing platforms and Internet-connected devices such as cell phones and PDAs continue to worm their way into our lives, more of these protocol-specific addressing schemes will continue to emerge.

To give a sense of how quickly these new address protocols are proliferating, Shirky observed that at the end of the year 2000, after 16 years of IP address accumulation, there were 23 million domain names in use. Napster created 23 million protocol-specific addresses in 16 months.

P2P doesn't care who you are or which computer you are using. All it cares about is that you want a file, and someone else has it, or vice versa. It's quick and dirty. And it works.

The Internet will likely never return to its former state of one address per machine or device, because such addresses are often applied to things other than machines, such as pieces of a single file spread out across a file-sharing network like Freenet (a P2P network designed to prevent censorship and ensure anonymity by fragmenting every file that it stores into encrypted chunks, which it then distributes across the hard drives of its users). 'P2P is designed to handle unpredictability,' writes Shirky, 'and nothing is more unpredictable than the humans who use the network.'[3]

Clay Shirky is the person who's done the most interesting and visionary thinking about P2P and its potential uses. He defines P2P as a set of applications that takes advantage of decentralized, unused resources at the less-connected 'edges' of the Internet, such as processing power on idle computers, partially empty hard drives and unemployed and insomniac users. In order to access these resources, which aren't even constantly connected to the Net and frequently change their IP addresses when they are connected, a P2P system must be equipped with the ability to operate without reliance on a central server, and will probably need its own system of assigning addresses as well.[4]

Shirky has a two-point checklist for determining if a system is P2P:

1. It must take into account that not all elements of the network will be connected at any given time, and that when they are connected, their addresses may change, and

2. It must assign a substantial degree of freedom and control to even the less powerful computers at the peripheries of its network.[5]

In other words, P2P is a scavenger technology that works with and on resources that are usually ignored or abandoned. This reliance on fringe resources (small computers with only temporary Net connections) rather than powerful centralized computers can and does mean that P2P technologies are usually unconventional (and that their connections are sometimes unreliable), but in most cases the programmers of P2P software have developed ingenious methods of turning what had previously been deficits into assets.

For example, SETI@home <setiathome.ssl.berkeley.edu> and the Intel Philanthropic Peer-to-Peer program <www.intel.com/cure> use the idle cycles of running computers to crunch numbers for the greater good. Everyone has times when their computer is running but they're not actually using it, especially in an office setting, where many computer networks run all night. These peer-to-peer networks have found a clever way to utilize that idle time. Users who wish to participate in one of these projects download a screensaver program and install it on their machine. When the computer begins to idle, the screensaver kicks in and connects to a computer that assigns it a block of numerical data to process. When it's done processing that data (which takes about a full day), it sends a completed package back and requests another. In essence, the P2P software creates a vast 'virtual supercomputer' out of an indeterminate number of far-flung, low-powered desktop machines. The beauty of the system is that the data can be for anything—SETI@Home uses this system to analyze data from the Arecibo radiotelescope in the search for signs of extraterrestrial intelligence; the Intel Philanthropic Peer-to-Peer program analyzes research data from the fight against leukemia, Alzheimer's disease, Type II diabetes and Mad Cow disease.

Gnutella and other file-sharing networks go a step further than the philanthropic P2P programs, according the status of file server to lowly PCs that usually act only as clients. People connected to SETI@home can't see each other, or share information between their computers, but users of Gnutella, AudioGalaxy and the other file-sharing networks can, and do, even though there's usually no central database of files on the network or even of computers connected to the network. Each user assigns a directory as accessible to the network, and anything in that directory can in theory be accessed and downloaded by anyone else on the network. If there are enough regular users with similar goals it doesn't matter that everyone isn't on all the time, or even that every part of the network can't see every other part, because there's sufficient redundancy to ensure that most of the same information is available most of the time (or something that's close enough to it that everyone goes away satisfied).

As profoundly different as P2P seems from 'the way things are done' right now on the Internet, in Shirky's view it will eventually become ubiquitous—and almost invisible—as its techniques are incorporated into the emerging new world of Web services like .Net and into the very the fabric of networking itself.

Rewiring or dewiring?

While Shirky argues that P2P is 'rewiring the Internet,' others take a less salutary perspective on the subject. In an article in *The Wall Street Journal's* interactive edition, for example, Lee Gomes suggests that much of the

As profoundly different as P2P seems from 'the way things are done' right now on the Internet, in Shirky's view it will eventually become ubiquitous—and almost invisible— as its techniques are incorporated into the emerging new world of Web services.

What's at stake is not a particular piece of software, or even a particular startup. It's the act of putting the computers at the 'fringes' of the Internet to work in the most efficient way.

hype around P2P has already gone sour, and that the technology will never really amount to much because of a lack of obviously lucrative business models.[6]

It's true that a number of startups based on P2P solutions for office networking, such as Popular Power and InfraSearch, have either folded completely or been acquired by larger companies and folded into existing projects. And it's also true that, to date, the dominant implementations of P2P have been fueled by either the illegal swapping of music (in the case of Napster, Gnutella, Morpheus et al.) or pure philanthropy (in the case of distributed computing projects like SETI@home).

But the problem is likely not P2P itself; it's the categorical mistake that venture capitalists and the popular press alike have made in thinking about P2P. As Dr. John Orwant, CEO of computer book publishers O'Reilly & Associates and editor in chief of *The Perl Journal*, says, 'P2P is not a technology; it is a mindset.'[7]

In other words, what's at stake is not a particular piece of software, or even a particular startup. It's the act of putting the computers at the 'fringes' of the Internet to work in the most efficient way. It's about using hitherto untapped—and in most cases, freely available—processing power. It's about having the flexibility to choose dynamically between centralized and decentralized.

Existing P2P systems aren't all that secure because they haven't had to be. As the Web services model develops and credible digital identifiers (like Microsoft's proposed Passport system) become widespread, P2P paradigms will begin to shift in that direction. But credible P2P systems are already in use.

Consider NextPage <www.nextpage.com>, a P2P content-sharing system used by Deloitte & Touche, among others. It provides a single interface to the hodge-podge of legacy systems that worldwide corporations such as Deloitte often have in abundance. (Legacy systems are the combinations of antiquated computers and software that house much of the data that's crucial to running the businesses of the world. These systems are frequently maintained in their original state due to the high cost of migrating the data over to new machines and/or new software, which means that someone has to figure out how to make them talk to today's computers.) NextPage is capable of pulling together relevant information despite the format in which it was stored. Unlike the garden-variety P2P systems, it's not cheap (it costs somewhere in the neighborhood of $85,000 for a 250-user license), but it works, and it's secure. As Orwant observes,

'They just don't get as much press, because let's face it: Ripping off [Metallica drummer] Lars Ulrich makes a much better story than sharing Excel spreadsheets to avoid the email data skew plaguing so many companies today.'[8]

The SETI@home Project is also a totally legitimate use of P2P, and a roaring success to boot. There are now 3 million users of the software, with thousands more signing up every day. This gives the project far more total computing power than the largest supercomputer ever built—so much power that SETI is now going to increase its processing to 20 times the amount of data that it's been running to date. If it doesn't, it's going to be in danger of running out of things for its users' computers to do. And in order to record data faster, SETI is installing a brand-new Linux-based (what else?) data recorder that's 10 times faster than the one they've been using.[9]

So P2P clearly has its uses, and likely has a future. But its past—and present—are mired in controversy, because the uses to which this new technology have been put are almost all antithetical to our existing ideas about intellectual property and copyright law.

A brief history of copyright

> *[An idea's] peculiar character, too, is that no one possesses the less, because every other possesses the whole of it. He who receives an idea from me, receives instruction himself without lessening mine; as he who lights his taper at mine, receives light without darkening me.*[10]
>
> —THOMAS JEFFERSON

Try an experiment for a moment. In the above paragraph, substitute the term 'digital file' for the word 'idea.' Thomas Jefferson would have loved peer-to-peer technology. At least, that's the argument that Siva Vaidhyanathan, the author of *Copyrights and Copywrongs: The Rise of Intellectual Property and How It Threatens Creativity*, made recently in an article on MSNBC.com.[11]

We have a tendency to regard our past history as monolithic, even our recent history. (All those marble busts and monuments don't help matters much.) But sometimes it's instructive to go back and look at the opposition that's always present at the inception of an idea, especially an idea as powerful as copyright. Vaidhyanathan's Cook's tour of the history of copyright is particularly useful in this respect.

Vaidhyanathan begins by noting that when copyright first saw the light of day, it was as a method of censorship. In 1557, Queen Mary issued a charter to the Stationers' Company, a printers' guild, giving them the sole right to legally produce books (and of course, those books had to be approved by agents of the Queen).

He contrasts this with the US system established in 1791, which 'grew to embody four safeguards':

1. A guarantee that all works would enter the public domain once the copyright term expired.

2. A collection of purposes that consumers could consider 'fair use,' such as limited copying for education or research.

3. The principle that after the 'first sale' of a copyrighted item, the buyer could do whatever he or she wants with the item, save distribute unauthorized copies for profit.

4. The concept that copyright protects specific expression of ideas, but not the ideas themselves.

From this perspective, copyright was not intended to bolster the notion of intellectual property rights so much as it was intended to guarantee the ongoing flow of ideas. The temporary monopoly on an idea that copyright extends to an author, argues Vaidhyanathan, should exist precisely long enough to provide him or her with the means and incentive to create further ideas. And no further.

Texts penned by the USA's founders support this interpretation. Vaidhyanathan contends that James Madison, who introduced the copyright and patent clause to the US constitution, 'did not engage in "property talk" about copyright … Copyright fulfilled its role for Madison because it looked forward as an encouragement, not backward as a reward.'

In Vaidhyanathan's opinion, the growing popularity of the term 'intellectual property' is a sign that copyright legislation has been skewed in favor of established authors with something to sell—and, more significantly, the corporations that often end up owning and licensing the work that they create—over the interest of audience members, researchers and less established creators. In contrast to a temporary monopoly that exists only long enough to encourage the production of other ideas, the notion of a 'property right' for ideas encourages thinking of them as something that should belong to an individual or corporation (and maybe even their heirs) in perpetuity. If, as I argued earlier, authors and other copyright holders have some legitimate grievances about how their work has been circulated online, they also have to realize that the same system that assigns them those rights also assigns limits to those rights.

As corporations grow large enough to become monopolies, or establish cartels that give them near-monopolistic status, they become less and less limited by the ordinary rules of the economy. With no effective competition, a monopolistic corporation never has to drop its prices, and, if it is essential to the economy (as many monopolies are), the demand for its goods doesn't drop significantly. To that end—ensuring that it remains the only option—a monopoly can use its copyrights and patents 'to create artificial scarcity by limiting access, fixing prices, restricting licensing, litigating, and intimidating potential competitors, misrepresenting the principles of the law and claiming a measure of authenticity or romantic originality.'

Sound familiar? It should. Madison and Jefferson knew what was coming, but they just didn't know that it would take so long for their warnings to become relevant. Or that, at the turn of the millennium, a controversial piece of legislation would tip the balance of copyright heavily in favor of those who would hoard ideas like things.

The DMCA

The Digital Millennium Copyright Act (DMCA) was passed in 1998, at the end of the 105th Congress of the United States. While it has its supporters, many people view it the same way that they view Monica Lewinsky's navy-blue cocktail dress—as a nasty relic that we'd rather had never seen the light of day.

The DMCA's roots go all the way back to 1993, when Clinton's nascent administration established a task force on the National Information Infrastructure. A white paper titled 'The Report of the Working Group on Intellectual Property Rights' followed two years later. It was a fairly general document, whose overall stance was that US copyright law as it existed was able to handle most digital issues that might arise. It did, however, recommend that the exclusive rights of copyright holders needed to be expanded to include transmission, that libraries should be allowed to make digital as well as print copies, and that devices designed to circumvent data protection needed some new restrictions.

Minor turf wars ensued between the Department of Commerce and Congress over who would get to set US copyright policy. Simultaneously, copyright advocates began to press for an expansion of the copyright term from the life of the author plus 50 years (75 years in the case of work for hire) to the life of the author plus 70 years (95 years for work for hire). The main rationale for this expansion was to harmonize US copyright laws with European laws, so that US copyright holders could have their works protected in Europe for as long as they were protected domestically. (European laws specified that US authors could not enjoy the full span of their copyright protection term unless the US term was of the same length.) This would eventually pass into US law in 1998 as the Sonny Bono Copyright Term Extension Act, making the late Bono notorious for something more than getting his ass dumped by Cher.

While the US government was hashing out the details of this white paper, the World Intellectual Property Organization (WIPO) was planning an international conference on copyright. A 1996 diplomatic conference held in Geneva resulted in some amendments to the WIPO Berne treaty aimed at developing international consensus on copyright issues, and in the further development of a second treaty dealing with the rights of the producers of sound recordings. The core issues that would find their way into the DMCA grew out of this meeting: anti-data-encryption circumvention laws, US copyright laws harmonized with European laws, and a limitation on ISP liability.

In 1998, Senator Orrin Hatch, the chair of the Senate Judiciary Committee, renamed the WIPO Treaty Implementing Legislation the Digital Millennium Copyright Act. Debate was intense, seesawing back and forth between the interest of creators and the interests of users. In the end, the bill was passed on October 28, 1998, but without any consensus on whether the purpose of its guidelines were focused on the notion of intellectual property protection or the notion of fair use.[12]

What the DMCA says

So what does the DMCA actually say? The answer is a fair amount; it's a complex piece of legislation. Following are summaries of some of its most important points. (The full act is available online in several locations, including <www.eff.org/IP/DMCA/hr2281_dmca_law_19981020_pl105-304.html>, and the Copyright Office's summary is at <www.loc.gov/copyright/legislation/dmca.pdf> in PDF form. There are many sites that analyze it in detail, including <www.arl.org/info/frn/copy/dmca.html>.)

The DMCA and cracking

The DMCA makes it officially illegal to manufacture, import, distribute or provide products or services for the purpose of circumventing technological data protection schemes, such as watermarking or encryption. Further, it's illegal to sell or circulate such products. If a product appears to lack legitimate commercial uses, it's history. Thus the fate of Napster.

Further, it's now illegal to crack any data protection scheme that's already in place. The significance of this provision is considerable, because while copyrights eventually expire, protection schemes do not. Will it remain illegal to crack encrypted files even after their copyright has expired? This provision also seems to dictate what sorts of hardware may be used to view digital media (but we'll look at this in greater detail when we discuss DeCSS, the program that cracked the DVD built-in data protection Content Scramble System).

Fortunately, the government hasn't been totally clueless on this matter. Due to the concerted efforts of lobbyists like the Electronic Frontier Foundation and many library organizations, Congress made this prohibition subject to a review by the Librarian of Congress, in consultation with the Register of Copyrights, every three years. If it starts to look like the use of data protection has severely limited access to any particular category of digital works—say, music—the Librarian can suspend the prohibition.

Do not remove this tag

If mattresses were protected under the DMCA, we'd all be in heaps of trouble. The DMCA prohibits the falsification, alteration or removal of 'copyright management information'—metadata that identifies the authors, copyright licensing information and so on for a given digital work. Once again, it's also illegal to knowingly sell or circulate works where this information is damaged, removed or forged. People who flout this provision can be sued criminally and civilly (though schools and nonprofits can't be criminally prosecuted, and, if they can demonstrate that their violations were committed in ignorance, they can be exempted from monetary damages as well).

Hard times for hardware

Hardware manufacturers are not exempt from the DMCA either. While they don't have to reinvent their technology every time someone invents

While copyrights eventually expire, protection schemes do not. Will it remain illegal to crack encrypted files even after their copyright has expired?

a new data protection scheme, they are nevertheless obligated to use the serial copy management system (SCMS), which ensures that it's possible to make only first-generation copies of digital media.

The DMCA and ISPs

The DMCA limits the liability of ISPs (Internet service providers) for copyright infringement perpetrated by its users. ISPs aren't financially liable for copyright infringements if they're just a conduit for the transmission or routing of pirated files, nor are they liable for copies made during automatic caching processes (which should come as a major relief to search engines such as Google ... as long as no corporation with deep pockets challenges this portion of the act). If someone accesses such cached material without the knowledge of the ISP, that's also fine, even if some sort of hyperlink or pointer to the material has been generated.

The DMCA also lays out a 'notice and takedown' system to deal in an efficient and orderly fashion with potential instances of infringement by ISP users. While copyright holders are required to use this system, it does provide a quick and expedient way to serve notice to alleged infringers that your copyright has been violated. If ISPs act quickly to deal with such notices, their financial liability for violations is limited considerably. The system also makes it much easier to obtain a subpoena to identify ISP users who post allegedly infringing material.

If the person or company that posted the offending file in the first place takes exception to the takedown notice, the DMCA also describes a procedure for counter-notification and the restoration of the file to the network.

The DMCA and the record companies

The DMCA had a lot to do with the end of the three-year-long MP3 party that raged on the Web until early 2001.

Until mid-1999, when the first big lawsuits against sites such as MP3.com (which had been amassing large libraries of downloadable music) started to appear, it was actually possible to find MP3s of popular music on the Web. Pre-DMCA, the larger online music sites had argued that there was a large degree of ambiguity over whether or not posting an MP3, or streaming a song over a system such as RealPlayer or Windows Media Player, meant that the poster and/or streamer had to pay royalties to record companies and recording artists. The DMCA, however, states that section

114 of the Copyright Act applies to streaming and webcasting, and it redefines certain types of programming as 'interactive services' subject to the copyright holder's exclusive rights.

DMCA issues

> 24. *Amount an eBook customer may be fined for a backup not permitted by the Publisher: $250,000*
> 25. *Amount of time that customer might spend in jail: 5 years*
> 29. *Average sentence for committing rape: 5 years[13]*
>
> —THE ANTI-DMCA INDEX

Fair use

Fair use and intellectual property protection exist in inverse proportion to each other—an increase in one means a decrease in the other. Many critics of the DMCA argue that it goes too far in the direction of rights protection, and that the category of fair use has been badly compromised.

A major problem is that the anti-circumvention clause of the DMCA means that even after a work is in the public domain, it can't be accessed legally from a copy that has been digitally protected. Digital protection schemes raise other issues as well—how is a library to cope with hypothetical digital works that automatically erase themselves after a given number of viewings, or a given time period? Or, more immediately, given the overall movement to a licensing paradigm from a sales paradigm for digital commodities, how can libraries continue to operate if they're required to pay ongoing licensing fees for digital works on deposit?

Databases

According to some analysts, the situation could also become worse, especially where databases are concerned.

Under conventional copyright laws, many databases do not qualify for copyright protection because the selection and arrangement of data is not necessarily a creative act in the legal sense. (Until 1991, when the Supreme Court decided in the Feist case that only databases in which some creative effort had been exerted were protected, databases had been protected legally under what was known as the 'Sweat of the Brow Doctrine.' It specified that if the owner had expended 'sweat'—effort—in the creation of the database, it was protected by law.[14]) Even when a database qualifies for copyright, it doesn't mean that the data *in* the database can't be used by another party in another context.

While the US was putting the DMCA together, it looked very carefully at the copyright protection for databases that had been implemented in the European Union in 1996. These regulations specify that any party that devotes substantial resources to the compilation of a database can legally prevent anyone else from extracting or reusing all or 'a substantial part' of the database's contents for a period of 15 years. Because spending more money on the database gives its creator the right to extend the term of copyright, the contents of a database in the EU can, in theory, be under indefinite protection. (This is directly antithetical to the argument that organizations such as the Public Library of Science have been making for the need for free, publicly accessible databases—see 'Blinded by Science' in the previous chapter).

The ramifications of such a law are considerable. Because database contents can be protected indefinitely, the concept of fair use disappears entirely. Databases protected by such legislation can actually be a drain on the existing contents of the public domain, as images or text are catalogued and sealed behind a barrier of revenue-generating copyright laws. While some might see this as a 'repurposing' of legacy material, others see it as a potentially huge erosion of the creative works that are publicly accessible.

Due in part to protests from members of the academic community, the section of the DMCA dealing with the protection of databases was deleted at the last minute. But at some point (likely not that far away) the legislation will undoubtedly reemerge, given the pressure from database creators who have argued that there's little incentive to create valuable databases without strong legal protection for them.

The shrinking public domain

Though the database section of the DMCA was dropped (if only temporarily), the extension of copyright terms for an additional 20 years creates a significant gap in works in the public domain—and means that further royalties must be paid. The adaptation of existing public domain works for proprietary platforms can also produce bizarre results ...

Case study: Electronic Alice

Consider the case of Adobe's adaptation of *Alice in Wonderland* for its new eBook Reader. The initial set of permissions attached to Adobe's Alice were restrictive in the extreme:

Under the 'Copy' heading, the permissions said: 'No text selections can be copied from this book to the clipboard.' Under 'Print,' it indicated: 'No printing is permitted on this book.' Under 'Lend,' users were told: 'This book cannot be lent or given to someone else.' Under 'Give': 'This book cannot be given to someone else.' And finally, under 'Read Aloud,' the permissions page asserted: 'This book cannot be read aloud.'[15]

It took Lawrence Lessig, a professor at Stanford Law School and a specialist in the issues surrounding digital intellectual property, to unravel what Adobe *really* meant by these clauses.

When Adobe says 'lend' it doesn't mean lend; it is referring to a function that enables users to forgo the rights to a book temporarily, while someone else has them. 'Give' does not mean give; when Adobe says 'give,' it is referring to a function that enables users to permanently forgo the rights to a particular book, when they 'give' it to someone else. And when Adobe says 'print' (as in 'No printing is permitted on this book'), it doesn't mean printing on the book; it apparently means printing of the book.[16]

As Lessig wryly suggests, this policy represents an entirely new use of the word 'permissions' because it doesn't actually allow one to do very much. While Adobe changed some of its permissions due to public protest (users are now permitted 'to copy 10 text selections every 10 days' and 'to print 10 pages every 10 days' and the book 'can be read aloud') the e-Alice still 'cannot be lent' and 'cannot be given.'

Lessig accords Adobe a large degree of slack, crediting it with the attempt to build 'into its code equivalents to the freedoms that exist in real space' rather than focus on creating a system that permits near-prefect control over copyrighted materials. He also applauds it for building its restrictions into its software rather than its hardware, which, he argues, will better enable the development of a diverse marketplace. Lessig's musings end with a call for an industry-wide striving for balance between the rights of creators and the rights of users, but with the corporate call for intellectual property control on one side and the advocates of the 'free' Internet on the other, the odds of his voice being drowned out in the ensuing mad tea party will be very high.[17]

Hobbles on scientific research: DeCSS

Unlike the video tapes that they're quickly replacing, Digital Video Discs (DVDs) have a built-in data protection system. It's called—as unimaginatively as you might expect—the Content Scramble System (CSS).

CSS is not exactly a copy protection system. In fact, it provides little or nothing in the way of protection against copying. What it *does* do is prevent DVDs from playing in 'unauthorized' players. In their wisdom, the designers of the CSS protocol divided the world up into numbered regions, with each region assigned a code. DVDs with one regional code won't play in DVD players that have a different regional code. The movie industry isn't afraid of people making bootleg players; rather, its concern is that mass illegal shipments of DVDs will find their way from one region into another before the film has been officially released on DVD there. (Of course, anyone with a DVD burner can [illegally] duplicate a CSS-protected DVD, and that duplicate will work just fine in any DVD player from the same region.)

As is often the case with encryption schemes, it wasn't too long before a group of smartass teenagers (who referred to themselves using the spooky-cool acronym MoRE—'Masters of Reverse Engineering') figured out how to crack CSS. In this case, the point man was 15-year-old Jon Johansen of Larvik, Norway. Johansen posted a link to the program on his father Per's Web site in November 1999, and it began to circulate on bulletin boards and in chat rooms. Somewhere between 20,000 and 30,000 people downloaded the program over the next few months. In January 2000, following up on charges filed by the Motion Picture Association of America (MPAA), the Norwegian police showed up, seized the family computers, and charged Johansens Jr. and Sr. under the European intellectual property laws for posting and advertising DeCSS and for cracking the CSS system (though this latter act was actually accomplished by a German friend of Johansen's).[18]

The Norwegian government wants to fine the Johansens and throw them in jail for two years. In the meantime, Johansen received Norway's most prestigious prize for high-school students, and has been courted by several large computer companies.

But why did Johansen and his friends build DeCSS in the first place? Not surprisingly, Johansen is a Linux user; the development of DeCSS was part of an attempt to build DVD support for Linux and other free operating systems.[19] (Since Linux was incapable of reading a DVD, Johansen and his friends had to compile their code as a Windows program in order to test it.[20])

In an interview with Linux World, Johansen said 'This had nothing to do with copying, because encryption does not prevent copying—which the DVD CCA [Copy Control Association] and MPAA are claiming. And everybody knows that even if something is encrypted you can still copy it if the reading of the data goes through decryption.' He also pointed out that reverse engineering (taking apart a commercial software product in order to understand its functions or to improve on it) is crucial not only to the process of creating alternatives to commercial software, but also to creating *compatibility with* commercial software, such as Microsoft Windows.[21] Moreover, Norway has a law that specifically allows reverse engineering to provide compatibility between computer programs.[22] The DMCA itself has a similar provision, which has forced DeCSS case prosecuters to rely on the argument that this 'is really about computer hackers and the tools of digital piracy.'[23]

The actual mechanics of copying a movie from a DVD bear out Johansen's claim. First of all, DeCSS was hardly the first tool capable of ripping images from DVDs; it was just the first one that functioned purely on the level of software (previous decryption programs relied on hardware to do the decrypting, and subsequently copied the video stream). More importantly, copying raw video onto a hard disk is a cumbersome process. Most DVDs contain between seven and nine files of one gigabyte in size. It's far cheaper for potential pirates to leave the data on the DVD and physically copy it than it is to fill up hard drives with movies, and much easier than laboriously chunking the movie down into smaller pieces in other file formats for online distribution or copying piecemeal onto CD-ROMs.[24] Even with newer digital compression schemes like DivX <www.divx.com>, which wasn't around in usable form when DeCSS was written, ripping movies is still a process that consumes large amounts of time and resources.

When someone finally did build a Linux DVD player, it was substantially indebted to the code that Johansen and his friends actually wrote. LiVid—the Linux Video Project <www.linuxvideo.org>—is actually a collection of related video and DVD-related subprojects. It contains segments of the code from DeCSS, and would have taken much longer to produce without it. You'd think DVD makers would have welcomed another entire class of computer users as prospective purchasers of DVDs, but the

Reverse engineering is crucial to not only the process of creating alternatives to commercial software, but also to creating compatibility with commercial software

film industry's reaction indicates that they're more concerned about the proliferation of player platforms breaking their monopoly on DVD hardware.

But the MPAA didn't stop its litigating with the Johansens. It went after a number of people who posted the software to their Web sites—or even linked to places where it could be found. The most prominent of these was Eric Corley, aka 'Emmanuel Goldstein,' publisher of the long-running hacker journal 2600. Early in 2000 his magazine was sued by the MPAA, first for posting the DeCSS software for download on its site, and then for simply linking to it once it had been physically removed from the site. By August the US District Court had delivered a 93-page ruling against 2600 that was subsequently appealed. That appeal is still in progress, and the case has featured none other than Edward Felten and Jon Johansen among its witnesses.

Not that the ruling slowed anyone in the pro-DeCSS community down. 2600 managed to obey the letter of the law by simply posting a plain-text list of URLs (not active links) that could be pasted into a browser window with one or two mouse clicks. DeCSS sites both inside and outside the US proliferated like mad.

One of the most interesting of these is the Gallery of DeCSS Descramblers <www-2.cs.cmu.edu/~dst/DeCSS/Gallery/index.html>, maintained by Dr. David S. Touretzky, a professor in the Computer Science Department at Carnegie Mellon University. The Gallery contains the DeCSS code in many different versions, including translations into haiku, film, dramatic readings and musical settings, printed T-shirts, and even as a prime number. Touretzky's purpose is to point to the absurdity of the ruling against the DeCSS code. He created a Web site to explore the following question—'If code that can be directly compiled and executed may be suppressed under the DMCA, as Judge Kaplan asserts in his preliminary ruling, but a textual description of the same algorithm may not be suppressed, then where exactly should the line be drawn?'—and, ultimately, he concludes that legally distinguishing computer code from other forms of written expression is untenable.[25]

To underline his conviction that the ruling is a threat to free speech as constitutionally defined, Touretzky has explicitly identified his site as an academic publication. But this is not just a matter of semantics; it's a decision with substantial real-world implications. In an interview with Salon, Touretzky stated:

The judge decided to invent a new category of speech that does not enjoy First Amendment protection. Besides the old standards (libel, fraud, obscenity, incitement to riot and copyright infringement), the court's new category is, essentially, 'anything that potentially threatens the profits of Time Warner and Disney.' That ought to scare the hell out of everyone. If the government can suppress information that is true fact—as opposed to speech that has a direct effect like inciting people to riot—then we're all in trouble.[26]

Nor is Touretzky alone in his concerns. The DeCSS and Edward Felten cases are only the beginning of the problems the DMCA poses for scientists and researchers. Though they've stopped threatening Felten and his associates with legal action, the SDMI and RIAA haven't really moved from their initial stance that the writing, delivering at a conference and distributing of an academic paper describing the reverse engineering of a data protection is just as illegal as the creation of software capable of cracking that scheme.

As a result, the DMCA affects not only scientists but academics, writers and journalists as well. Because it's possible to protect any form of data with digital encryption, it is therefore possible to use the DMCA to prevent people from viewing documents that they'd normally be able to access, such as annual reports, the results of surveys revealing scandalous or unpopular results and scientific research with results that prove unfavorable to those who commissioned the research. This legislation is dangerous precisely to the extent that it removes corporations from public accountability.[27]

Implications for cryptography

The scientists most directly affected by the DeCSS ruling are cryptographers and computer security experts. Cryptography (protecting data by translating it into a cipher that can be decoded only by those who have the correct key) isn't just about protecting private conversations from prying eyes; it's essential to the ongoing success of sectors of our society that may seem surprising at first—sectors as diverse as e-commerce and the human rights community. Commercial sites need systems to guarantee their customers that crucial data such as credit card numbers and other personal identifiers are well protected. Without the ongoing efforts of cryptographers to ensure that secure systems continue to improve and that potential breaches are patched, a successful future for e-commerce would be a dubious proposition at best. Ditto for the success of human

Because it's possible to protect any form of data with digital encryption, it is therefore possible to use the DMCA to prevent people from viewing documents that they'd normally be able to access.

rights activists. Without the ability to protect the names and vital information of potential rights abuse victims, or to credibly communicate bulletins to each other (which requires digital signatures), the task of human rights workers would be much more difficult.

During the 2600 trial, several prominent cryptographers submitted briefs expressing their misgivings about how the DMCA rules will affect their profession. While the DMCA ostensibly accounts for the exceptions necessary to conduct serious cryptographic and security-related research, the cryptographers who submitted the brief state that 'in the cramped interpretation of the District Court, the "good faith encryption research" exception applies to virtually no one,' and that 'not only will they be prevented from testing the strength of existing cryptosystems, cryptographers will be hamstrung when publishing mathematics that might also be used to cryptographically protect copyrighted material.'[28]

The brief ends with a call for openness:

Only in an open environment, where cryptographers ... can perform tests in a peer review of encryption technologies, can cryptographers or the public place trust in those that pass the review. While the District Court likens publication of DeCSS to dissemination of the combination to a bank's safe, is the bank more secure if its lock succumbs to the first visitor who twiddles the knob to zero, despite that combination's never being published? Cryptographic research can steer users of encryption, including publishers, away from such weak locks.

Reverse engineering

If the plight of the cryptographers doesn't move you, consider that other kinds of scientists will be affected by the DMCA. Most computer scientists and various and sundry engineers, programmers and so on will occasionally find that they have to reverse-engineer a piece of software. There are several reasons for this, including learning how to make the program work with other software, fixing bugs in the program itself or simply trying to ascertain how the program operates. Needless to say, all these actions are potential violations of the DMCA.

As is the case with cryptography, the DMCA's exception clause for reverse engineering is far too limiting to be of real use, because it only allows for the attempt to make the program operate with other software (interoperability). Moreover, the DMCA makes it illegal to disseminate information obtained during the reverse-engineering process, even in an academic context.

The demonizing of libraries

Are librarians members of a weird fringe cult poised on the brink of some kind of orgiastic, information-based digital apocalypse? Apparently, parts of the Association of American Publishers think so. Letting people borrow books for free, after all, is wildly subversive and perhaps even anti-American. Judith Platt, a spokeswoman for the AAP, says 'They [librarians]'ve got their radical factions, like the Ruby Ridge or Waco types,' who want to share all content for free.[29] Roll in the tanks, folks: I've heard enough.

Much of the usefulness (and *raison d'être*) of libraries relies heavily on the availability of public-domain works, which places them at odds with the publishing community in an explicit way. Librarians lobbied long and hard to get exemption from the 20-year term extension of the DMCA.

Some modernizing concessions were included in the DMCA. Though standard library practice calls for three copies of any deposited work—an archival copy, a master copy and a use copy—a 1976 law prohibited libraries from making more than one copy of a work. The DMCA has amended the earlier law to allow for contemporary practice and a limited digitization of texts.

As is the case with ISPs, the liability of libraries for unwittingly transmitting digitized copies of copyrighted works has some limitations. But these limitations should prevent further cases like *Kathleen R vs. City of Livermore*, in which the parent of a child who used computers at a public library to download porn off the Net sued the library to force the installation of blocking software on the library's computers. The plaintiff argued that the use of public funds to pay for children's access to pornography constituted a 'waste of public funds,' that the library's refusal to block Net access constituted a 'nuisance' and that they were liable for the use of computers on their premises. The parent lost in the trial court, and appealed. The parent lost again in the California Court of Appeal.[30]

Distance education

Educational markets are the bread-and-butter of many companies that rely on digital licensing. With expanded protection for digital intellectual property, it's reasonable to assume that there should be expanded exemptions for schools, libraries and other institutions offering electronic distance education services to allow them to continue to operate ... but there aren't.

Are librarians members of a weird fringe cult poised on the brink of some kind of orgiastic, information-based digital apocalypse? Apparently, parts of the Association of American Publishers think so.

All these examples focus on what *could* happen if the DMCA continues to exist unmodified. This is not to suggest that the existence of legislation hasn't already had a significant impact on the Internet in particular and contemporary society in general. Let's backtrack for a moment and look at the two most important DMCA-related events to date: the ongoing Dmitri Skylarov case and the history of Napster itself.

Oh, those Russians: Dmitri Skylarov

On July 16, 2001, at a hackers' convention in Las Vegas, 26-year-old Russian programmer and PhD student Dmitri Skylarov was arrested under the DMCA on charges of distributing a product designed to circumvent copyright protection measures.

Skylarov works for a company called ElcomSoft, makers of a little piece of software with a big name, the Advanced eBook Processor (AEBPR). This software, which only works on legitimately purchased eBooks, permits eBook owners to translate from Adobe's secure eBook format into the more common Portable Document Format (PDF). This would allow the owners of eBooks to do the following, all of which can be prevented by the original format:

1. read it on a computer or PDA other than the one on which the eBook was first downloaded

2. continue to access a work that you've purchased when the 'original' version downloaded is not accessible because of hard disk failure or incompatibility with the operating system of the computer on which the eBook was first downloaded

3. guarantee forward compatibility for the file if the particular device for which the eBook was purchased becomes obsolete

4. print out an eBook to read it on paper

5. read an eBook on an alternative operating system such as Linux (Adobe's format works only on Macs and MS-Windows PCs)

6. loan it to a friend

7. copy snippets of a work to include in a school project, a critique, academic research or a parody

8. have your computer read your eBook out loud (i.e., with text-to-speech software), which is particularly important for visually-impaired people[31]

Starting to sound like the DeCSS case, isn't it? The legal issues may appear similar: does circumventing copy protection allow consumers their fair use rights under U.S. copyright law, or does it simply make it easier to pirate Adobe eBooks?

There is a major difference, however. The DeCSS and Felten cases were civil lawsuits, with private entities suing each other for the cessation of activities and financial compensation. The Skylarov case, on the other hand, involved a criminal charge, and could have resulted in a prison sentence. (Note: During the final editing of this book, criminal charges against Sklyarov were dropped, provided he agreed to testify against his employer ... though he will likely testify *for*.[32] Curiouser and curiouser.

The matter was complicated further because Skylarov is a Russian national, and Russia has no law similar to the DMCA. An FAQ on the EFF's Web site says,

The general presumption is that acts of copyright infringement and related alleged crimes which occur completely outside of the US cannot be litigated under US copyright law unless Congress intended the particular law to apply outside of US territory. It's not clear that Congress intended the anti-circumvention provisions of the DMCA to apply to acts done outside of the US.[33]

Jennifer Granick, clinical director at the Stanford Law School Center for Internet and Society, observes that 'the DMCA says that companies can use technology to take away fair use, but programmers can't use technology to take fair use back. Now the government is spending taxpayer money putting people from other countries in jail to protect multinational corporate profits at the expense of free speech.'[34]

If Skylarov were convicted on charges of trafficking and conspiracy to traffic in a copyright circumvention device, he would have faced 25 years in prison and a potential fine of up to $2,250,000. ElcomSoft corporation still faces the same potential fine.

Until the charges were dropped, Skylarov was in a bizarre limbo. Adobe Systems, who brought the initial complaint against Skylarov, withdrew their complaint due to a blizzard of negative publicity, and, along with the Electronic Frontier Foundation, were actually recommending Skylarov's release because they no longer saw it as being in the best interests of the industry[35] (or their relations with the public, in all likelihood). But because this was a criminal case, prosecution continued without their support until the charges were dropped.

'The DMCA says that companies can use technology to take away fair use, but programmers can't use technology to take fair use back. Now the government is spending taxpayer money putting people from other countries in jail to protect multinational corporate profits at the expense of free speech.'

Napster was the
flashpoint for the
current interest
in P2P.

Facing the music: A brief history of Napster

There's no doubt that Napster was the flashpoint for the current interest in P2P. By now, everyone knows the early history: founded in May 1999, Napster was the brainchild of Shawn Fanning, then an undergraduate at Northeastern University who was looking for an easy way for himself and his dorm roommate to share MP3s with their friends. After a single term where he found himself working on the Napster code more than his studies, he dropped out, incorporated the company, and moved it to Redwood City, California.

By early 1999, the recording industry had already decided that MP3s were a big problem. Though the format itself has always been legal—and zealously defended by its inventors at the Fraunhofer Institute <www.iis.fhg.de/amm/index.html>, who, to complicate matters, are now beginning to seek licensing fees for the use of their invention—its contents are often duplicates of commercial music, which many parties consider to be illegal. In October 1998 the RIAA had filed a lawsuit against Diamond Multimedia, makers of the Rio portable MP3 player. Though the RIAA lost that suit in June 1999, by that point Napster had presented a bigger fish to fry.

In December 1999, when the RIAA filed suit, it seemed that everyone who had an interest in the music business descended on Napster in a massive lawsuit: Universal Music (Seagram Co. Ltd), BMG (Bertelsmann AG), Sony Music Warner Music Group and EMI Group (AOL/Time Warner). In April 2000, musicians Metallica and Dr Dre weighed in with suits of their own against Napster ... and Yale, Indiana University and USC for not blocking access to it.

Many Metallica fans saw this gesture as more than slightly hypocritical, as the band has maintained a designated taping area for fan 'bootlegs' at its live concerts for years. Initial statements from motormouth Metallica drummer Lars Ulrich were also met with considerable skepticism. 'It is sickening to know that our art is being traded like a commodity rather than the art that it is,' read the initial Metallica press release, to which The Industry Standard reporter Michelle Goldberg replied, 'Wait a minute—isn't Metallica's problem that its music *isn't* being treated as a commodity, i.e., as something that needs to be paid for?'[36] Subsequent parodies of the band's legal hijinks, such as the ongoing, excruciatingly funny 'Napster Bad!' series at Camp Chaos <www.campchaos.com>, coupled with the frenzied rate at which Metallica MP3s continue to circulate on Gnutella and elsewhere, indicate a seriously disgusted fan base.

Since then, suing Napster has become something of a national pastime. In March 2001, EMusic (a subscription-based downloading company) and the producers of the Grammy Awards filed separate suits, the former claiming that Napster was letting its users trade songs that it had the license to distribute, and the latter attacking Napster for letting a bootlegged performance by Elton John and Eminem appear on the system.

In late July 2000, Judge Marilyn Hall Patel issued an injunction ordering Napster to remove all copyrighted songs from its system. Two days after the injunction, Napster appealed the order to the 9th Circuit Court of Appeals on the grounds that it would prevent it from operating. The order was stayed until late in the trial, though the RIAA asked the 9th Circuit Court of Appeals to reinstate the injunction in October 2000.

At this point something happened that seemed surprising at the time, but is utterly predictable in retrospect. Bertelsmann AG and Napster announced that they had formed an alliance to develop a subscription-based P2P system, and that once the service had launched, Bertelsmann would be dropping out of the lawsuit.

The RIAA and the other labels were guardedly optimistic about this turn of events. Hilary Rosen, CEO of the RIAA, said:

This case has always been about sending a message to the technology and venture capital communities that consumers, creators and innovators will best flourish when copyright interests are respected ... It has never been about peer-to-peer technology itself, which can be implemented legitimately, as today's announcement confirms.[37]

Executives from the four remaining major record labels in the lawsuit were invited by Bertelsmann and Napster to participate in the creation of a new service, but the labels remained standoffish into the new year. AOL/Time Warner officials said they were waiting to see a valid business model; and Vivendi Universal CEO Jean-Marie Messier said his company wouldn't settle with Napster if a court ruled against them, because he felt confident that they could get better terms from the ruling. Speculation was (and remains) that what's keeping the other labels from settling is equity in Napster itself. The Napster brand name still carries a lot of cachet and user recognition, though the audience, which once numbered over 8.5 million users daily, has dropped drastically because of the lawsuit (a matter I'll return to later, when we examine the fallout of this case).[38]

On February 12, 2001, the party was over. The 9th Circuit Court of Appeals ruled that Napster knew its users were violating copyright laws while using its P2P service. The smoking gun was a memo by Napster's co-founder Sean Parker stating that Napster employees needed to remain ignorant about the 'real names' of the users because 'they are exchanging pirated music.'[39]

In early March, District Judge Marilyn Patel gave Napster five days to outline plans to begin policing its network. The entire burden wasn't placed upon the file-sharing company itself, as the injunction called for dividing the responsibilities for policing the system between Napster and the RIAA—the RIAA had to identify violations, and Napster was to have three days to filter the song off of its system. But by the end of the month lawyers from the RIAA were grousing that Napster was dragging its heels, and that most of the 675,000 songs and 8 million files that the industry had identified hadn't been removed.[40]

Despite the RIAA's complaints, Napster was doing a lot to remove offending songs from its network, including rewriting its software. The drop in the service's traffic rates speak for themselves. A Webnoize study said that the average number of songs shared per person dropped from 220 in March 2001 to 37 the following month, and that the overall number of songs traded dropped from an estimated 2.79 billion in February to 1.59 billion in April.[41]

In early June it became evident that deals were being made as well. Napster announced penning an agreement with MusicNet, a music licensing company set up by Bertelsmann/BMG, Warner Music Group, EMI Group and RealNetworks. According to the Standard, this deal gave Napster access to approximately 40% of the global music market, contingent on its reinvention of itself as a paid music service.[42] Sony and Vivendi, the holdout record companies, had already set up Duet, a potential rival service, but are apparently in talks with MusicNet to join forces.[43]

But as good as this news was, it didn't make any of Napster's legal woes go away. No one dropped out of the lawsuit, and its users were continuing to flee like rats leaving a sinking ship.

Napster was finally ordered to cease its operations by Friday, July 28, 2001. On Sunday, July 1, Napster went down, ostensibly because of difficulties with its new file identification technology and its authentication database. This occurred only four days after Napster had locked out all previous versions of its software and required users to download a new version. A few days later, Judge Patel ruled that the service had to stay down until it could prevent unauthorized songs from appearing on its network. Metallica and Dr Dre settled out of court for an undisclosed sum of money, though they seem to have lost more than a few fans in the process.

The last bit of the old 'free' Napster disappeared when Napster announced plans to abandon MP3s altogether. The new-look Napster will split its offerings between a proprietary '.nap' format, which it will use for the music it has licensed from independent music labels, and the MusicNet proprietary format. Napster is working on software that will convert users' MP3s to the new .nap format before putting them online, which should help them to ensure compliance, but raises questions about whether or not consumers will be interested.[44]

Napster subsequently lost its appeal to the 9th Circuit Court of Appeals, leaving as its only option an appeal to the US Supreme Court. Late in September, the beleaguered company announced a major breakthrough— an agreement to pay $26 million in damages to publishers and songwriters, plus future royalties to music publishers amounting to one third of the royalties that Napster will pay to content owners (a substantially better deal than publishers get for offline music). Once again, though, the labels are continuing with their own litigation.

Some analysts remain puzzled by this deal, because Napster has yet to announce what its subscription fees will be when it relaunches, or how much of its revenue will go to the owners of the music itself. Aram Sinnreich of Jupiter research says '[The deal] says absolutely nothing about what business model [Napster] is using. It sidesteps the issue of how you can have a royalty model based on a percentage of revenue' that can support the kind of subscription levels Napster is planning.[45]

As of this writing (end of September 2001), Napster remains down for the count.

The last bit of the old 'free' Napster disappeared when Napster announced plans to abandon MP3s altogether.

7 Life after Napster

As the Napster saga illustrates, the future of peer-to-peer file-sharing is entwined, for better or worse, with copyright law.

—FRED VON LOHMANN

The passing of the first incarnation of Napster has changed many aspects of life online, and particularly those issues that prospective P2P businesses must consider before they hang out their virtual shingle.

One of the most cogent analyses to date is lawyer Fred von Lohmann's white paper 'IAAL: Peer-to-Peer File Sharing and Copyright After Napster.' (The acronym 'IAAL' is geek humor at its most abstruse: 'IANAL' is a standard abbreviation for 'I Am Not A Lawyer'; Lohmann, on the other hand, actually *is* a lawyer.) von Lohmann describes in detail both the kinds of infringement that a P2P system is likely to commit and the best ways to avoid making those infringements, making this document useful for everyone from engineers to potential investors.[1]

Lohmann's first observation is that any act of P2P file-sharing 'inevitably implicates copyright law.' Because they are 'fixed' works—i.e., they can be stored in a specific form—digital files usually qualify for copyright status from the moment of their creation. The act of sharing those files over a network constitutes reproduction, distribution and possibly even 'performance' (under US copyright law, merely transmitting a copyrighted work to the public is a performance). If the files aren't in the public domain, or the copyright owner hasn't given explicit permission for their use in this manner, or the sharing doesn't constitute fair use, then a royalty has to be paid, or an infringement has been committed.

The people who swap copyrighted files commit what is known as *direct infringement*, because they are trading copyrighted works. Napster and other companies that maintain P2P networks aren't guilty of direct infringement because they don't store the files themselves—their users do. All they do is provide the connections between users. But copyright law also provides for other, more circuitous kinds of infringement: *contributory infringement* and *vicarious infringement*. The Napster case was the first application of these types of infringement to a P2P system.

A *contributory infringer* must not only have knowledge that a direct infringement has taken place, but must also somehow aid and abet that infringement. Napster's internal e-mails, combined with promotional shots of the service in use listing copyrighted files, the use of the service by its own executives and a list of infringing songs provided by the RIAA, established that they had knowledge of the infringements. Their provision of the facilities for song swapping constituted aiding and abetting the infringement.

A *vicarious infringer* is someone who 'has the right and ability to supervise the infringing activity and also has a direct financial interest in such activities.' Both requirements have been interpreted very loosely in the Napster case. In the eyes of the court, the ability to ban users from the system constituted control, and the potential to expand their user base by allowing infringement was enough to equal a direct financial benefit. It's also worth knowing that ignorance is not bliss, because knowledge of the infringing activities is not required to establish vicarious infringement.

'Any act of P2P file-sharing 'inevitably implicates copyright law.'

Best defenses

So what's a poor P2P company to do if it's taken to court? von Lohmann suggests three possible defenses.

No direct infringement

This is the least likely of the three possible defense strategies, because it relies on proving that there's no indirect infringement by way of arguing that there's no *direct* infringement. Because P2P networks are so diffuse and difficult to monitor, this may be almost impossible to prove, except in cases where there's a proprietary file type and explicit monitoring process in place (though even in such a case, it's possible to 'wrap' illegal files inside shells that look like other, more innocuous file types).

If a company can
control direct
infringement but
doesn't because
it's financially
benefiting from it,
the fact that there
are non-infringing
uses for the tech-
nology isn't worth
a spit in the wind.

The Betamax defense

Napster defendants had originally hoped to use the 1983 Betamax defense, in which the Supreme Court stated that as long as a technology had 'substantial noninfringing uses' it couldn't be outlawed.

The Napster case has eviscerated much of the usefulness of this defense, because the court found that it can't be used in relation to vicarious infringement. In other words, if a company can control direct infringement but doesn't because it's financially benefiting from it (especially after someone has provided the company with the knowledge that infringement is taking place), the fact that there are non-infringing uses for the technology isn't worth a spit in the wind.

Safe harbors

Under the DMCA, Section 512 of the Copyright Act provides a series of small loopholes for online service providers in the event of copyright infringement by their users (I mentioned these earlier when talking about an ISP's liability for the infringements committed by its customers). These exceptions work in the following cases: if the service provider has cached the files; if it has passed them through its network in a transitory fashion; if it is unwittingly storing files on behalf of users; or if it has somehow pointed to such material via hyperlinks or a similar method. In addition, the service provider must meet the following conditions:

- the adoption and reasonable implementation of a policy of terminating the accounts of subscribers who are repeat infringers, and it must notify its users of the same

- the use of 'standard technical measures' that have been widely implemented on the basis of industry-wide consensus

- designation of a 'copyright agent' to receive notices of alleged copyright infringement, register the agent with the Copyright Office, and place relevant contact information for the agent on its Web site

- willingness to remove or disable access to the infringing material upon receiving notification of infringement from a copyright owner

- a genuine unawareness of infringement, not just a willingness to turn a blind eye

- the ISP must not receive a direct financial benefit from infringing activity if they're capable of controlling it[2]

Because this law was drafted shortly before the P2P explosion, most P2P services will have difficulty qualifying under their restrictions. For that matter, Web caching as practiced by Google and Akamai may also constitute an infringement, depending on who decides to sue and when ... which only shows that the law will probably be playing a frustrating game of catch-up with software development for the foreseeable future.

Don't infringe

The best defense for a company against being sued is to not conduct business in such a way that will get them sued in the first place. To this end, von Lohmann provides a number of suggestions.

First, and most obviously, try to build a P2P system with non-infringing uses, and don't infringe directly yourself by storing files for users, or using someone else's trademark in your company name (Apple Soup has already been forced by Apple Computer to change its name to FlyCode). Sometimes, as in the case of Hotline, the pirates will find ways of using the system anyway. But if a company can establish out of the gate that there are legitimate uses for their software, they're probably going to be all right—at least until they receive a cease-and-desist letter from someone who knows their copyrights are being infringed. In any event, it's prudent not to build the revenue stream around anything that's potentially an infringement.

Second, potential P2P providers have two options for dealing with their user base, neither of which is particularly palatable: total control or total anarchy. The former means that everything is above board, but provides little incentive for users other than those within closed corporate environments. The latter means that there's precious little possibility of producing anything like a conventional business plan out of it—Gnutella marches on, but it's unlikely that anyone will make much money off of it ... certainly not AOL, who disowned their mutant offspring long ago (see page 155).

Next, to avoid vicarious liability, it's probably smarter to conceive of a P2P model where the product is marketed as a stand-alone piece of software rather than a service. A company that isn't selling a service has no users to monitor, and therefore less responsibility. Companies like BearShare, which make software capable of searching Gnutella, are probably banking hard on this one.

Plausible deniability of the actions of your end-users goes hand-in-hand with this. If a P2P product does have illegal uses, it's not wise to advertise or acknowledge them. This also means that spyware that reports back on users can create problems. Sure, it's marketable information, and may lead to advertising revenue, but what good is it if it provides enough information to scupper a plausible deniability defense?

Openness is also an advantage. If a particular P2P system develops its software on an open-source model, and the code becomes widely distributed, it will be difficult for anyone to launch a suit against the software's copyright holder based on notions of financial benefit or control. (LimeWire, the makers of one of the most popular Gnutella clients, has just open-sourced their software at Limewire.org). It would be possible, in fact, to open-source the potentially litigious bits of code and base a business model around another proprietary section of the same product, such as the search engine or the advertising module. This modular approach also makes it possible to limit the kinds of controlling actions that a court might order a company to take.

The Napster aftermath: All your base redux

Unless we approve, your idea will not be permitted. It will not be allowed.[3]

—ATTR. RIAA CEO HILARY ROSEN

So who were the losers in the great online music debate? The answer seems to be just about everyone, with the possible exception of the record labels.

Whether or not sales of CDs are down because of music file-sharing in general and Napster in particular is a subject of hot debate. A 2000 study by retail tracker SoundScan suggested that CD sales near universities—acknowledged hotbeds of file sharing—dropped 4% over the previous two years ... but that the industry itself saw overall growth of about 20% during the same period.[4]

But there's more than one way to read data (or, to use the famous coinage, to lie with statistics). C|Net reports that 'the drop in college music store sales was more pronounced in 1998 than in 1999—a year before Napster was written,' and suggests that the advent of online retail is also cutting into sales through bricks-and-mortar stores. Further, the drop in sales of CD singles, cassettes and cassette singles has more to do with the preference for digital technology and full-length albums over overpriced singles than it does with file sharing.[5] Another difficulty in assessing whether file sharing has a negative impact on record sales is that, as with software companies, music companies tend to see pirated copies as lost revenue, whereas these wouldn't necessarily translate into direct sales if the means to pirate weren't available.

The International Federation of the Phonographic Industry (IFPI) says that CD piracy grew by 25% in 2000, and estimates that one out of three recordings sold worldwide is pirated, for a grand total of 1.8 billion illegal recordings (CDs and cassettes) sold over the course of the year. While the IFPI blames the increase in illegal CD copies on cheaply available CD burners and organized crime, it also refers to the Internet as a '100 per cent pirate medium.'[6] That's it: in the eyes of the IFPI, you're ALL criminals. Even you, Mom. Sorry.

Musicians are usually the first to complain about the business side of the music business. And, sure enough, as soon as it was obvious that Napster was down for the count, the temporary alliance that had been struck between the labels and (some) songwriters broke up, and the normal chaos returned. At a May 2001 Congressional hearing on digital music, while label execs were busy extolling the virtues of their own proprietary P2P systems (MusicNet and Duet) the songwriters and music publishers accused the labels of attempting to short-shrift them on copyright payments.

The process of paying royalties to musicians is complicated because of the vast number of publishing agencies and the lack of any central clearing house.[7] But many musicians are arguing that centralization is the problem.

What's wrong with the music industry

The plethora of new online music services in the late 90s offered the potential for an interesting, diverse competitive market. Briefly, it was possible to conceive of a world where the artists were in control, selling music directly to the consumers and bypassing the conglomerates that keep prices high and products scarce. That was the vision of musicians like Chuck D of Public Enemy, Courtney Love of Hole, producer Steve Albini and countless others working in alternative music or trying to break in (or out) of the big-league labels.

Chuck D's Web site Rapstation <www.rapstation.com>, drawing its philosophy in equal parts from Malcolm X, Marshall McLuhan and the Wachowski brothers, bears the banner 'The Revolution will not be Televised,

Briefly, it was possible to conceive of a world where the artists were in control, selling music directly to the consumers and bypassing the conglomerates that keep prices high and products scarce.

it will be Digitized, Break free from the Matrix, the New Music Industry is Here!' Rapstation is a heady, optimistic mix of MP3s, streaming music, links to music listening and recording tools, and written polemic on the need for artistic independence. Chuck himself publicly debated Lars Ulrich of Metallica during the Napster lawsuit, frequently speaks publicly on related issues and testified before Congress in May 2000 about the salutary effects of the Internet on music as a small business.

Courtney Love's speech to the Digital Hollywood conference on May 16, 2000, was more vituperative. Briefly (because the speech itself is quite lengthy and full of her trademark weird digressions) her position is that while Napster-style piracy is a problem, major label recording contracts are worse. Love presented a budget breakdown for a hypothetical new band, showing how little of the profits actually go to the artists and how much goes to the labels. (This is the least interesting section of Love's speech, because it's basically a crib of Steve Albini's classic rant 'The Problem with Music,' which ends with the line 'Some of your friends are probably already this fucked.'[8])

But there are a few interesting and useful observations in Love's speech. She understands that the real strengths of P2P are its distribution system and users' ability to pick and choose from the tracks an artist has produced.[9] And unlike many people in the music industry, Love sees P2P as an opportunity for artists to regain control over their music licenses and to get their work to music listeners. Nor is she worried about a resultant drop in sales: 'I'm not scared of you previewing my record. If you like it enough to have it be a part of your life, I know you'll come to me to get it, as long as I show you how to get to me, and as long as you know that it's out.' Artists, she reasons, provide a service, like waiters. And most people don't stiff the waiter. 'I live on tips. Giving music away for free is what artists have been doing naturally all their lives.'

There are also more musicians than you'd think who are squarely on the side of an even greater degree of openness. Bands such as Negativland <www.negativland> have been championing royalty-free sampling and online distribution since long before there was anything like P2P. Their Web site features a wealth of information about the history of copyright law and their various entanglements with it as a result of producing their own brand of sample-based music.

Bands that wish to distribute their music freely have begun to take lessons from the free software community, and have developed similar licenses based on the GPL. The Electronic Frontier Foundation's Open Audio License <www.eff.org/IP/Open_licenses/20010421_eff_oal_1.0.html> has recently received a lot of attention for precisely these reasons.

Janelle Brown of Salon suggests that the ultimate losers in the Napster trial were the music listeners:

The recording industry's vision of the future is one in which we will all be paying $2.50 for every digital single we download or $.25 for every streaming song we hear—and you'd better forget about ever swapping those MP3s with your friends or, God forbid, an All-Metallica-All-The-Time radio station accessible through your Web browser. Innovation is being sledge-hammered out of existence by legal threats and buyouts. It's all about control—and right now, consumers are set to lose what little gains the Internet offered them.[10]

But is this true? Certainly the online environment is less open than it was even a year ago. There is now a lot of interest in record company circles in various technologies for spying on the traffic on P2P networks. 7 am News <7amnews.com> recently posted screenshots of a piece of software called Media Tracker that collects data such as machine addresses of clients using P2P networks (as well as IRC chat rooms and newsgroups, which most people who trade files have assumed the record companies have forgotten about, or don't know about) and adds the information it gathers to an infringement database. (Actually, some Gnutella clients, like BearShare, are also capable of tracking and time-stamping the IP addresses of any machine that makes a query of the machine on which it's running.) Presumably, lists of these addresses will be sent to ISPs, along with DMCA-prescribed cease-and-desist letters requiring that the users be banned.

To a certain extent, this is already happening in the United States. Both the Motion Picture Association of America and independent P2P 'bounty hunters' like MediaForce have been sending cease-and-desist letters to ISPs, asking them to terminate services to consumers found to have been downloading music. Some ISPs, such as DirecTV Broadband, Adelphia and Excite@Home, have been either cutting off directly or issuing warnings to their customers. Others, like Verizon, have emphatically refused to play along, stating that copyright law does not require them to monitor the contents of their customers' hard drives, and calling the requests to do so a 'drastic remedy that infringes on people's rights and speech.' A more cynical take might be that they're simply worried about losing customers, since someone who's been cut off from one ISP can simply move to another.[11]

**The record
companies can't
possibly sue
everyone, and even
if they did, they
would risk further
alienating the
people who are
supposed to be
buying their CDs.**

It will be interesting to see whether this is at all effective; the success of the tactic will depend on how long ISPs keep logs of the addresses they temporarily assign each user. The growing use of firewalls that mask the addresses of particular machines may also prove frustrating. The sheer number of people involved in file trading may be the largest roadblock— the record companies can't possibly sue everyone, and even if they did, they would risk further alienating the people who are supposed to be buying their CDs.

MP3s themselves are under siege as Napster and the new record-company-owned P2P nets develop proprietary formats. The forthcoming next-generation Microsoft operating system, Windows XP, had an MP3 encoder in its early beta versions, but it's been removed from the shipping version in favor of the Windows Media Player, which apparently features some rights management capabilities. Speculation is that this is an attempt to corral the audio player market in the same manner that Microsoft wrested the browser market away from Netscape.[12]

While RIAA Senior Communications VP Amy Weiss has noted that litigation is not an effective business model,[13] the rest of the RIAA is behaving as though it is. In early October 2001, the RIAA launched copyright infringement lawsuits against MusicCity.com, Grokster and Consumer Empowerment that are similar to the one that was launched against Napster.[14] But while the RIAA may be able to stop companies from building businesses based on file-sharing by dragging them through the courts, many observers still believe that the record companies will always be one step behind the pirates.

It looks like there will be changes on the physical CD front as well. Record companies are beginning to experiment with encryption schemes ... if unsuccessfully.

Wounded pride

In early 2001 the Charley Pride CD *A Tribute to Jim Reeves* was released with much hoo-ha because of its use of an encryption product produced by SunnComm of Phoenix, Arizona. Hacked copies showed up on the Net soon after, and have remained in heavy circulation on Gnutella (not so much because people like Charley Pride, but for the same reason that bootlegging Metallica tracks became so popular after they launched their lawsuit against Napster—out of spite).[15]

Michael Jackson has recently followed suit, releasing his new single 'You Rock My World' in a copy-protected version. While the CD works in normal audio CD players (so far), when put in the CD drive of a computer it spins continuously, in the same manner as a blank or corrupted disc would. The technology works through the inclusion of 'bad' audio correction codes, or intentional errors; normal audio CD players aren't sensitive enough to pick them up, but CD-ROM drives will. Critics argue that some CD players *will* have trouble reading these discs, that the discs will degrade faster as a result of this sort of meddling, that someone will eventually crack the protection (as happened with computer software in the 80s) and that in any event, they have the right to listen to their music on their computers if they want to. One wag noted that he didn't mind all that much because the new song isn't apparently as good as Jackson's earlier, audible work anyway.[16]

Copy protection, round 3

Out of curiosity, I just ran a quick check on Gnutella. The new Michael Jackson single is all over it like tattoos on Tommy Lee.

This fact alone won't stop the industry's experiments with copy protection. Generic boy band NSync's new album, *Celebrity*, is being sold with at least three different levels of copy protection: extra-strong in Germany, slightly weaker safeguards in the US, and no protection at all on the UK version. After testing the discs, the *New Scientist* reported that all three discs played on the commercial CD players they used, though Sony and Phillips players required about 30 seconds to read the German discs. While the UK and US versions of the discs played fine in the CD-ROM drive of a Windows box, the German version would not. Both the UK and US versions permitted the making of copies with a CD burner, but once again, the German version wouldn't cooperate, nor could its files be ripped to MP3s or copied to MiniDisc. The article concludes with the observation that all such copy protection systems can be circumvented very simply with only a slight quality loss by connecting the analog output of a CD player to the analog input of a digital recorder or PC sound card—perhaps the strongest indication that any copy protection scheme is an inconvenience at best for those truly determined to copy digital music.[17]

On a larger scale, Vivendi Universal group is planning to release all its new CDs with copy protection. AOL Time Warner and Bertelsmann are considering similar moves.[18]

Though details remain scarce about exactly how this sort of protection will work, one likely scenario is that CDs in the near future will contain two sets of files: a copy-protected set that will play on conventional music players and a set of files in a proprietary digital audio format that can be played on computers, but not swapped or duplicated. The most likely candidate for the proprietary format is (long, frustrated pause) Microsoft's Windows Media Audio (WMA). Which once again would put Microsoft back in the catbird seat, in control of the management of the majority of circulating audio files, just sitting back and soaking up the licensing fees. In this brave new future, evidently, smaller established online audio companies such as RealNetworks, not to mention Mac and GNU/Linux users, are SOL.

Even though this technology is in its infancy, consumers are already irate. SunnComm, makers of the market-leading copy protection schema, are already being sued, along with Denver-based Fahrenheit Entertainment, for misleading consumers by failing to include an adequate disclaimer on packaging for the copy-protected CDs. The lawsuit seeks an injunction against the two companies that would require them to provide adequate privacy notices on the CD case and keep them from tracking consumer habits.[19]

SunnComm's CEO Peter Jacobs, an admitted Napster user, says he sees his company's technology as a deterrent or 'speed bump' rather than a definitive end to digital copying. And he seems to be aware that many of the proposed copy protection systems stomp all over the notion of 'fair use' with big jackbooted feet.

Ours is the only copy-protection scheme that doesn't violate fair-use rights ... We allow (people) to make copies for their own personal use: for their computer, for their compilation disc and for their MP3 player, so they can have portable use of their music. The only fair use that's left—and it's not fair use at all—is the 'fair use' of sending thousands of copies to file-sharing services to be copied hundreds of thousands or millions of times.[20]

Will something like Jacobs is proposing become the industry standard? Jupiter Research analyst Aram Sinnreich says 'I think the reality here is that none of these [CD copy-protection] techniques is going to be successful in the long term ... They're fraught with technical difficulties, and if they did surmount those, they would meet with a severe consumer backlash.'[21]

What do *I* think? People will find ways to bootleg digital files, even if they have to hold microphones up to their speakers to do it—but something tells me it's never going to be that difficult ever again.

This is one side of the story. There are plenty of other people who believe that while the consumers might have lost the online audio battle, they certainly haven't lost the war. And now they may be spoiling for a real fight.

Pro-P2P

Many analysts believe that the RIAA and the record companies completely bobbled the ball on the whole subject of file sharing. Forrester Research's Jeremy Sharrard, author of 'The Digital Copyright Standoff,' is one of them. Based on his interviews with over 30 authorities on the subject of digital copyright, he believes that tens of millions of people have already come to the conclusion that because music was free on Napster it should stay that way, and that convincing anyone otherwise will be a very tough sell.[22]

Sharrard also believes that Congress will be unwilling to step in and legislate against music file-sharing (just as they were unwilling to legislate against pornography on the Web). This is partly because the Internet is in such a constant state of change that premature legislation could prevent legitimate technologies from taking root, and can limit the possibility of a more diverse market. After the conclusion of the Napster trial, Senator Orrin Hatch stated, 'Pro-competitive marketplace solutions that provide for a significant on-line offering of popular music delivered to consumers through an entity not controlled by the labels is the type of positive synergy I have long hoped to see.'[23] It's also partly because, as in the case of the DMCA, it's possible that rights management technologies could prevent some aspects of fair use of digital files as well as create violations of users' privacy.

The unlikelihood of legislation has implications in turn for other content-based industries such as book publishing, television and film, though they won't be vulnerable to quite the same extent as the music industry. This is partly due to lower demands for illegal digital copies (in the case of books) and partly due to the current bandwidth bottleneck that limits the size of files that can be easily shared (though the ongoing development of technologies such as the DivX video compressor may change that as well).

In the face of ongoing 'free' circulation of music online, Sharrard presents one possible business model for generating revenue: using free

Tens of millions of people have already come to the conclusion that because music was free on Napster it should stay that way, and that convincing anyone otherwise will be a very tough sell.

content to drive increases in subscriptions for service providers like AOL and MSN. AOL in particular will have the advantage of being affiliated with Warner Music, one of the larger record labels (though the label itself may not be all that enthused about distributing its content for free ... at least not initially).

Eben Moglen, chief legal counsel for the Free Software Foundation, makes a similar (if more polemic) argument in his article 'Liberation Musicology.' Far from seeing the closing of Napster as a victory for the record companies, Moglen sees it as the beginning of the end of all the cultural oligopolies that have controlled the publishing industry for the last century.[24]

In Moglen's view, the record companies had an opportunity to retain the 60-million-plus people in the original Napster user base—if they'd opted to make a deal. Instead, by forcing Napster to shut down, they in effect educated those people that there were other places online to get free music, like Morpheus, Kazaa, Gnutella, IRC chat rooms and so on. And what's more, they've created a situation where litigation is nearly impossible: 'Suddenly, instead of a problem posed by one commercial entity that can be closed down or acquired, the industry will be facing the same technical threat, with no one to sue but its own customers. No business can survive by suing or harassing its own market.'

Like most other thinkers on the subject of P2P, Moglen recognizes that what makes it work is its overwhelmingly effective distribution system—which could spell the end of big corporate music companies since it renders their owner-distributor function superfluous. But he also believes that

composers, songwriters and performers have everything to gain from making use of the system of unowned or anarchistic distribution, provided that each listener at the end of the chain still knows how to pay the artist and feels under some obligation to do so, or will buy something else—a concert ticket, a T-shirt, a poster—as a result of having received the music for free.

Moglen sees the possible emergence of 'hundreds' of new business models—there won't be one tailor-made solution for all artists and content providers, but people will find imaginative new ways to proceed.

And what about the record companies, ad agencies, promoters and consultants? 'They will have to become suppliers of services in the production and promotion of music ... or find new jobs.' Media pundit and official Slashdot in-house journalist Jon Katz concurs. 'Clearly the music industry's panicky and greedy overreaction will prove one of the most dunder-headed, short-sighted responses in recent business history. The industry couldn't have been more off-base, dishonest or greedy.'[25]

Katz also views the end of Napster as more of an opportunity than a tragedy—a chance to develop new markets rather than a death knell for intellectual property. He advances a three-step model for the business of putting culture online, whereby the Net initially connects customers with new art; then, through the process of introduction and word-of-mouth, creates interest in new cultural and informational offerings; and finally provides a means for companies of tracking consumer taste through digital marketing research. Katz sees this as a new opportunity for civics, because P2P applications could also work in the context of education, business and politics.

Katz provides statistics to back up his claims, citing a Jupiter Research study that found that 45% of people who download music are more likely to increase their music purchases than people who don't download, and that 71% of Napster users said they'd pay to download an entire album. In other words, musicians and other artists have probably made more money from the people who download than from those who don't. Accordingly, the corporations that make up the music industry should be supporting P2P and file-sharing rather than trying to sue the pants off of anyone with a file-sharing startup company.

What's at stake is the loyalty of the next generation of consumers. The recording industry is blithely alienating the people who might have otherwise been buying their products tomorrow by making their universities block their Gnutella, Morpheus and Bearshare access today. Encouraging them to sample different kinds of culture now, argues Katz, is the best way to ensure that they'll be interested in trying new venues and products in the future.

One more thing: 'Aside from these new findings,' writes Katz, 'the Napster experience also suggests that when it comes to dealing with the Net, businesses often have no idea what's good for them.'

Internet columnist Robert Cringely (you gotta love a guy who calls his column 'I, Cringely' and gives it a tagline like 'Caught on a planet of peril, he dared challenge its monster rulers ...') also plays devil's advocate on the issue of file-sharing. He begins with this analogy: most public transit agencies in the US claim that their ticket sales account for only 10–15% of their total revenues (the rest coming from government subsidy

Musicians and other artists have probably made more money from the people who download than from those who don't. Accordingly, the corporations that make up the music industry should be supporting P2P and file-sharing rather than trying to sue the pants off of anyone with a file-sharing startup company.

Napster, the first killer app of the new millennium, basically kept PC sales afloat during the 2000 Christmas quarter.

and advertising), and that since the cost of printing the tickets and paying people to sell them accounts for at least 15% of operating expenses, it would ultimately make more sense to simply run subways, buses and other forms of public transit for free. The benefits of the service are obvious, and people pay for it through taxation anyway. Eliminating the bureaucracy makes everyone's lives easier.

Does the argument map onto file-sharing? Cringely thinks so. Napster, the first killer app of the new millennium, basically kept PC sales afloat during the 2000 Christmas quarter. Yes, PC sales dropped for the first time ever during a Christmas season, but the carnage could have been much worse if people weren't hyped about getting online, downloading MP3s and burning them to CD-ROM (CD-ROMs and assorted peripherals did extraordinarily well that season, totaling $20 billion in sales). Napster was averaging 800,000 users at any given time, 24/7—far higher numbers than any of the TV networks can boast. Cringely lays it all out in big capital letters that even the dopiest money-grubbing executive should be able to understand: 'Napster is such a big killer app that the PROFITS on the sale of Napster-related or -inspired PC hardware and software were more than the SALES of the very music industry Napster feeds on.' It would have been a relatively simple procedure to slightly increase the tax on blank CD-ROMs and burners, 'and suddenly you have $1 billion or so to pay to artists, writers, and publishers in the exact proportions specified by the Napster servers. That $1 billion is approximately equal to the entire profits of the recording industry, and it is $1 billion they aren't getting now.'[26]

But greed got in the way. The record industry wanted all the marbles. Napster is still down, and while it may relaunch as a paid commercial service one day, it may never regain its vast original audience.

So what's the state of the file-sharing universe right now?

Spreading the nutty goodness

Alive and well, thank you very much.

Gnutella and its cousins—Morpheus, Kazaa, Freenet, IRC chat rooms, Hotline, Usenet and so on—are operating full-bore. New interfaces for existing systems, such as LimeWire, BearShare and OpenNap, provide newer and better access, while people are also devoting time to figuring out how to make the networks and servers work more efficiently. Portals like

Zeropaid <www.zeropaid.com> provide information about where to go, how to get there and what you'll find when you do.

Gnutella has been the most frequently discussed of the new P2P systems, because on so many levels it seems virtually unstoppable. It was invented in March 2000 by Justin Frankel and Tom Pepper of Nullsoft, makers of the wildly popular WinAmp MP3 player (and a division of AOL). Ostensibly, Gnutella was designed for sharing recipes, but is capable of sharing any sort of digital file: music, of course, which remains its dominant use, but also executable programs, e-books, movie clips and full-length films. When the first betas of Gnutella were posted on the Web, horrified higher-ups in AOL realized the implications and killed the project immediately. But they had already opened Pandora's Box (and as the name suggests, Gnutella would have eventually been released under the GPL, so perhaps its proliferation was inevitable in any case). The protocol was promptly reverse-engineered (probably by a programmer named Brian Mayland, but there may have been others) and the explosion in Gnutella client software began.

Gnutella software turns each computer connected to the network into a 'servent'—a combined client, server and network. As Gene Kan et al. describe it in their article on Gnutella, the software creates a giant, network-wide 'cocktail party' game of pass-the-message, shuttling individual search requests back and forth within a constantly shifting web of connected machines.[27] Requests stay on the machines they pass through for a certain amount of time, so that queries can be picked up as new computers are added to the net and begin to extend their own net of searches. Over time, the faster machines migrate to the center of the network, forming a sort of extemporaneous network backbone.

But that isn't Gnutella's only innovation; it also uses the http protocol to transfer files, just like Web pages. In essence, Gnutella is another World Wide Web, but one where the pages and servers change constantly. And because the search strings in Gnutella are so basic, each system is free to interpret those searches as it best knows how (which makes Gnutella an ideal candidate for a platform for some sort of new, unorthodox search engine).

And, unlike Napster, there's no central database, no controlling company. And no one to sue.

Gnutella is not without its problems, and it experienced significant growing pains when users began to desert Napster *en masse* and began looking for another place to share files. People developed a number of ingenious solutions to help the network scale (adapt to an increasingly large number of users) better: host caches and host catchers that list starting-off places for people just connecting to the network (and varying them to prevent congestion) and 'superpeers' or reflectors to strengthen the network's signals in the same way that an actual server might. BearShare has even developed a mode known as 'Defender,' which allows for the establishment of temporary configurable servers that act as proxies connecting slower users to the rest of the Gnutella network via users with faster connections, and even providing their own chat systems. The end result is a more robust network.[28]

While Gnutella may be around for a long time—because it will be very tricky (but not impossible) to shut down—other networks will invariably follow. But Gnutella isn't the only game in town.

Geek.com reported recently that in August 2001 over 3 *billion* files were traded by 15 million people over various P2P networks. At Napster's highest traffic levels, in February, 'only' 2.79 billion files were traded. The top four services were FastTrack, AudioGalaxy, iMesh, and Gnutella. MusicCity's Morpheus and KaZaA (both of which use the same software created by FastTrack) are the hot up-and-comers, with 3 million new users between them since June.[29]

But by the end of November the gaze of the legal machine had already shifted to KaZaA; a Dutch court ordered them to stop users of their software from sharing files within a span of two weeks. Impossible, said KaZaA, which could be facing daily fines of up to 100,000 guilders (US$40,240) if it can't manage the estimated 20 million people who downloaded the software. When it becomes obvious that even if KaZaA goes under, history will repeat itself—someone will reverse-engineer the software and the network will continue unabated, like Gnutella—this may be the case that forces another approach. As usual, The Register nails it on the head: 'The answer to that is talk to the music industry and figure out a way of licensing the content that users are sharing.'[30]

And what of MusicNet, the much-touted legitimate alternative launched by RealNetworks, Bertelsmann, AOL/Time Warner and the EMI Group? The good news is that it's apparently quite fast. The bad news is that the model of 'use' that this coalition has in mind for music lovers is the most reprehensible form of perpetual rental. If you download a song from MusicNet, you can listen to it—only on the machine to which you downloaded it—for 30 days. If you want to keep 'using' it, pay for another month ... and so on. For the moment, songs can't be copied to a portable music player or purchased for permanent use. A $10 subscription fee for one month gives you the right to download about 75 songs, roughly six CDs full of stuff. Keeping that music around for a year comes to about $20 a CD. Keeping them for another year means you've now paid $40 for the privilege of a hard drive of music you don't own and can't transfer to another machine or burn. Considering that the companies are doing no packaging and shipping at all, and everyone and his dog knows that CD prices are already grossly overinflated, how can anyone reasonably expect that consumers would be attracted to such a service?[31] Add to that the fact that the selection on MusicNet is limited to a handful of labels (to get access to all the majors alone, you'd have to subscribe to MusicNet and PressPlay, which has only the music of the Sony/Universal catalog) and you have a product with all the visceral appeal of a Spam sandwich with no mustard.

What will the RIAA's next move be? Trying to block the production of bootleg digital files at the source by lobbying for disabling technology on sound cards or hard drives? Haranguing ISPs to boot people downloading from Gnutella off their service? Something in tandem with Microsoft's recently patented 'Digital Rights Management' operating system?[32] The only certainty is that they won't roll over and play dead in the face of the ongoing download bonanza. In some respects, even a weak but ubiquitous form of copy protection will accomplish one thing for the RIAA—it will make it possible under the DMCA to prosecute people who circumvent that protection to rip MP3s.

The latest-breaking news is that, just before Christmas 2001, Universal announced plans to be the first of the major labels to release a copy-protected CD in the US, and to have all of its CDs copy-protected by 2002. The form of protection Universal is testing renders CDs that use it unplayable on Macs, DVD players, game consoles and probably some CD players as well.[33] In other words, the industry really doesn't care what you think. Happy holidays, folks.

Potlatch: A Festivus for the rest of us

What beautiful potlatches the affluent society will see—whether it likes it or no—when the exuberance of the younger generation discovers the pure gift. The growing passion for stealing books,

Even a weak but ubiquitous form of copy protection will accomplish one thing for the RIAA—it will make it possible under the DMCA to prosecute people who circumvent that protection to rip MP3s.

Time for a little perspective.

First, as Edward Felten's experiments suggest, the problem of media piracy will probably never go away. It's simply too easy to circumvent the current generation of encryption—and the kids will always be one step ahead of the industry, because that's the way of the world.

Second, the entertainment industry's current attempts to bludgeon consumers into line with Old Testament-style righteousness is not sustainable. Their pockets are deep, but ultimately they'll need to get back to the business of churning out pablum and relining said pockets, because, to paraphrase one industry spokesperson, prosecution is not a business model. Not to mention the fact that it's simply not in their best interests to have their customers hating them even more than they already do.

On top of everything else, the very landscape of the industry is changing. The record companies themselves are being swallowed by larger entertainment conglomerates—Warner music is now owned by AOL, and CBS has been owned by Sony for years. In many cases, the efforts of the entertainment industry to police their content are already conflicting with the interests of other, potentially more profitable parts of these conglomerates: those parts that make the hardware (say, Sony's hardware division) and run the networks that provide the content to the consumers (like AOL proper). At some point, the people at the top will demand a reconciliation.

And the big five labels aren't the only show in town anymore—far from it. Maverick artists like Chuck D, Courtney Love and Negativland are just the beginning of what will likely be a small but ongoing trickle of people defecting from major label culture, disillusioned with the way they do business. And, like Chuck D and Negativland, these artists will find other ways to distribute their music, direct to the consumer. Alternative infrastructures will begin to appear, tiny quasi-gift economies which, with the help of the Net itself, could eventually carry the day.

It's time for everyone to unclench a little. The industry's current control frenzy must pass; every moment they spend punishing consumers for liking their products too much is a moment that could have been employed in constructing an attractive alternative (and, as MusicNet demonstrates, there's a long-ass way to go on that front). If the Internet is becoming the new radio/TV, why not look to these older industries for revenue models? Small taxes on ISPs and recordable media stand a much stronger chance of working than tracking everything on a song-by-song basis—there's too much data, and the networks they exist on (Gnutella, etc.) are barely there at all.

So here's the answer to the problem: let people trade their songs. As I've been arguing from the outset of this book, it's possible and helpful to view waste as part of a successful business practice. Potlatch can't be stopped, but its energy can occasionally be channeled into other useful things, like customer loyalty and hardware revenues.

In any event, it's not mass consumer revolt that the entertainment industry needs to fear, but something much worse: indifference. As the Napster incident demonstrated all too clearly, when the cops show up, the party is perfectly capable of moving somewhere else.

If the Internet is becoming the new radio/TV, why not look to these older industries for revenue models?

CONCLUSION: ASS, GAS OR GRASS ...

... no one rides for free.

—1970S BIKER T-SHIRT

Complex little word, 'free' is.

Most of the issues that I've discussed in this book are far from resolved—in fact, many of them may remain perpetually in flux as new gift economies emerge and are in turn squelched or absorbed into the mainstream of networked culture. Some of them, however, have turned some major corners recently. Following are the latest developments, and some tentative conclusions.

File sharing

After 15 months of legal wrangling with Napster and tens of millions of dollars in legal bills, the RIAA is left with a situation that's worse than what they started with. 'It may have been that the music industry would have been better off following other strategies,'[1] said Webnoize analyst Matt Bailey. 'The strategy of trying to close down peer-to-peer file-sharing networks hasn't worked.'

If anything, Bailey is grossly understating the situation. More files are being swapped than ever, and the sizes of those files suggest a rapid increase in the sharing of movies and software programs. At the beginning of August 2001 the average size of swapped files was 4.8 megabytes—the length of a four-minute song. By the end of the month the average file size was 5.2 megabytes, which indicates that the interest of the average user is moving toward sharing things other than songs—snippets of porn films and action sequences from popular movies like *The Matrix* (video files are substantially larger than music files because they contain more information).[2]

As with most open-sourced technologies, file-sharing software is rapidly improving—and in some respects has already eclipsed Napster. New P2P clients are capable of automatically resuming interrupted transfers and simultaneously accessing many identical versions of a file to speed up the downloading process.

In their zeal to crush the competition in the courts, the record companies have neglected to provide a positive alternative by developing

P2P services that people will want to use. And until they do so, they'll pay the price: a recent Webnoize survey of 3,981 US-based college-age Web users found that 62% say they will continue to access MP3 music files through the existing non-commercial P2P services—or even e-mail, if they have to —and don't plan to stop.[3]

Many analysts believe the only way the record companies can win is through an even greater degree of largesse and expenditure than the free networks provide. Senior Webnoize analyst Ric Dube calls this 'super-serving' customers, which means free giveaways, access to exclusive online events, virtual backstage passes, pre-release access to new songs, real-world discounts on CDs and concert tickets and so on.[4]

Once it's been established that commercial networks can offer more than the free ones, it should be possible to establish a tiered subscription system similar to cable TV, where users pay for successively more deluxe levels of service. As the Internet moves into an era of 'Web services,' this approach may actually work.

... But that's a big 'once.' Ingenious new ways to swap files keep appearing all the time, because that's what software buyers want. The newest versions of popular instant messaging services from AOL, Yahoo and (yes) Microsoft all now have file-sharing capabilities. Users can designate a folder or folders on a hard drive as 'shared' by anyone on one of their designated 'buddy lists.' These buddies can then search one another's hard drives for files (yes, it's a security nightmare to boot). While the Terms of Service for Yahoo and Microsoft's IM clients specify that illegal swapping is *verboten*, the companies are playing both sides of the fence, trying to grab the interest and drive space of the market by flirting with a legal gray area.

Poor old Napster itself continues to get no respect. After laying off 15% of its employees in late October 2001,[5] the beleaguered parent of today's crop of file-sharing apps announced that it would not be relaunching its service until 2002 at the earliest. While Napster's CEO maintains that the delay is due to the need to collect a 'critical mass' of content, analysts suspect that it has more to do with settling the remaining lawsuits pending against the company.[6] The big question that remains is whether any users will still be around to notice when the new, legit Napster reopens for business.

Many analysts believe the only way the record companies can win is through an even greater degree of largesse and expenditure than the free networks provide.

Son of DMCA: The SSSCA

It's also beginning to look like ongoing efforts to legislate a solution to the intellectual property crisis are bogging down in the mire. Many Internet users were living in dread of the arrival of the Security Systems Standards and Certification Act (SSSCA), which many people refer to as the DMCA Part 2.[7]

The pet project of Senator Fritz Hollings, chair of the Senate Commerce Committee, the SSSCA would make the creation, marketing or distribution of any kind of computer equipment that does not include and utilize government-approved digital rights management technologies a civil offense. Further, the SSSCA makes distributing copyrighted material that has been stripped of copy protection—or that even has a network-attached computer capable of disabling copy protection—into a federal offense, with punishments of up to five years in prison and $500,000 in fines. The icing on the cake is that the early draft of the bill gave the entire tech industry 18 months to decide on a copy-protection standard or have one established by government mandate.

Not only is the bill's implementation time laughably short, but its consequences could be disastrous to many segments of the high-tech sector. For starters, the SSSCA would effectively render all existing Free Software illegal. If the bill's proscriptions were taken literally, many sectors of the entire computer industry would grind to a halt as they struggled to 'legalize' their operations by inserting likely ineffectual rights management technologies into devices that in many cases wouldn't actually require their use on a daily basis.

Criticism of the SSSCA has been vociferous. Jessica Litman, a law professor at Wayne State University who specializes in intellectual property, says 'Forgetting all the reasons why this is bad copyright policy and bad information policy, it's terrible science policy.'[8]

While some media companies, including Disney, heartily endorse the SSSCA, many of the big software and media companies, including Microsoft, Intel, IBM and Compaq, have recently begun voicing their opposition.

At a press conference clearly aimed at pre-empting the introduction of the bill, Ken Kay, the executive director of the Computer Systems Policy Project, a trade group that includes IBM, Intel, Dell Computer, Motorola and others, stated that 'this legislation would be an unwarranted intrusion

FREE

by the government into the commercial marketplace ... [it] would freeze technology ... [and] force government to pick winners and losers.'[9]

As of this writing, the first hearings on the bill have been postponed because of mounting public opposition, and the bill may be rewritten before it's introduced. But there's little doubt that, as with most monster movies, the SSSCA, or something very much like it, will be back again soon to make life difficult for all of us.

GNU/Linux gets an MBA

GNU/Linux is working ... hard.

The open monopoly

A fall 2001 report by Forrester Research found that, out of Global 2500 IT executives surveyed, 56% said their companies were using open-source software.[10] (Even though Free Software is in the ascendancy, it's remarkable that 56% of IT executives even know what 'open source software' *is.*)

Based on these findings, Petr Hrebejk and Tim Boudreau argue that Microsoft's closed monopoly on the software world is on the brink of being replaced with something they call an 'open monopoly.'[11]

Microsoft's monopoly, they contend, was the result of factors such as patents and other restrictions on source code that made it difficult for prospective new software vendors to enter the market, as well as factors that made it difficult for customers to choose alternatives, such as the cost and inconvenience of switching operating systems. In addition, because the cost of reproducing commercial software goes down as the market for it increases, and every new copy sold further decreases the ability of other companies to compete, an existing software monopoly tends to become stronger over time.

Yet these conditions of market dominance only hold as long as the competition uses the same business model that made the monopoly possible in the first place. The Free Software movement has completely shattered that expectation, rendering the usual business strategies (fair and unfair alike) useless against it.

Like the recording industry, Microsoft has made some noises about trying to legislate the problem away ... but there is no clear enemy, no one to sue. Microsoft is in a position not unlike the US during the opening years of the Vietnam War—just starting to clue in to the fact that none of its tools and tactics will be much use in this unfamiliar new terrain.

Hrebejk and Boudreau believe (for no particular reason they mention) that the Microsoft vs. Free Software conflict will result in a world where Free Software predominates.

In the end, there will be a monopoly again. The one-winner principle still applies. To [the big software-using companies], the world will not change greatly whether open-source or proprietary software is running the world's computers. The end result will still be decreasing average costs, and the same barriers to entering the market will still apply.

The modularity of Free Software makes it easier for small interests to develop niches in which they can compete. Customers can either seek out a solution from the pool of likely candidates or tailor software to their specific needs by working directly with the developers (a much more affordable proposition in the world of open source than in the world of commercial software applications). In all likelihood, companies will be able to choose between various public licensing schemes as well.

While I agree that the days of one company dominating the software market are probably over, I think a much more likely scenario is the emergence of a spectrum ranging from the totally free to the totally commercial. a wild variety of software options

Forked paths

This emergence of a diversified market is already well underway. Companies like Sun, which has split its productivity suite into the completely open OpenOffice and the more commercial StarOffice, are exemplary. A forked but parallel development stream allows for all the advantages of GNU/Linux bazaar-style development as well as a supported commercial product that can be marketed under a reputable brand name. It also makes it possible to charge for part of a company's activities and products rather than relying on Free Software mystique to supply the revenue stream.

IBM's interest in Linux is another indication that the future of the software market will be a spectrum of free/open source/commercial possibilities rather than an open monopoly. Over the course of 2001, Big Blue has invested nearly $1 billion into GNU/Linux services, software, partnerships, hardware and the community itself.[12] And as revolutionary as their 'Love, Peace & Linux' campaign looks, it's unlikely that we'll see employees abandoning themselves to orgies of sex, drugs and Quake deathmatch tournaments in the IBM office towers of the world. Dan Frye, head of IBM's GNU/Linux development team, says 'We are going to remain a mixed proprietary/open source software company ... We will continue to make billions off proprietary software ... We are not going to be a pure open source company—ever.'[13] That's right, IBM's in it for the money—and that's okay.

As a manufacturer of 'big iron' systems, IBM's primary interest in GNU/Linux is for server applications and large-scale business computing (though they do make GNU/Linux available on their desktop systems as well). Steve Solazzo, head of GNU/Linux marketing for IBM, says 'The majority of current marketplace activity is on server-based deployments, so that really is where we're spending most of our time.'[14] Because of its close relationship to Unix, which is still the enterprise computing environment *par excellence*, many executives are more ready to accept GNU/Linux on their servers and mainframes than they are on its desktops.

What's more, key members of the GNU/Linux community—such as the development team for the kernel itself—are working hard to curry the favor of the corporate sector, and to convince them that GNU/Linux hackers can also be serious businesspeople.

Their efforts appear to be working. A recent *Wired* article reported that '20 percent of companies responding to a 2000 study were using Linux to support a database; 10 percent were using Linux for a major app, such as CRM—double the figures from 1999.'[15]

One of the major GNU/Linux conversion success stories currently making the rounds is Amazon.com. The online bookseller changed its back-end services from a proprietary Unix system to a GNU/Linux system, trimming $17 million dollars off of its $71 million IT budget in the process.[16] Another is Intel, makers of the Pentium processors that power most PCs. Intel's recent abandoning of a proprietary Unix system in favor of a P2P-based Intranet that runs on GNU/Linux servers has saved them about $200 million dollars this year.[17]

In both of these cases, GNU/Linux exists as the server component of a complex mix of commercial and free software. And this is probably how it will be for the foreseeable future. Microsoft may play by a zero-sum game that sees any victory other than its own as a loss, but GNU/Linux doesn't work that way. Any adoption of GNU/Linux is a recognition that the world is a vast and complex place, and that there is more than one solution to any problem. As GNU/Linux servers begin to enter the

> Any adoption of GNU/Linux is a recognition that the world is a vast and complex place, and that there is more than one solution to any problem.

corporate world, the GNU/Linux desktop may come along for the ride ...
and end up propagating like jackrabbits in Australia.

—chance Linux will be on (Corporate.world's desktops

Just when you thought it was safe
to surf again ...

On October 25, 2001, more or less concurrently with the release of its
Windows XP operating system, Microsoft made some changes to its portal,
MSN.com. Specifically, they incorporated code to lock out practically
every browser other than recent builds of Internet Explorer and MSN
Explorer, and only the most recent generation of Netscape. (For a complete
list of affected browsers, see <www.theregister.co.uk/content/6/
22441.html>.) Ironically, at least one of those browsers—Opera—not
only rendered the site perfectly, but did so faster than Explorer itself.[18]

Now, it's not like there's a lot to see on MSN at the moment, but as I've
been pointing out, that could all change with .Net. And when 'Web services'
becomes the new buzzword, Microsoft wants to be the one controlling
the access to those services through their browser. Netscape/Mozilla has
known for a long time that the key to future applications will be through
the browser; Microsoft may have arrived at the party late, but they've done
everything in their power to ensure that they'll be the only ones with beer
to sell after closing time.

In any event, the geeks of the world were righteously pissed. Tim
Berners-Lee, the father of the Web himself and a key member of the W3
consortium that sets standards for Web applications, came forward to say,

I have fought since the beginning of the Web for its openness: that anyone can
read Web pages with any software running on any hardware. This is what
makes the Web itself. This is the environment into which so many people have
invested so much energy and creativity. When I see any Web site claim to be
only readable using particular hardware or software, I cringe—they are pining
for the bad old days when each piece of information needed a different program
to access it.[19]

Berners-Lee went on to observe that while no one browser perfectly
implements all the W3C's standards, many browsers that follow those
standards to a scrupulously high level, including Opera and Amava, the
W3C's own browser, had been locked out. He also pointed out that running
MSN's front page through the free W3C Validator Service <validator.

w3.org> demonstrates without a doubt that Microsoft isn't following W3 standards, despite their claims to the contrary.

By the end of the same day that they began the lockout the egg-faced monopoly reversed its position. Bob Visse, the MSN director of marketing, said 'The [MSN] experience may be slightly degraded [for users of other browsers] simply because they don't support the standards we support closely, as far as the HTML standard in those browsers.'[20]

Early evidence suggests that Microsoft's much-touted Passport system will need a lot of work before it's capable of doing the work that Microsoft claims—i.e., managing the unified electronic IDs of the world's computer users (200 million people have already signed up for some form of service that utilizes Passport). Early in November 2001, a software developer named Marc Slemko (a founding member of the Apache Foundation, which maintains the GNU/Linux Apache server that powers most of the Internet) demonstrated that it was possible to steal everything in users' Passport profiles—including their credit card numbers—simply by getting them to open a Hotmail message. 'It is very clear that either Microsoft does not have sufficient resources in place to properly review the security of their services and software, or that they are aware of the shortcomings but decided that attempting to gain market share was more important than their users' security,' Slemko said.[21]

The big news while I was finishing the final edits of this book, in early November 2001, was that Microsoft and the US government had reached a tentative settlement of the massive antitrust suit that has been running for years now. The official press release reads, in part, as follows:

The proposed Final Judgment includes the following key provisions:

Broad Scope of Middleware Products—The proposed Final Judgment applies a broad definition of middleware products which is wide ranging and will cover all the technologies that have the potential to be middleware threats to Microsoft's operating system monopoly. It includes browser, e-mail clients, media players, instant messaging software, and future new middleware developments.

Disclosure of Middleware Interfaces—Microsoft will be required to provide software developers with the interfaces used by Microsoft's middleware to interoperate with the operating system. This will allow developers to create competing products that will emulate Microsoft's integrated functions.

Disclosure of Server Protocols—The Final Judgment also ensures that other non-Microsoft server software can interoperate with Windows on a PC the same way that Microsoft servers do. This is important because it ensures that

Early evidence suggests that Microsoft's much-touted Passport system will need a lot of work before it's capable of doing the work that Microsoft claims.

Microsoft cannot use its PC operating system monopoly to restrict competition among servers. Server support applications, like middleware, could threaten Microsoft's monopoly.

Freedom to Install Middleware Software—Computer manufacturers and consumers will be free to substitute competing middleware software on Microsoft's operating system.

Ban on Retaliation—Microsoft will be prohibited from retaliating against computer manufacturers or software developers for supporting or developing certain competing software. This provision will ensure that computer manufacturers and software developers are able to take full advantage of the options granted to them under the proposed Final Judgment without fear of reprisal.

Uniform Licensing Terms—Microsoft will be required to license its operating system to key computer manufacturers on uniform terms for five years. This will further strengthen the ban on retaliation.

Ban on Exclusive Agreements—Microsoft will be prohibited from entering into agreements requiring the exclusive support or development of certain Microsoft software. This will allow software developers and computer manufacturers to contract with Microsoft and still support and develop rival middleware products.

The proposed Final Judgment also includes key additional provisions related to enforcement:

Licensing of Intellectual Property—Microsoft also will be required to license any intellectual property to computer manufacturers and software developers necessary for them to exercise their rights under the proposed Final Judgment, including for example, using the middleware protocols disclosed by Microsoft to interoperate with the operating system. This enforcement measure will ensure that intellectual property rights do not interfere with the rights and obligations under the proposed Final Judgment.

On-Site Enforcement Monitors—The proposed settlement also adds an important enforcement provision that provides for a panel of three independent, on-site, full-time computer experts to assist in enforcing the proposed Final Judgment. These experts will have full access to all of Microsoft's books, records, systems, and personnel, including source code, and will help resolve disputes about Microsoft's compliance with the disclosure provisions in the Final Judgment.[22]

How long will this all stay in effect? According to *The New York Times*,

The tentative settlement calls for a five-year consent decree between the government and Microsoft governing the company's conduct, according to people involved in the talks, with the possibility of a two-year extension if the company violates the agreement. To try to ensure enforcement, a three-member advisory committee of independent experts would be set up.[23]

But just because a settlement is in the works with the government doesn't mean that everyone is happy. Dan Gillmor of the *San Jose Mercury News* pulled out all the stops, calling the judgment 'a love letter to the most arrogant and unrepentant monopolist since Standard Oil' and 'an invitation to keep on plundering and whacking competition in the most important marketplace of our times, the information marketplace.'[24] Gillmor believes that not only does the settlement fail to require Microsoft to refrain from doing what eight federal judges found illegal, but it provides no substantial penalties for the illegal acts they have committed or any correctives with teeth. 'A couple of the measures, such as giving computer makers modestly more freedom, might have made a difference five years ago,' writes Gillmor. 'They are close to meaningless today, given the pervasiveness of the monopoly.'

Even in government, there are rumbles of dissent. From the perspective of the state attorneys general representing the 18 states that joined in the federal suit, the Bush administration's proposed remedies are much too lenient and difficult to enforce. The federal government has rejected most of the recommendations from consumer and industry groups for sanctions with any likelihood of actually changing Microsoft's behavior, such as unbundling Internet Explorer and Windows Media Player from Windows XP; opening up Microsoft's file formats (such as the Word '.doc' document format); placing Explorer into the public domain; or requiring Microsoft to develop licensing that would allow other companies to merge Windows into their own products. And what's more, the proposed Final Judgment actually allows Microsoft to avoid having to admit that they did anything wrong.[25]

Making the situation even worse, there's no guarantee that even the mild sanctions in this settlement will make it through to the final version of the judgment. The Register reports that Microsoft has managed to secure opt-outs for itself from the only provisions in the judgment that really matter: those concerning the disclosure of APIs (Application Program Interfaces—the tools that provide the necessary tools and protocols for building a program that will work well with a given operating system and other programs). On November 3, Microsoft secured an explicit agreement whereby, despite what the original text of the judgment says, it doesn't have to disclose any of its APIs.

Gillmor believes that not only does the settlement fail to require Microsoft to refrain from doing what eight federal judges found illegal, but it provides no substantial penalties for the illegal acts they have committed or any correctives with teeth.

The small print in Section J 1 of the 'Prohibited Conduct' notes:
'No provision of this Final Judgment shall:
1. Require Microsoft to document, disclose or license to third parties:
(a) portions of APIs or Documentation or portions or layers of Communications Protocols the disclosure of which would compromise the security of anti-piracy, anti-virus, software licensing, digital rights management, encryption or authentication systems, including without limitation, keys, authorization tokens or enforcement criteria;
or (b) any API, interface or other information related to any Microsoft product if lawfully directed not to do so by a governmental agency of competent jurisdiction.'[26]

In essence, this clause allows Microsoft to sidestep sharing anything with anyone if they can make a case that their security would be affected.

But it's possible that the states may not tow the government line—they're entitled to challenge the ruling when it's presented to the federal court for public hearings, and they can also attempt to continue their antitrust lawsuits against Microsoft without the federal government. In late October, the state of California announced that it was retaining prominent lawyer Brendan Sullivan on behalf of the 18 states in the case. That move was widely seen as foreshadowing a possible split between the Justice Department and the states. And there's also the host of other parties that have lined up to take a poke at Microsoft.

I had not intended this book to be a target painted on Microsoft's giant corporate ass, really. As I describe in the Afterword, I was a loyal paying Microsoft customer for most of a decade. And I believe that the future of software is not an either/or proposition, partly because of emerging practice (as mentioned above), and partly because of theory (a gift economy can never entirely replace a restricted economy). But confronted once again with a situation where Microsoft is blocking valid open standards and not adhering to them itself while pointing accusatory fingers in all directions, any sane person has to ask how this kind of behavior is possible from a corporation that has just definitively lost a major antitrust suit.

For the foes of Microsoft, Robert Cringely's predictions for 2002 paint a glum picture:

Microsoft will make itself a part of every deal, everywhere, no matter what happens with its anti-trust case ... That is because, in addition to having deep pockets, Microsoft owns the start page, the defaults, the windowing environment, and the content standards. It turns out they also own the traffic, the audience management, and if you're watching closely what they're doing with Windows Media, they're going to force you to pay licenses to show your own content on-line.[27]

If, as Linus Torvalds has always half-joked, the implicit goal of Linux is 'world domination,'[28] there's a long, long way to go for free-as-in-speech software. On the other hand, if the goal is world *subversion*—gift-economics-based cultural guerrilla warfare in the name of providing alternatives to corporate monoculture—the task at hand seems not only less daunting, but even possible. Under such conditions, one takes one's victories where one can find them, even (maybe especially) from the world of free-as-in-beer.

DeCSS: Free speech for free beer

A court finally came out and said what the geeks have been claiming all along: code is speech ... free speech.

And ironically, it was said in the context of a free-beer argument. On November 1, 2001, the California appeals court handling the DeCSS case overturned an earlier ruling barring people from publishing the code for the program. The court wrote: ~ can publish code

Like the CSS decryption software, DeCSS is a writing composed of computer source code which describes an alternative method of decrypting CSS-encrypted DVDs. Regardless of who authored the program, DeCSS is a written expression of the author's ideas and information about decryption of DVDs without CSS. If the source code were compiled to create object code, we would agree that the resulting composition of zeroes and ones would not convey ideas.

That the source code is capable of such compilation, however, does not destroy the expressive nature of the source code itself. Thus, we conclude that the trial court's preliminary injunction barring Bunner from disclosing DeCSS can fairly be characterized as a prohibition of pure speech.[29]

As speech, computer code is protected by the Constitution of the United States. If this decision is upheld, it will mean that people can still be prosecuted for posting pirated or cracked otherwise illegal software, but they will nevertheless have the right to post such material before it's judged as legal or illegal. To block the right to publication itself, the court ruled, would fall under the category of 'prior restraint' (a category of activity that's usually ruled as unconstitutional; the US Supreme Court has never upheld a prior restraint):

As speech, computer code is protected by the Constitution of the United States.

The movie industry's 'statutory right to protect its economically valuable trade secret is not an interest that is "more fundamental" than the First Amendment right to freedom of speech,' the judges wrote. Nor is it 'on equal footing with the national security interests and other vital governmental interests that have previously been found insufficient to justify a prior restraint.'[30]

While the case is still in a pretrial stage, and the ruling can nevertheless be appealed to a higher court, this decision means that legal minds are beginning to take seriously the arguments being advanced by the programming community.

IAAMOAC (I am a member of a civilization)

If we are all doomed to be either courteous slaves or liberated barbarians, what's the point?

—DAVID BRIN

When trying to suss out a middle route between the digital cryptocowboys on the one side and the corporate and government milquetoasts on the other, science fiction writer David Brin in his essay 'Getting Our Priorities Straight' found himself reaching all the way back to the Greek myth of Akademos—a farmer granted the gift of a garden (the 'academe') in which he could say anything he wanted to without fear of reprisal from the gods.[31]

Because the Greek gods were a shifty, backbiting, petty lot (i.e., not unlike real people), Brin found himself wondering exactly what was protecting Akademos and the others in his garden from the gods themselves. It either had to be a very substantial physical barrier—which would have made the garden cramped, sunless and unpleasant—or something else, an equalizing factor that would allow Akademos to make the gods keep their promise.

In retrospect, it seems obvious: that factor was knowledge. (What else would you find in the academe?—besides a profound lack of social skills, I mean.) In combination with accountability, knowledge provides a better defense of free speech and a free commons than the walls and trenches built by those who would wall off the commons for their own profit or build walls around themselves to keep the eyes of authority off of their actions, legal or otherwise.

The other thing that becomes obvious when viewed in this light is that the goal of knowledge plus accountability is openness. And yes, Virginia, that also means open as in 'open source.' It takes a certain arrogance to say, like Richard Stallman, that there is a moral imperative to using Free Software, but screw it, let's make the leap. We all make moral judgments every day; we're just usually too scared to admit to them. And it's not like the commercial software companies of the world in general and Microsoft in particular present anything even remotely like a compelling alternative example of good citizenship. If Free Software suits your business model, great. Call it 'open source' if that feels more credible. Mix it up with commercial products. Make money. Wonderful. But respect the values that that software represents.

If you *really* want free speech, you can have it. Sometimes, like the present, you have to experience some inconvenience, and even fight for it (to paraphrase my favorite Scandinavian metal band, ride hard, shoot straight, and speak the truth). In some cases, you can even have your free speech for nothing. If you're lucky enough to be around for one of those moments when the gift economy reigns, break out the free beer kegs, and we'll have a party. But in exchange for that freedom, you have to be accountable for not just what you say—or what you program, because it amounts to the same thing—but also how you license, distribute and run that program. You are a member of a civilization (read 'network', if you like), and therefore accountable to each and every other member of that civilization. As Brin writes, 'In the long run, what use is a civilization unless it gently helps us become so smart, diverse, creative and confident that we choose—of our own free will—to be decent people?'[32]

Or, as every Spiderman cartoon used to begin: 'With great power comes great responsibility.'

AFTERWORD: WINDOWS 95 OR BETTER?

The instructions said 'Windows 95 or better,' so I installed Linux.

—GEEK FOLK SAYING

My name is Darren, and I am a user of GNU/Linux and the Mac OS. I have been Windows-free for ten months [polite applause follows]. What made me kick the Microsoft habit? The Blue Screen of Death.

The BSOD

When most people buy their computer, the operating system is already installed. While some people may add a new program from time to time, most leave the operating system alone. They never, ever, patch it, update it, modify it or (gasp) change it entirely. So on a societal level, there's only a dim kind of awareness—like knowing that the Galapagos Islands exist, but not knowing where to find them on a map—that there's a galaxy of alternatives to Windows, including Mac OS X, GNU/Linux, BeOS, BSD Unix and Solaris, to name only a few.

But in almost all cases, the operating system that's installed on a newly purchased computer is some flavor of Microsoft Windows. I was a loyal, paying Windows user for most of a decade, even to the extent that I regularly poked fun at my Mac friends, warning them not to spill any granola on my keyboard. Among older and wiser geeks, such debates about operating systems are often referred to as 'holy wars,' because (a) the participants usually waste vast amounts of energy trying to foist personal value choices and cultural attachments onto others in the guise of objective technical evaluations, and (b) although much carnage ensues, the differences between the two opposing terms really aren't all that vast.

Sometimes, though, there are things worth fighting about. Minor technical differences are one thing ('You say Trash Can, I say Recycle Bin'), but when significant technical shortcomings come hand-in-hand with questionable corporate philosophy and draconian licensing schemes, it's time to start looking for real alternatives.

Enter the Blue Screen of Death, epitome of the computer culture that Microsoft has created. When a Windows program crashes (which is alarmingly often), the crash often happens in such a way that it brings down the entire operating system. The hapless user, having done something innocent, such as launching a game or inserting a CD into his drive, is confronted with a flat blue screen filled with white text announcing that, in all likelihood, the only option for proceeding is to reboot and run some utilities in an attempt to repair the damage that the crash has created.

In a Windows world, the BSOD is a fact of life. Power users will often see it several times a day. And as computers become an increasingly large part of the urban environment, the BSOD has begun popping up everywhere: bank machines, pixel-powered billboards, airports, train stations. While the BSOD is butt-ugly, it's not so much the aesthetic affront of the thing that's the problem—it's what it represents. Every crash means many minutes (or hours) of lost work, damaged documents, and teeth-grinding frustration.

And while Microsoft doesn't set out to write deliberately bad software, they can get away with selling sloppy code because they dominate the market. Because few people know that there *are* alternatives to Windows, it's simply not in Microsoft's interest to fix any problems that aren't drastically threatening their monopoly. As Henry Ford said during the early days of automobile production, you can have any color car you want, as long as it's black.

Linus built my hotrod

But there *are* alternatives to Windows. This book was written with Free Software. The 'free as in speech' kind. It was surprisingly easy to make the switch, and it's getting easier all the time.

If you want to buy a PC with GNU/Linux already installed, you can do it. Many retailers, from large companies to corner-store computer shops, are selling shiny new PCs complete with various Linux distribution 'flavors' included. (Due to customer demand, Dell still factory-installs and supports Red Hat Linux on its entire line of PowerEdge servers and some of its Precision workstations, despite its plans to drop Linux earlier in 2001.[1]) When a computer arrives with a modern GNU/Linux graphic user interface such as Ximian or KDE preinstalled and raring to go, it's really not that much harder to run than Windows or even the Mac OS ... and many people argue that it's much more stable and powerful than either. Individual programs may crash from time to time, but they rarely bring down the entire system or require rebooting to restart them. Many GNU/Linux users leave their computers on for months at a time, and even a clueless newbie like me can manage to go several weeks in a row without encountering any significant problems.

This book was written with Free Software. The 'free as in speech' kind.

But because GNU/Linux is capable of wringing the untapped potential out of older hardware that would be annoyingly sluggish under Windows, its most frequent use these days is for after-purchase installations. For the last decade I've been a slave to Moore's Law (which states that the number of transistors per integrated circuit will double every 18 months), replacing my computer hardware about every two years just to keep up with the power of the average computer system, never mind the bleeding edge. By early 2001, my Pentium II 333 box was ready for the glue factory—or so I thought.

Having transferred most of my real work to a Mac laptop the previous year, all I was really running on my Windows machine were some Internet apps and a hard drive full of violent and time-consuming video games (i.e., the best kind). I'd been reading Slashdot (a major GNU/Linux watering hole <www.slashdot.org>) avidly for about two years, and was ready to bite the Linux bullet. The question was which distribution to choose. There are many good ones, each with different features to recommend it—Debian, SuSe, Red Hat, Caldera, VALinux, Mandrake and Slackware all score highly (Linux World News maintains a much longer list <lwn.net/2001/0719/dists.php3>)—and I wanted to select one quickly without getting caught up in the religious issues surrounding which one was superior.

GNU/Linux distros are easy to come by, because they're often bundled with other products as a value-add feature (and unlike AOL CDs, they're occasionally useful for something more than putting your coffee on). Looking around the piles of high-tech rubble that litter the floor of my office, I can see a SuSe disc, a TurboLinux disc, a Libranet/Debian disc, Corel Linux and Red Hat. Initially, I spent a lot of time playing with Libranet Linux <www.libranet.com>, a small Canadian distribution based on Debian (the geek distro of choice because of its close ties to the GNU Project <www.gnu.org>). Libranet is aimed at the desktop user who wants a full suite of productivity applications without having to deal with the complexity of a full Debian distribution. While Libranet is great, I finally settled on Red Hat 7.1, the most recent version of the most popular Linux distribution, because of its wider support community and ease of installation and maintenance.

The Red Hat install routine has an edge over Libranet for neophyte users because of its graphic user interface, which is no more complex or intimidating than a Windows install. You can even automate the disk partitioning (the underlying indexing system that divides up available hard disk space and tells your computer where your programs and other files are located), which is the scariest part of most GNU/Linux installations. Red Hat systems are also easy to maintain. Their software package management system, RPM, is so good that it's been adopted by many other GNU/Linux distributions as a standard. Red Hat's Web site <www.redhat.com> will even automate much of the process of updating, for those who wish to avoid the issue altogether. They also offer user support on a subscription basis, which beats the hell out of having some acne-faced squint telling you to RTFM (Read the Fucking Manual) every time you post a query to a user's mailing list.

But nice as the big red box and the little transparent Red Hat logo stickers are, Red Hat's slick packaging is of little use for more than the first day in your life as a Linux user. The manuals aren't good for much except throwing at the nearest cat, and wouldn't make a satisfactory impact in any event. If obtaining documentation is your primary concern, you'd be better off buying one of those gargantuan commercial GNU/Linux manuals with a CD-ROM bound into the back. If I had to do it again, I'd probably try out Mandrake Linux as well, which is even easier to set up than Red Hat.

The real reason for a Linux neophyte to settle on a modern Linux distro like Red Hat or Mandrake is not merely the ease with which they can be maintained, but the importance of supporting a commercial Linux distribution in the marketplace. Red Hat posted its first quarterly profit in May 2001, after losing $3.7 million the previous year,[2] demonstrating that selling support for free software is as viable a proposition as selling software itself. The big commercial distros also employ many of the key developers of the operating system, ensuring that GNU/Linux as a whole continues to grow and evolve.

A star is born—again

But the choices don't end once you've selected a distribution. Linux is an embarrassment of riches. You also have to select a desktop and applications to run.

The bulk of *Free* was written in GNU/Linux StarOffice 5.2, Sun Microsystems's powerful (if eccentric) productivity suite, with occasional forays into Corel WordPerfect for Linux and various and sundry less

> **The real reason for a Linux neophyte to settle on a modern Linux distro like Red Hat or Mandrake is not merely the ease with which they can be maintained, but the importance of supporting a commercial Linux distribution in the marketplace.**

powerful text editors, including KDE's KWord and AbiWord. (Okay, every now and then I'd cheat a little and take my Mac laptop and a beer out onto the deck. I'm only human.)

The transitions between the various word processor environments were relatively painless. Barring a few snags, like inadvertently installing the Spanish version of StarOffice instead of the English one (¡Yo quiero StarOffice!), the mechanical side of the writing went reasonably smoothly. Most aspects of word processor interfaces were standardized long ago, and even complex features like styles and tracking changes usually work seamlessly. Odds are that if a word processor can read your files—a less frequent occurrence than you might imagine—you'll be able to figure out how to make it work without pulling too many hairs.

StarOffice, which began in 1993 as a word processor for Windows and OS/2, is the last best hope for cracking the dominance of the Microsoft Office suite in the workplace. StarOffice handles Microsoft Office word processing, presentation files and all but the most complex spreadsheets with ease and grace. There are currently versions of StarOffice for GNU/Linux, Windows and Solaris, Sun's operating system.

For most of its existence, StarOffice was free but commercially licensed software. But in July 2000, in an unprecedented moment of largesse, Sun open-sourced the StarOffice source code—all 9 million lines of it.[3] This represents the single biggest contribution to the open source code base in history. At the same time, the OpenOffice.org site was launched to serve as the coordination point for the source code, file formats and application programming interfaces for OpenOffice, the 'development' version of StarOffice (which remains a commercial product).

The birth of OpenOffice doesn't mean the death of StarOffice—far from it. Sun will continue to produce commercial versions of StarOffice using the OpenOffice.org sources, while funneling all code changes and improvements that it makes back to the OpenOffice project. What Sun gets in return is the loyalty of a huge community of debuggers, developers and users who'll develop its product for free, because it's in their interest as members of the Free Software community to do so, and provide a user base that includes people who will gladly pay for support, manuals and other Sun products.

OpenOffice is still in development, and the daily builds (the 'work-in-progress' draft versions that the developers upload for those interested in monitoring the development of the program's code) aren't suitable for use by anyone except the very brave and the very foolish. The StarOffice 6.0 beta is out, however, and it has already made some significant improvements over the original StarOffice interface by ditching the annoying 'desktop' environment and built-in browser and separating the suite's different capabilities into distinct applications. This more intuitive approach to the interface, combined with the decision to move to an open, easily translatable XML-based file format along with the crucial ability to read and produce usable MS Office files, gives the nascent suite a fighting chance as the dark-horse competitor for MS Office.

If, as part of future antitrust remedies, Microsoft is forced to open its jealously guarded APIs (Application Program Interfaces—the routines and protocols that allow software applications to speak to the operating system, and to each other) and file formats, it will become even easier to swap documents back and forth from Windows to GNU/Linux. 'Microsoft's lock-in on its Office file formats is arguably at least as important to their monopoly position as their control of the operating system itself,' says Tim O'Reilly, founder and CEO of computer book publisher O'Reilly and Associates.[4] 'The availability of StarOffice under the GPL will give Linux a boost on the desktop, but more importantly, the wide availability of StarOffice Suite's code for reading and writing Microsoft Office formats will allow other open source projects to provide compatible functionality as well. Open data is the other side of the open-source coin.'

From the perspective of many contemporary business models, the act of giving away 9 million lines of solid code might seem like unforgivable squandering. But as I've suggested, such 'squandering' may be an unavoidable part of the corporate growth cycle—and it may have rewards that we haven't been able to identify until very recently.

The anti-Mac

GNU/Linux rules the world of server appliances—the machines on which the Internet is built. As the recent waves of Internet worms have demonstrated, Microsoft's NT servers have all the stopping power and integrity of a wet brown paper bag. So GNU/Linux boxes are solid, appropriate tools for software engineers, system administrators and other people who write and work with real code on a daily basis, but are they of any use to the rest of us? Can you use them to play MP3s, run games, manage spreadsheets, surf the Net and watch movies?

From the perspective of many contemporary business models, the act of giving away 9 million lines of solid code might seem like unforgivable squandering. But as I've suggested, such 'squandering' may be an unavoidable part of the corporate growth cycle.

Yes, of course you can. But the design philosophy behind GNU/Linux—when it's coherent at all, which is not very often—is frequently different from the ones that underpin Windows and the Mac OS. And let's face it; GNU/Linux is no miracle cure for all that ails the world of computers. Different OSes accomplish similar tasks in different ways, and with differing degrees of success. Which one you choose depends on your priorities.

Back in 1996, Sun Microsystems engineers Don Gentner and Jakob Nielsen wrote a paper titled 'The Anti-Mac Interface,' not because they disliked or didn't use Macs, but because they wanted to explore some possibilities for working with computers that were different from either Apple's famous (and still-dominant) Human Interface Design specifications or the standard Unix command-line driven environment.[5] Gentner and Nielsen envisioned a world where there would be a large number of relatively sophisticated computer users connected together by a network, and that these people would need to manipulate large quantities of complex information objects (i.e., files that contain or link to large amounts of text and images) on a regular basis.

In such an environment—the environment that is beginning to develop now—both command-line interfaces and graphic user interfaces fall short in certain respects. Plain text doesn't convey enough information about the contents of particular files. For example, there's no way to know what a file with a generic name like 'book' contains, or even what software is required to run it. A graphic user interface may provide you with more information about particular files by assigning an icon that looks like a little piece of paper, maybe with a special logo attached to it that identifies it as an Adobe Acrobat file. But GUIs make repetitive tasks (such as translating the e-book into variety of formats) more difficult, because to most users it's not immediately obvious how to write a script to carry them out—a job that would be much easier under a command-line interface.

In order to solve such difficulties, Gentner and Nielsen proposed an interface that would have the following qualities:

A central role for language

Graphics have their uses, but the abstraction of words makes a more powerful sort of relation with data possible. 'Language lets us refer to things not immediately present, reason about potential actions, and use conditionals and other concepts not available with a see-and-point interface. Another important property of language missing in graphical interfaces is the ability to encapsulate complex groups of objects or actions and refer to them with a single name ... Finally, natural languages can cope with ambiguity and fuzzy categories.' The anti-Mac interface wouldn't necessarily be a 'natural language' environment, but it would be more flexible than an old-fashioned command line, and would be able to 'negotiate' with the user to determine exactly what she wants. The result might be something like the text-adventure computer games from the mid-80s, or like being inside an early-90s MUD (multi-user-dimension).

A richer internal representation of objects

Anyone who recognized the name 'Jakob Nielsen' probably did so because of his current status as a usability guru. It should come as no surprise, then, that even back in 1996 Nielsen was extremely interested in metadata. The Anti-Mac interface would utilize file formats that provide a much better sense of what sort of information individual files contain, probably by using a markup language such as XML, which would also allow for automated extraction of that information (such as author names, addresses and keywords).

A more expressive interface

Screen size, resolution, color depth and pricing have improved dramatically since 1996. With all the screen real estate that a 19-inch monitor affords, it's theoretically possible to take the internal representation of information described above and display it in a way that allows users to locate what they need rapidly and to sort it effectively.

A larger pool of expert users

GUIs are great for initiating novice computer users. But as our culture becomes increasingly computerized, and new generations are raised with computers as familiar objects, there will be less need to initiate people slowly into the use of complex operating systems. In fact, Gentner and Nielsen predict that people raised with computers will demand more powerful and more complex interfaces than those currently available. (This goes a long way toward explaining the '15-year-old-hacker' phenomenon.)

Shared control

A networked environment means sharing data, and that means abrogating a certain amount of the control that users have over their computers. Giving up a bit of control means that you can benefit from the knowledge and skill of others, and that repetitive or boring tasks, such as updating your software, can be handled by computer 'agents' (little programs that automate repetitive tasks, or walk you through the process of how to accomplish them quickly and easily. 'Clippy,' Microsoft's infamously annoying Office assistant, is an example of a poorly implemented agent).

Joakim Siegler, an engineer for Ximian (a GUI desktop suite built on Gnome, one of the two major graphic environments for GNU/Linux), recently picked up the Anti-Mac gauntlet in an article on the Avogato software development site.[6] He rightly points out that the design tendencies in much of the existing free software point toward something like the Anti-Mac Interface (the same could be said of Mac OS X).

- GNU/Linux GUI environments like KDE or Gnome are less rooted in visual metaphors than is the pre OS-X Mac.

- Users are always opening terminal windows to run programs from command lines.

- GNU/Linux is justifiably famous for its networked information-sharing tools, like Apache.

- Many GNU/Linux applications, such as KWord, the KDE Word processor, use the XML standard as the basis for their file formats.

- GNU/Linux is nothing if not geared toward expert users.

Where the GNU/Linux interface still needs work is in the graphic representation of information objects. Linux is arguably a more language-oriented interface than Windows or the Mac OS, but it doesn't have the flexibility or interactivity that Gentner and Nielsen describe (for that matter, no software that exists at the moment does). Siegler also notes that the whole area of agents needs further exploration, and may even provide the 'holy grail' of a revenue model for free software companies—the software would be provided for free, and access to the agent would work on a subscription basis, much like Red Hat's current Update Agent system. Exactly how much control users are willing to give up to such agents is also open for debate, as the controversy around Microsoft's .Net project continues unabated (see Chapter 3 for more on .Net).

Different tools are appropriate for different types of users, or even the same user in a different situation. Operating systems like GNU/Linux demonstrate that graphics and text doesn't have to be an either/or proposition. As a synthesis between a command-line driven interface like DOS or Unix and the all-graphic (pre-version X) Mac OS, GNU/Linux offers both a comfortable 'tidepool' for beginning users, and all the power and flexibility that any hacker could ever want or need.

Making GNU/Linux not suck

If the battle for control of the computer environment was a season of *Survivor*, would GNU/Linux already be off the island? Some people seem to think so ... even some people in the GNU/Linux community.

A large part of the debate hinges on the 'Linux on the Desktop' question. As Miguel de Icaza, chief developer on the Ximian Gnome desktop and Mono projects writes in his polemical call to arms, 'Let's Make Unix Not Suck,' 'Do not be confused. The majority of people do not use computers to do programming, nor to learn how to use [arcane little programs like] nroff, nor to run a web server. The majority of people use computers to simplify their lives, to communicate with people, to get work done, or to have fun.'[7] With Gnome in general and Ximian in particular, de Icaza sees his task as breaking out of the 'technology for its own sake' mindset that tends to dominate programming communities, and actually getting free technology to the nonprogramming community for use on a daily basis.

de Icaza deals directly with the holy war problem (Unix-based systems vs. Mac and/or Windows) by pointing out that 'people focus on their strengths and ignore their flaws when it comes to anything that is dear to them. Even worse, when comparing with another competing entity, they focus on their weaknesses and ignore their strengths.' Noting that the key components of a successful operating system are not just open development models and concerted efforts to deal with specific problems (things the GNU/Linux community does well) but also policy formation and code reuse (things that GNU/Linux doesn't do so well), he points to Microsoft's Internet Explorer (gasp) as an example of successful software design.

The Unix/Linux ideal is a system built of small executable components that use common libraries and components. Such components are usually developed independently, but should work together to produce the illusion

GNU/Linux offers both a comfortable 'tidepool' for beginning users, and all the power and flexibility that any hacker could ever want or need.

of integrated applications. Presenting a standard list of GNU/Linux applications for end users, including Netscape, GhostView, XDVI, Acrobat, Mathematica, Maple, Purify, FrameMaker and StarOffice, de Icaza notes that the only components these programs share are a couple of libraries. Explorer, on the other hand, consists of a series of independently developed components (an HTML engine, an XML engine, the toolbars, configuration menus and so on) that work extremely well together *and* can be called on by other parts of the Windows operating system.

It's clear that there's lots of work to be done to make the GNU/Linux desktop run smoothly, but will that work happen? An admittedly pessimistic 2001 editorial on LinuxPlanet <www.linuxplanet.com> suggested that the demise of the Eazel project <www.eazel.com> (an initiative begun by former Apple and AOL employees to make GNU/Linux safe for the rest of us), combined with Corel's inability to practically give away the desktop-oriented Corel Linux, are serious indications that there currently isn't an acceptable rate of return on corporate development of a GNU/Linux desktop environment.[8] Without corporate champions, the editorial suggests, GNU/Linux desktop development rates will slow to a crawl. And this is a problem—a big problem—because Windows and the Mac OS can mop the floor with any GUI contender that GNU/Linux can currently put in the ring with it:

One of the problems in being a Linux user is the need to figure out exactly what tools are usable in their present release and which tools merely show a great amount of promise. Sadly, I'd submit that most Linux desktop tools—like KOffice, like Evolution, like AbiWord—aren't really usable in their present release. ... You cannot ask users to compromise when you want them to switch operating systems, and you need to be realistic about how things work. Let's face it: at the present time there's nothing under Linux that works as well as Microsoft Office. Period.

Emily Dresner-Thornber, a freelance writer and professional programmer who has used Linux since 1994 to serve files to the Internet and render graphics, concurs in 'What Linux Must Do to Survive.' Whatever else she does in GNU/Linux, Dresner-Thornber writes in Word 2000, running on Windows 98. 'The nail in the coffin,' she writes, 'was that my fallback, the greatest of bloated text programs, EMACS, just doesn't do it for me anymore. It was a pain before Word became a useful program and it is a pain today.'[9]

What makes Dresner-Thornber's article interesting is that instead of carrying on in the sackcloth-and-ashes mode of the LinuxPlanet editorial, she offers a list of constructive suggestions for the qualities she believes Linux will need to survive.

Easy install routines

I've already addressed this matter, and its role in my decision to run with Red Hat or Mandrake. But the point goes double for Dresner-Thornber, who wants nothing more complicated in her install routine than two big buttons—a red one for setting up workstations, and a blue one for servers. 'Anything else is too hard ... No more cylinders. No more manual formats of hard drives. No more hyper-customization of the system on install. No more choices. Just two big buttons and be done with it because, in the end, fewer people care than anyone cares to admit.'

An end to the beta versions

GNU/Linux programmers are justifiably proud of the accuracy of the versioning systems that identify their software releases, but the versions never end. The 'simple' act of trying to update a single program can turn into a rat's nest of RPMs and tarballs and source code that needs to be compiled and library files and bug reports that would create a strong desire in almost anyone to avoid any interface more complicated than WebTV. 'Nothing kills adoption of software or an operating system faster than a lack of confidence, and lack of real releases is squashing confidence like a bug. People should never have to patch their kernel by hand, they should never have to upgrade their major software let alone build it from source, and they should never, ever, ever have to go to a site in Madagascar to get their code,' writes Dresner-Thornber. 'Nuff said.

Readable documentation

There's an interesting difference of opinion as to whether or not GNU/Linux is well documented. In 'The Cathedral and the Bazaar,' open source theorist Eric Raymond refers to the 'stunning variety, quality and depth of Linux documentation.'[10] True, there's a lot of it, and the fact that it's possible to run the GNU/Linux 'man' command with a program name attached to it and generally obtain any result at all is no small feat (think about the last time you used the Windows Help system). But as Dresner-Thornber notes, 'The thing about Linux documentation is that it backs the oft-blabbered fallacy that engineers, as a whole, cannot communicate

> **'People should never have to patch their kernel by hand, they should never have to upgrade their major software let alone build it from source, and they should never, ever, ever have to go to a site in Madagascar to get their code,'** writes Dresner-Thornber. **'Nuff said.**

with the outside universe and those that can have some sort of strange gift from the Heavens.' Many existing GNU/Linux manuals are arcane, or fragmentary, or incomplete, which renders what should be simple tasks far more complicated than they need to be. While online support resources for GNU/Linux are growing in number and quantity, tracking down the information you need can be a lengthy, frustrating process.

A unified user experience

To paraphrase Jello Biafra, with GNU/Linux, the freedom of choice you have demanded is now mandatory. The GNU/Linux system is configurable to a fault. You can run your system from one of a variety of shell prompts, or from one of a variety of desktops. Or both. Or all of the above. Factor in all the configuration options for all these environments and what you've got is a completely heterogeneous computing experience. This is fine for power users, but a poor argument for general adoption. Neophytes need a stable, homogeneous tidepool to begin their GNU/Linux computing— and it needs to be the same one that other neophytes use. Providing a single shell and a single crash-proof windows manager with minimal configurable options, argues Dresner-Thornber, will boost GNU/Linux's credibility and ease its entry into mainstream computing.

Technical standards

In the world of computing, sets of standards for coding, interface, documentation and release schedules are the fuel that powers widespread adoption. 'The core problem with Linux,' writes Dresner-Thornber, 'is what gives it the rabid appeal to the geek set: it allows programmers to do anything they want in the system, to the system, without thinking about the end user. To this end, trying to get standardization is much like herding cats.' Apple has standards. However much they change and/or ignore them, Microsoft also has standards. Parts of GNU/Linux, such as KDE and Ximian, have standards. But there is a tremendous amount of resistance to the adoption of rigid standards in many parts of the GNU/Linux community, because to the users, standards represent creeping corporatization. If GNU/Linux is to achieve its stated goal of World Domination, they argue, it must do so without becoming the thing it opposes.

... Which, as Drensner-Thornber notes, leaves the GNU/Linux vs. Everything Else holy war at an impasse. If the GNU/Linux status quo continues, 'the rogue programmers will win, because they are many and vocal. Standardization will never come to pass, and Linux will continue to be what it is today: a little brother to the Big UNIX operating systems and a fabulous toy for hackers everywhere. It is an impossible force to stop.'

About a year earlier than Dresner-Thornber's article, a research note from the Gartner Group titled 'Will Linux Be Viable Competition for Windows Desktops?' drew many of the same conclusions, especially where standards are concerned.[11] While the GNU/Linux star is on the rise, Windows has attained the status of 'nonsubstitutable infrastructure.' That is, for most businesses, switching from Windows to another operating system would involve considerable expense; it has strong third-party and vendor support; it serves as the scaffolding on which other technologies depend ... and the organization that produces it has achieved a level of total or near-total internal standardization. 'The lack of standards in the Linux community, coupled with a lack of key productivity applications and with Unix complexity, will continue to make Linux a poor choice for the mainstream business productivity user.'

So what will happen to GNU/Linux if it doesn't become more coherent? The Gartner Group document presents three scenarios, the most likely being that it will remain an alternative operating system, holding about 5% of the desktop computing market by 2004. In order to convert more Windows users than that, the document argues, GNU/Linux would have to develop a killer app (probably an office suite) important enough to justify a mass user conversion. One factor making such a scenario unlikely is the open nature of GNU/Linux licensing: 'Any application that can be created under Linux can easily be ported to Windows, thus obviating any advantage.'

However, there are other factors than technical issues involved in learning to use GNU/Linux—social factors. And they can be far more discouraging.

GNU/Linux goes Hole Hawg

In a short and highly entertaining treatise on operating systems titled *In the Beginning ... Was the Command Line*, science fiction writer Neal Stephenson (author of *Cryptonomicion* and *Snow Crash*) presents an analogy for GNU/Linux that, while shedding some light on the nature and purpose of the operating system, also buys into a certain kind of geek machismo that is one of the major factors in keeping GNU/Linux from broader success.

Scorn for the
technically inept
may be one of the
most formidable
roadblocks to the
eventual
acceptance of
GNU/Linux by the
larger world of
computer users.

During the phase of his career that most writers refer to as 'gaining life experience' (i.e., the part where you can't actually make your living from writing), Stephenson worked in construction. One of his regular tools was the Hole Hawg, a drill made by the Milwaukee Tool Company. Stephenson describes it as 'a cube of solid metal with a handle sticking out of one face and a chuck mounted in another.' That's it. Not pretty at all ... but astonishingly powerful. In order to combat the drill's counter-torque, its user requires a separate side 'handle' that consists of a one-foot piece of threaded galvanized pipe that screws into the drill's side.[12]

Stephenson relates several workplace safety horror stories about himself and his coworkers being flung around like the proverbial frog in a blender by the drill's mighty motor on those instances when its bit jammed. 'The Hole Hawg,' he notes, 'is like the genie of the ancient fairy tales, who carries out his master's instructions literally and precisely and with unlimited power, often with disastrous, unforeseen consequences.'[13] As Georges Bataille might have said, it's all in fun until someone loses an eye.

... You can see where this is going. The Hole Hawg is Stephenson's analogy for GNU/Linux. Like most geeks, Stephenson comes away slightly intoxicated by the superpowers that his tools have bestowed on him:

Pre-Hole Hawg, I used to examine the drill selection in hardware stores with what I thought was a judicious eye, scorning the smaller low-end models and hefting the big expensive ones appreciatively, wishing I could afford one of them babies. Now I view them all with such contempt that I do not even consider them to be real drills—merely scaled-up toys designed to exploit the self-delusional tendencies of soft-handed homeowners who want to believe that they have purchased an actual tool.[14]

Unfortunately, the scorn that Stephenson expresses for less robust drills than the Hole Hawg is sometimes analogous to the scorn that many GNU/Linux types express for other operating systems ... along with their programmers and users.

Sometimes, as in the Bastard Operator from Hell <bofh.ntk. net/Bastard. html> column on The Register <www.theregister.co.uk/ content/30/ index.html>, that scorn is nothing more than the source of a few cheap belly laughs for the disenfranchised IT workers of the world. But that scorn for the technically inept may be one of the most formidable roadblocks to the eventual acceptance of GNU/Linux by the larger world of computer users.

Rob Malda, aka CmdrTaco, the head honcho at Slashdot, recently posted a long rant beginning with the following statement: 'Linux won't ever be accepted as a truly mainstream OS by most vendors. The reason for this is quite simply the users. And I'm not talking about everyone, I'm talking about the 31337 h4x0r ['elite hacker'] kids with the bad attitude. They're posting right here on this system, intermixed with others who often share the attitude, but also have a bit more civility.'[15] Malda then relates the story of encountering a group of particularly foul-mouthed and aggressive Linux users on a Hewlett Packard Web board while looking for a driver for his scanner. His conclusion is interesting, because it could apply to the Hole Hawg as easily as it could to using Linux: 'I'm not saying drop the attitude. Linux is a superior operating system to the one that HP usually supports [i.e., Windows]. But that attitude is a double edged sword. If wielded childishly, it will hurt us all.'

Brian Proffitt of LinuxReview concurs:

When presented with a calm, reasonable-sounding statement from a large corporation versus sarcastic rants and flames from a bunch of apparent malcontents who do nothing all day but argue why Microsoft is an evil entity instead of stipulating exactly why their product is better, I will guarantee you that the average listener is going to give far more weight to the calm, reasonable-sounding statements every single time.[16]

White hat penguins

By and large, though, as GNU/Linux gains more users, and those users begin to air their inevitable questions, the community seems to be rising to the occasion.

Despite the attitude, the arcane documentation, and the difficult (if powerful) software itself, good help is available for the newbie. A growing number of members of the GNU/Linux community are realizing that a vital part of convincing people that your software is worth using is being nice to them and providing useful answers when they ask questions.

By inventing the NHF, or 'Newbieized Help File,' Linuxnewbie <linuxnewbie.org> has gone a long way toward meeting that need. The 'NHF on NHFs' (how thoughtful) begins as follows:

We the newbies of the Linux community, in Order to form a more perfect Union, establish better documentation, insure cross-platform understanding, provide for the common computer user, promote the general goodness of Linux and other OSs, and secure the Blessings of Linus to ourselves and our Posterity, do ordain and establish this Website for the Linux Newbies.

The core concept of Linuxnewbie is that NHFs are written mostly by other newbies who have figured problems out for themselves. Their language is simple and direct, and free of hostility or attitude. The only shortcoming, as with any other help system for Linux, is that coverage of all possible topics is sketchy, because there's so much information to be gathered.

Fighting Penguin <fightingpenguin.net> is a site with a similar mandate, as their motto ('Finally, good Linux help') suggests. They maintain an easily navigated database of the top GNU/Linux software, along with an index of command references and a series of help forums. Unfortunately for them, the hit counter at the bottom of their home page, which tabulates the number of hits from different operating systems, showed at the time of this writing that about twice as many Windows users as GNU/Linux users were reading their pages.

But is desktop usability *really* the direction that GNU/Linux should take to World Domination? A noted GNU/Linux hacker named Bero, who maintains his own distribution as well as working on KDE for Red Hat, believes that the direction Linux should take

strongly depends on what you want to do—I personally want to eliminate the need for non-free OSes, which means usability (and thereby KDE) needs the most attention at the moment. But then, things like scaling down to embedded devices and up to high-end servers are not exactly useless either ...[17]

The idea of Linux in embedded devices is worth exploring further, because it's already here.

Little Linuxes

Industry pundits are always predicting the death of something or other. Lately, it's been the death of the PC. An article from the BBC in February 2001 is typical: 'There has been some speculation that the real reason for falling profits at Dell and other computer companies is that nobody wants to buy PCs anymore.'[18] PC sales have slowed for a number of reasons—the market is saturated, the desktop units that people have in their possession already do pretty much everything that normal people could wish to do with a computer, and the economic downturn has shifted people's priorities to more pressing matters, like paying their rents and mortgages and putting food on the table.

But while our interest in the computers on top of our desks is waning, computers are creeping in to all sorts of other places: PDAs, automobiles, TV set-top boxes, cell phones, Web pads, Internet audio components, wrist watches, robots, servers and cameras. This is what's known as 'pervasive computing,' or the 'embedded' OS market, because the operating systems for these devices are frequently stored as part of the hardware, and can't be accessed by consumers using normal means (though hacking embedded operating systems has turned into a hobby for many people—check out <digita.mame.net/> for examples of Doom and other classic video games running in the viewfinder LCD of a Kodak digital camera).

And many of these tiny computers are powered by scaled-down versions of GNU/Linux. Pervasive computing is one area where GNU/Linux really has its shit together. The Embedded Linux Consortium <www.embedded-linux.org>, an organization of over 120 members from companies ranging from Global 100 firms to startups, with 23 corporate parents, is working hard to become a standards organization and thus to reduce fragmentation and confusion in the field. Their FAQ contains the following statement:

A reliable standardized platform will undoubtedly gain developer interest as fragmentation and forking concerns abate. As the platform gains API's in areas like Java, GUI, real-time, footprint, high availability and more, developer interest will increase rapidly. The key, we think, is interoperability. Since interoperability is difficult and expensive to achieve on a cross-platform basis, a unified Linux standard is likely to be very appealing and very competitive.[19]

This is sound thinking based on community organization on a grassroots level. Nor is the ELC alone: Linux Devices <www.linuxd evices.com>, The Embedded Linux Journal <embedded.linuxjournal. com>, All Linux Devices <alllinuxdevices.com> and a host of others provide a steady stream of news about developments in the field. If the unified desktop itself is about to dissolve into myriad other devices, GNU/Linux will already be there to power them.

Case Studies: Linux on the Desktop
City of progress

Despite all the hand-wringing and breast-beating on the issue of GNU/ Linux on the desktop, there are people and organizations here and now that make it work, big time.

If the unified desktop itself is about to dissolve into myriad other devices, GNU/Linux will already be there to power them.

Take the entire staff of the city of Largo, Florida, for example: 800 users running 400 devices, all of it powered by Red Hat Linux 7.1 with a KDE 2.1.1 desktop. These devices aren't PCs, but 'thin clients' or terminals connected to a central server—each boots in seconds, and runs its software off of a central server. The clients cost about $750 US each (cheaper units are available, but the city decided to stick with this particular high-end model because they already had several hundred of them), and the server cost about $9,500 US to build.

System Administrator Dave Richards and his 10-person tech support staff run the whole show. Richards states that there's no way that a Windows NT system could be maintained as cheaply as their Linux environment, in terms of human resources, hardware cost and software licensing fees.

If the city had opted for individual Windows boxes, Richards says, he and his IT staff would be 'doing nothing but running around fixing PCs all day.' If the city had chosen a Windows server solution, he says they'd have had to run 'a substantial server cluster' instead of a single machine, because 'NT [or 2000] gets flaky when you run more than 40 clients, while Linux can handle hundreds.'

Richards estimates that hardware savings alone are in the range of about $300,000 per year, 'just to stay current, not to increase productivity,' if they ran Windows (this is based on having to replace about 33% of their hardware each year).

Largo currently uses a mix of free and proprietary productivity software, including WordPerfect, Excel and Balsa (a GPLed e-mail client). Balsa is about to be replaced with Insight, a proprietary e-mail client. Why not Outlook? Because the total licensing costs for Insight will be about $85,000, while the costs for Outlook would be around $450,000. Richards plans to migrate the city staff to the OpenOffice suite as soon as possible— within six months to a year is their current estimate. Why not MS Office? Richards estimates the total cost of installing, licensing and maintaining MS Office to be around $1.5 million over a six-year cycle, compared with a $100,000 cost for the same period for OpenOffice.

And how are the users faring? Very nicely, thank you. The only transition glitches have been on the level of people needing to memorize new shortcut keystrokes, or learning that they're aren't allowed to load 'politically incorrect' desktop images onto their machine because they work in a public building, or learning that they don't have to back up their data every night because (a) the server handles backup automatically, and (b) the system isn't going to crash anyway, because it's GNU/Linux.[20]

GNU/Linux as best practice: ICLEI

The International Council for Local Environmental Initiatives (ICLEI) <www.iclei.org> is an international environmental agency for local governments, with a total membership of over 350 cities, towns and counties worldwide. ICLEI's mission is textbook 'think global, act local'— to build and serve a worldwide movement aimed at improving global environmental conditions and encouraging sustainable development. ICLEI's function as an information clearinghouse for a diverse global audience makes the use of the World Wide Web a natural, and its politics, together with the financial dictates of running an NGO, make GNU/Linux a natural choice for the operating system that stitches all the pieces together.

Stuart Baird, the WWW Coordinator for ICLEI, has been running the ICLEI systems on GNU/Linux for almost two years now. Like most engineers, Baird seems to enjoy getting his hands dirty; the ICLEI Web server, international e-mail server and main database are currently running Mandrake Linux 8 on a collection of plain-vanilla PCs that Baird has chopped, channeled and tweaked to achieve peak performance for minimal cash outlay.

What's more, half of the employees in the office of the ICLEI World Secretariat in Toronto happily run GNU/Linux on their desktops. The office network currently consists of 11 GNU/Linux boxes running a KDE desktop over Mandrake, plus an assortment of 11 Windows 98 and ME boxes, and two legacy Macs (this is the way of the world: years ago, ICLEI was an all-Mac shop, and switched to PCs for cost reasons).

Baird and one part-timer maintain this network with little difficulty. As system administrator, Baird can address most configuration issues for the Linux machines over the office LAN using the Linuxconf utility, without requiring users to temporarily abandon their desks or disrupting workflow.

The initial reason for ICLEI's switch to GNU/Linux was cost. Baird reasons that a new mid-powered Windows machine doubles in price after purchasing the licensing for even the most basic MS software setup for office work (i.e., some flavor of Windows, MS Office Professional Edition, a virus scanner and utilities—and this was before the onset of the new and more restrictive Office XP licensing schemes). So for the last year and a half, ICLEI adopted a policy to begin all new staff on GNU/Linux systems, assuming that it would be far easier to achieve such a switch through attrition and new hires than by addressing the conventional 'you can have my Windows when you pry it from my cold dead hands' attitude head-on.

As part of the interview process, prospective ICLEI employees are seated in front of a GNU/Linux workstation and asked to perform a series of simple tasks, such as locating files, sending e-mail, and so on. Not only does this exercise prove that there isn't all that much difference in usability between a Windows system and a contemporary GNU/Linux system, it also conditions new employees to expect to deal with GNU/Linux as a matter of course. Existing staff could (and did) volunteer to switch OSes as well; Baird provided a little incentive by dangling a few small tech perks such as sound and video cards for those willing to take the plunge (though I saw no sign at ICLEI of the usual office Quake network).

Since 90% of the day of an average ICLEI employee involves word processing, spreadsheets and e-mail, ICLEI opted to give its GNU/Linux users StarOffice 5.2 (Baird himself uses a more recent build of OpenOffice; the Windows users, of course, use Word, Excel and Outlook Express). While there was some resistance to the (soon-to-be-obsolete) StarOffice integrated desktop, users at ICLEI appreciate its tightly coordinated calendaring, scheduling and e-mailing features.

When it comes to sharing files around the office, there are few difficulties because of StarOffice's efficient conversion filters.

As with most Linux converts, ICLEI has philosophical and ideological reasons as well as financial ones for using GNU/Linux. With members worldwide, including many members in developing countries, ICLEI can't really rationalize imposing closed, proprietary standards. Since sharing information is such an important part of their mandate, the adoption of open standards seems a good and necessary step. 'Our content is primary,' says Baird. 'There's no reason not to convert Word documents into HTML, which is not only open, but can then be indexed by search engines.' (The ICLEI best practices database is written in MYSQL, which produces HTML pages on the fly.)

Organizations such as ICLEI are the foot soldiers in the battle for the recognition of Free Software and open standards as viable options for the office environment. After all the shouting and propagandizing and posturing, any remaining questions about the efficacy of GNU/Linux can be quickly dispersed by simply observing that GNU/Linux works, both as a server and on the desktop, right here, right now.

APPENDIX: FREE SOFTWARE LICENSES
GNU General Public License

Version 2, June 1991

Copyright © 1989, 1991 Free Software Foundation, Inc.

59 Temple Place, Suite 330, Boston, MA 02111-1307, USA

Everyone is permitted to copy and distribute verbatim copies of this license document, but changing it is not allowed.

Preamble

The licenses for most software are designed to take away your freedom to share and change it. By contrast, the GNU General Public License is intended to guarantee your freedom to share and change free software—to make sure the software is free for all its users. This General Public License applies to most of the Free Software Foundation's software and to any other program whose authors commit to using it. (Some other Free Software Foundation software is covered by the GNU Library General Public License instead.) You can apply it to your programs, too.

When we speak of free software, we are referring to freedom, not price. Our General Public Licenses are designed to make sure that you have the freedom to distribute copies of free software (and charge for this service if you wish), that you receive source code or can get it if you want it, that you can change the software or use pieces of it in new free programs; and that you know you can do these things.

To protect your rights, we need to make restrictions that forbid anyone to deny you these rights or to ask you to surrender the rights. These restrictions translate to certain responsibilities for you if you distribute copies of the software, or if you modify it.

For example, if you distribute copies of such a program, whether gratis or for a fee, you must give the recipients all the rights that you have. You must make sure that they, too, receive or can get the source code. And you must show them these terms so they know their rights.

We protect your rights with two steps: (1) copyright the software, and (2) offer you this license which gives you legal permission to copy, distribute and/or modify the software.

Also, for each author's protection and ours, we want to make certain that everyone understands that there is no warranty for this free software. If the software is modified by someone else and passed on, we want its recipients to know that what they have is not the original, so that any problems introduced by others will not reflect on the original authors' reputations.

Finally, any free program is threatened constantly by software patents. We wish to avoid the danger that redistributors of a free program will individually obtain patent licenses, in effect making the program proprietary. To prevent this, we have made it clear that any patent must be licensed for everyone's free use or not licensed at all.

The precise terms and conditions for copying, distribution and modification follow.

Terms and conditions for copying, distribution and modification

0. This License applies to any program or other work which contains a notice placed by the copyright holder saying it may be distributed under the terms of this General Public License. The "Program", below, refers to any such program or work, and a "work based on the Program" means either the Program or any derivative work under copyright law: that is to say, a work containing the Program or a portion of it, either verbatim or with modifications and/or translated into another language. (Hereinafter, translation is included without limitation in the term "modification".) Each licensee is addressed as "you".

    Activities other than copying, distribution and modification are not covered by this License; they are outside its scope. The act of running the Program is not restricted, and the output from the Program is covered only if its contents constitute a work based on the Program (independent of having been made by running the Program). Whether that is true depends on what the Program does.

1. You may copy and distribute verbatim copies of the Program's source code as you receive it, in any medium, provided that you conspicuously and appropriately publish on each copy an appropriate copyright notice and disclaimer of warranty; keep intact all the notices that refer to this License and to the absence of any warranty; and give any other recipients of the Program a copy of this License along with the Program.

    You may charge a fee for the physical act of transferring a copy, and you may at your option offer warranty protection in exchange for a fee.

2. You may modify your copy or copies of the Program or any portion of it, thus forming a work based on the Program, and copy and distribute such modifications or work under the terms of Section 1 above, provided that you also meet all of these conditions:

    (a) You must cause the modified files to carry prominent notices stating that you changed the files and the date of any change.

    (b) You must cause any work that you distribute or publish, that in whole or in part contains or is derived from the Program or any part thereof, to be licensed as a whole at no charge to all third parties under the terms of this License.

    (c) If the modified program normally reads commands interactively when run, you must cause it, when started running for such interactive use in the most ordinary way, to print or display an announcement including an appropriate copyright notice and a notice that there is no warranty (or else, saying that you provide a warranty) and that users may redistribute the program under these conditions, and telling the user how to view a copy of this License. (Exception: if the Program itself is interactive but does not normally print such an announcement, your work based on the Program is not required to print an announcement.) These requirements apply to the modified work as a whole. If identifiable sections of that work are not derived from the Program, and can be reasonably considered independent and separate works in themselves, then this License, and its terms, do not apply to those sections when you distribute them as separate works. But when you distribute the same sections as part of a whole which is a work based on the Program, the distribution of the whole must be on the terms of this License, whose permissions for other licensees extend to the entire whole, and thus to each and every part regardless of who wrote it.

Thus, it is not the intent of this section to claim rights or contest your rights to work written entirely by you; rather, the intent is to exercise the right to control the distribution of derivative or collective works based on the Program.

In addition, mere aggregation of another work not based on the Program with the Program (or with a work based on the Program) on a volume of a storage or distribution medium does not bring the other work under the scope of this License.

3. You may copy and distribute the Program (or a work based on it, under Section 2) in object code or executable form under the terms of Sections 1 and 2 above provided that you also do one of the following:

(a) Accompany it with the complete corresponding machine-readable source code, which must be distributed under the terms of Sections 1 and 2 above on a medium customarily used for software interchange; or,

(b) Accompany it with a written offer, valid for at least three years, to give any third party, for a charge no more than your cost of physically performing source distribution, a complete machine-readable copy of the corresponding source code, to be distributed under the terms of Sections 1 and 2 above on a medium customarily used for software interchange; or,

(c) Accompany it with the information you received as to the offer to distribute corresponding source code. (This alternative is allowed only for non-commercial distribution and only if you received the program in object code or executable form with such an offer, in accord with Subsection b above.) The source code for a work means the preferred form of the work for making modifications to it. For an executable work, complete source code means all the source code for all modules it contains, plus any associated interface definition files, plus the scripts used to control compilation and installation of the executable. However, as a special exception, the source code distributed need not include anything that is normally distributed (in either source or binary form) with the major components (compiler, kernel, and so on) of the operating system on which the executable runs, unless that component itself accompanies the executable.

If distribution of executable or object code is made by offering access to copy from a designated place, then offering equivalent access to copy the source code from the same place counts as distribution of the source code, even though third parties are not compelled to copy the source along with the object code.

4. You may not copy, modify, sublicense, or distribute the Program except as expressly provided under this License. Any attempt otherwise to copy, modify, sublicense or distribute the Program is void, and will automatically terminate your rights under this License. However, parties who have received copies, or rights, from you under this License will not have their licenses terminated so long as such parties remain in full compliance.

5. You are not required to accept this License, since you have not signed it. However, nothing else grants you permission to modify or distribute the Program or its derivative works. These actions are prohibited by law if you do not accept this License. Therefore, by modifying or distributing the Program (or any work based on the Program), you indicate your acceptance of this License to do so, and all its terms and conditions for copying, distributing or modifying the Program or works based on it.

6. Each time you redistribute the Program (or any work based on the Program), the recipient automatically receives a license from the original licensor to copy, distribute or modify the Program subject to these terms and conditions. You may not impose any further restrictions on the recipients' exercise of the rights granted herein. You are not responsible for enforcing compliance by third parties to this License.

7. If, as a consequence of a court judgment or allegation of patent infringement or for any other reason (not limited to patent issues), conditions are imposed on you (whether by court order, agreement or otherwise) that contradict the conditions of this License, they do not excuse you from the conditions of this License. If you cannot distribute so as to satisfy simultaneously your obligations under this License and any other pertinent obligations, then as a consequence you may not distribute the Program at all. For example, if a patent license would not permit royalty-free redistribution of the Program by all those who receive copies directly or indirectly through you, then the only way you could satisfy both it and this License would be to refrain entirely from distribution of the Program.

If any portion of this section is held invalid or unenforceable under any particular circumstance, the balance of the section is intended to apply and the section as a whole is intended to apply in other circumstances.

It is not the purpose of this section to induce you to infringe any patents or other property right claims or to contest validity of any such claims; this section has the sole purpose of protecting the integrity of the free software distribution system, which is implemented by public license practices. Many people have made generous contributions to the wide range of software distributed through that system in reliance on consistent application of that system; it is up to the author/donor to decide if he or she is willing to distribute software through any other system and a licensee cannot impose that choice.

This section is intended to make thoroughly clear what is believed to be a consequence of the rest of this License.

8. If the distribution and/or use of the Program is restricted in certain countries either by patents or by copyrighted interfaces, the original copyright holder who places the Program under this License may add an explicit geographical distribution limitation excluding those countries, so that distribution is permitted only in or among countries not thus excluded. In such case, this License incorporates the limitation as if written in the body of this License.

9. The Free Software Foundation may publish revised and/or new versions of the General Public License from time to time. Such new versions will be similar in spirit to the present version, but may differ in detail to address new problems or concerns.

Each version is given a distinguishing version number. If the Program specifies a version number of this License which applies to it and "any later version", you have the option of following the terms and conditions either of that version or of any later version published by the Free Software Foundation. If the Program does not specify a version number of this License, you may choose any version ever published by the Free Software Foundation.

10. If you wish to incorporate parts of the Program into other free programs whose distribution conditions are different, write to the author to ask for permission. For software which is copyrighted by the Free Software Foundation, write to the Free Software Foundation; we sometimes make exceptions for this. Our decision will be guided by the two goals of preserving the free status of all derivatives of our free software and of promoting the sharing and reuse of software generally.

No warranty

11. BECAUSE THE PROGRAM IS LICENSED FREE OF CHARGE, THERE IS NO WARRANTY FOR THE PROGRAM, TO THE EXTENT PERMITTED BY APPLICABLE LAW. EXCEPT WHEN OTHERWISE STATED IN WRITING THE COPYRIGHT HOLDERS AND/OR OTHER PARTIES PROVIDE THE PROGRAM "AS IS" WITHOUT WARRANTY OF ANY KIND, EITHER EXPRESSED OR IMPLIED, INCLUDING, BUT NOT LIMITED TO, THE IMPLIED WARRANTIES OF MERCHANTABILITY AND FITNESS FOR A PARTICULAR PURPOSE. THE ENTIRE RISK AS TO THE QUALITY AND PERFORMANCE OF THE PROGRAM IS WITH YOU. SHOULD THE PROGRAM PROVE DEFECTIVE, YOU ASSUME THE COST OF ALL NECESSARY SERVICING, REPAIR OR CORRECTION.

12. IN NO EVENT UNLESS REQUIRED BY APPLICABLE LAW OR AGREED TO IN WRITING WILL ANY COPYRIGHT HOLDER, OR ANY OTHER PARTY WHO MAY MODIFY AND/OR REDISTRIBUTE THE PROGRAM AS PERMITTED ABOVE, BE LIABLE TO YOU FOR DAMAGES, INCLUDING ANY GENERAL, SPECIAL, INCIDENTAL OR CONSEQUENTIAL DAMAGES ARISING OUT OF THE USE OR INABILITY TO USE THE PROGRAM (INCLUDING BUT NOT LIMITED TO LOSS OF DATA OR DATA BEING RENDERED INACCURATE OR LOSSES SUSTAINED BY YOU OR THIRD PARTIES OR A FAILURE OF THE PROGRAM TO OPERATE WITH ANY OTHER PROGRAMS), EVEN IF SUCH HOLDER OR OTHER PARTY HAS BEEN ADVISED OF THE POSSIBILITY OF SUCH DAMAGES.

END OF TERMS AND CONDITIONS

How to apply these terms to your new programs

If you develop a new program, and you want it to be of the greatest possible use to the public, the best way to achieve this is to make it free software which everyone can redistribute and change under these terms.

To do so, attach the following notices to the program. It is safest to attach them to the start of each source file to most effectively convey the exclusion of warranty; and each file should have at least the "copyright" line and a pointer to where the full notice is found.

One line to give the program's name and an idea of what it does.

Copyright © yyyy name of author

This program is free software; you can redistribute it and/or modify it under the terms of the GNU General Public License as published by the Free Software Foundation; either version 2 of the License, or (at your option) any later version.

This program is distributed in the hope that it will be useful, but WITHOUT ANY WARRANTY; without even the implied warranty of MERCHANTABILITY or FITNESS FOR A PARTICULAR PURPOSE. See the GNU General Public License for more details.

You should have received a copy of the GNU General Public License along with this program; if not, write to the Free Software Foundation, Inc., 59 Temple Place, Suite 330, Boston, MA 02111-1307, USA.

Also add information on how to contact you by electronic and paper mail.

If the program is interactive, make it output a short notice like this when it starts in an interactive mode:

Gnomovision version 69, Copyright (C) year name of author

Gnomovision comes with ABSOLUTELY NO WARRANTY; for details type 'show w'. This is free software, and you are welcome to redistribute it under certain conditions; type 'show c' for details.

The hypothetical commands 'show w' and 'show c' should show the appropriate parts of the General Public License. Of course, the commands you use may be called something other than 'show w' and 'show c'; they could even be mouse-clicks or menu items—whatever suits your program.

You should also get your employer (if you work as a programmer) or your school, if any, to sign a 'copyright disclaimer' for the program, if necessary. Here is a sample; alter the names:

Yoyodyne, Inc., hereby disclaims all copyright interest in the program 'Gnomovision' (which makes passes at compilers) written by James Hacker.

signature of Ty Coon, 1 April 1989

Ty Coon, President of Vice

This General Public License does not permit incorporating your program into proprietary programs. If your program is a subroutine library, you may consider it more useful to permit linking proprietary applications with the library. If this is what you want to do, use the GNU Library General Public License instead of this License.

GNU Lesser General Public License

Version 2.1, February 1999

Copyright © 1991, 1999 Free Software Foundation, Inc.

59 Temple Place, Suite 330, Boston, MA 02111-1307 USA

Everyone is permitted to copy and distribute verbatim copies of this license document, but changing it is not allowed.

[This is the first released version of the Lesser GPL. It also counts as the successor of the GNU Library Public License, version 2, hence the version number 2.1.]

Preamble

The licenses for most software are designed to take away your freedom to share and change it. By contrast, the GNU General Public Licenses are intended to guarantee your freedom to share and change free software—to make sure the software is free for all its users.

This license, the Lesser General Public License, applies to some specially designated software packages—typically libraries—of the Free Software Foundation and other authors who decide to use it. You can use it too, but we suggest you first think carefully about whether this license or the ordinary General Public License is the better strategy to use in any particular case, based on the explanations below.

When we speak of free software, we are referring to freedom of use, not price. Our General Public Licenses are designed to make sure that you have the freedom to distribute copies of free software (and charge for this service if you wish); that you receive source code or can get it if you want it; that you can change the software and use pieces of it in new free programs; and that you are informed that you can do these things.

To protect your rights, we need to make restrictions that forbid distributors to deny you these rights or to ask you to surrender these rights. These restrictions translate to certain responsibilities for you if you distribute copies of the library or if you modify it.

For example, if you distribute copies of the library, whether gratis or for a fee, you must give the recipients all the rights that we gave you. You must make sure that they, too, receive or can get the source code. If you link other code with the library, you must provide complete object files to the recipients, so that they can relink them with the library after making changes to the library and recompiling it. And you must show them these terms so they know their rights.

We protect your rights with a two-step method: (1) we copyright the library, and (2) we offer you this license, which gives you legal permission to copy, distribute and/or modify the library.

To protect each distributor, we want to make it very clear that there is no warranty for the free library. Also, if the library is modified by someone else and passed on, the recipients should know that what they have is not the original version, so that the original author's reputation will not be affected by problems that might be introduced by others.

Finally, software patents pose a constant threat to the existence of any free program. We wish to make sure that a company cannot effectively restrict the users of a free program by obtaining a restrictive license from a patent holder. Therefore, we insist that any patent license obtained for a version of the library must be consistent with the full freedom of use specified in this license.

Most GNU software, including some libraries, is covered by the ordinary GNU General Public License. This license, the GNU Lesser General Public License, applies to certain designated libraries, and is quite different from the ordinary General Public License. We use this license for certain libraries in order to permit linking those libraries into non-free programs.

When a program is linked with a library, whether statically or using a shared library, the combination of the two is legally speaking a combined work, a derivative of the original library. The ordinary General Public License therefore permits such linking only if the entire combination fits its criteria of freedom. The Lesser General Public License permits more lax criteria for linking other code with the library.

We call this license the "Lesser" General Public License because it does Less to protect the user's freedom than the ordinary General Public License. It also provides other free software developers Less of an advantage over competing non-free programs. These disadvantages are the reason we use the ordinary General Public License for many libraries. However, the Lesser license provides advantages in certain special circumstances.

For example, on rare occasions, there may be a special need to encourage the widest possible use of a certain library, so that it becomes a de-facto standard. To achieve this, non-free programs must be allowed to use the library. A more frequent case is that a free library does the same job as widely used non-free libraries. In this case, there is little to gain by limiting the free library to free software only, so we use the Lesser General Public License.

In other cases, permission to use a particular library in non-free programs enables a greater number of people to use a large body of free software. For example, permission to use the GNU C Library in non-free programs enables many more people to use the whole GNU operating system, as well as its variant, the GNU/Linux operating system.

Although the Lesser General Public License is Less protective of the user's freedom, it does ensure that the user of a program that is linked with the Library has the freedom and the wherewithal to run that program using a modified version of the Library.

The precise terms and conditions for copying, distribution and modification follow. Pay close attention to the difference between a "work based on the library" and a "work that uses the library". The former contains code derived from the library, whereas the latter must be combined with the library in order to run.

GNU lesser general public license terms and conditions for copying, distribution and modification

0. This License Agreement applies to any software library or other program which contains a notice placed by the copyright holder or other authorized party saying it may be distributed under the terms of this Lesser General Public License (also called "this License"). Each licensee is addressed as "you".

    A "library" means a collection of software functions and/or data prepared so as to be conveniently linked with application programs (which use some of those functions and data) to form executables.

    The "Library", below, refers to any such software library or work which has been distributed under these terms. A "work based on the Library" means either the Library or any derivative work under copyright law: that is to say, a work containing the Library or a portion of it, either verbatim or with modifications and/or translated straightforwardly into another language. (Hereinafter, translation is included without limitation in the term "modification".)

    "Source code" for a work means the preferred form of the work for making modifications to it. For a library, complete source code means all the source code for all modules it contains, plus any associated interface definition files, plus the scripts used to control compilation and installation of the library.

    Activities other than copying, distribution and modification are not covered by this License; they are outside its scope. The act of running a program using the Library is not restricted, and output from such a program is covered only if its contents constitute a work based on the Library (independent of the use of the Library in a tool for writing it). Whether that is true depends on what the Library does and what the program that uses the Library does.

1. You may copy and distribute verbatim copies of the Library's complete source code as you receive it, in any medium, provided that you conspicuously and appropriately publish on each copy an appropriate copyright notice and disclaimer of warranty; keep intact all the notices that refer to this License and to the absence of any warranty; and distribute a copy of this License along with the Library.

   You may charge a fee for the physical act of transferring a copy, and you may at your option offer warranty protection in exchange for a fee.

2. You may modify your copy or copies of the Library or any portion of it, thus forming a work based on the Library, and copy and distribute such modifications or work under the terms of Section 1 above, provided that you also meet all of these conditions:

   (a) the modified work must itself be a software library.

   (b) you must cause the files modified to carry prominent notices stating that you changed the files and the date of any change.

   (c) you must cause the whole of the work to be licensed at no charge to all third parties under the terms of this License.

   (d) if a facility in the modified Library refers to a function or a table of data to be supplied by an application program that uses the facility, other than as an argument passed when the facility is invoked, then you must make a good faith effort to ensure that, in the event an application does not supply such function or table, the facility still operates, and performs whatever part of its purpose remains meaningful.

   (For example, a function in a library to compute square roots has a purpose that is entirely well-defined independent of the application. Therefore, Subsection 2d requires that any application-supplied function or table used by this function must be optional: if the application does not supply it, the square root function must still compute square roots.) These requirements apply to the modified work as a whole. If identifiable sections of that work are not derived from the Library, and can be reasonably considered independent and separate works in themselves, then this License, and its terms, do not apply to those sections when you distribute them as separate works. But when you distribute the same sections as part of a whole which is a work based on the Library, the distribution of the whole must be on the terms of this License, whose permissions for other licensees extend to the entire whole, and thus to each and every part regardless of who wrote it. Thus, it is not the intent of this section to claim rights or contest your rights to work written entirely by you; rather, the intent is to exercise the right to control the distribution of derivative or collective works based on the Library. In addition, mere aggregation of another work not based on the Library with the Library (or with a work based on the Library) on a volume of a storage or distribution medium does not bring the other work under the scope of this License.

3.   You may opt to apply the terms of the ordinary GNU General Public License instead of this License to a given copy of the Library. To do this, you must alter all the notices that refer to this License, so that they refer to the ordinary GNU General Public License, version 2, instead of to this License. (If a newer version than version 2 of the ordinary GNU General Public License has appeared, then you can specify that version instead if you wish.) Do not make any other change in these notices.

   Once this change is made in a given copy, it is irreversible for that copy, so the ordinary GNU General Public License applies to all subsequent copies and derivative works made from that copy.

   This option is useful when you wish to copy part of the code of the Library into a program that is not a library.

4.   You may copy and distribute the Library (or a portion or derivative of it, under Section 2) in object code or executable form under the terms of Sections 1 and 2 above provided that you accompany it with the complete corresponding machine-readable source code, which must be distributed under the terms of Sections 1 and 2 above on a medium customarily used for software interchange.

   If distribution of object code is made by offering access to copy from a designated place, then offering equivalent access to copy the source code from the same place satisfies the requirement to distribute the source code, even though third parties are not compelled to copy the source along with the object code.

5.   A program that contains no derivative of any portion of the Library, but is designed to work with the Library by being compiled or linked with it, is called a "work that uses the Library". Such a work, in isolation, is not a derivative work of the Library, and therefore falls outside the scope of this License.

   However, linking a "work that uses the Library" with the Library creates an executable that is a derivative of the Library (because it contains portions of the Library), rather than a "work that uses the library". The executable is there-fore covered by this License. Section 6 states terms for distribution of such executables.

   When a "work that uses the Library" uses material from a header file that is part of the Library, the object code for the work may be a derivative work of the Library even though the source code is not. Whether this is true is especially sig-nificant if the work can be linked without the Library, or if the work is itself a library. The threshold for this to be true is not precisely defined by law.

   If such an object file uses only numerical parameters, data structure layouts and accessors, and small macros and small inline functions (ten lines or less in length), then the use of the object file is unrestricted, regardless of whether it is legally a derivative work. (Executables containing this object code plus portions of the Library will still fall under Section 6.)

Otherwise, if the work is a derivative of the Library, you may distribute the object code for the work under the terms of Section 6. Any executables containing that work also fall under Section 6, whether or not they are linked directly with the Library itself.

6. As an exception to the Sections above, you may also combine or link a "work that uses the Library" with the Library to produce a work containing portions of the Library, and distribute that work under terms of your choice, provided that the terms permit modification of the work for the customer's own use and reverse engineering for debugging such modifications.

You must give prominent notice with each copy of the work that the Library is used in it and that the Library and its use are covered by this License. You must supply a copy of this License. If the work during execution displays copyright notices, you must include the copyright notice for the Library among them, as well as a reference directing the user to the copy of this License. Also, you must do one of these things:

(a) Accompany the work with the complete corresponding machine-readable source code for the Library including whatever changes were used in the work (which must be distributed under Sections 1 and 2 above); and, if the work is an executable linked with the Library, with the complete machine-readable "work that uses the Library", as object code and/or source code, so that the user can modify the Library and then relink to produce a modified executable containing the modified Library. (It is understood that the user who changes the contents of definitions files in the Library will not necessarily be able to recompile the application to use the modified definitions.)

(b) Use a suitable shared library mechanism for linking with the Library. A suitable mechanism is one that (1) uses at run time a copy of the library already present on the user's computer system, rather than copying library functions into the executable, and (2) will operate properly with a modified version of the library, if the user installs one, as long as the modified version is interface-compatible with the version that the work was made with.

(c) Accompany the work with a written offer, valid for at least three years, to give the same user the materials specified in Subsection 6a, above, for a charge no more than the cost of performing this distribution.

(d) If distribution of the work is made by offering access to copy from a designated place, offer equivalent access to copy the above specified materials from the same place.

(e) Verify that the user has already received a copy of thes materials or that you have already sent this user a copy.

For an executable, the required form of the "work that uses the Library" must include any data and utility programs needed for reproducing the executable from it. However, as a special exception, the materials to be distributed need not include anything that is normally distributed (in either source or binary form) with the major components (compiler, kernel, and so on) of the operating system on which the executable runs, unless that component itself accompanies the executable.

It may happen that this requirement contradicts the license restrictions of other proprietary libraries that do not normally accompany the operating system. Such a contradiction means you cannot use both them and the Library together in an executable that you distribute.

7. You may place library facilities that are a work based on the Library side-by-side in a single library together with other library facilities not covered by this License, and distribute such a combined library, provided that the separate distribution of the work based on the Library and of the other library facilities is otherwise permitted, and provided that you do these two things:

    (a) Accompany the combined library with a copy of the same work based on the Library, uncombined with any other library facilities. This must be distributed under the terms of the Sections above.

    (b) Give prominent notice with the combined library of the fact that part of it is a work based on the Library, and explaining where to find the accompanying uncombined form of the same work.

8. You may not copy, modify, sublicense, link with, or distribute the Library except as expressly provided under this License. Any attempt otherwise to copy, modify, sublicense, link with, or distribute the Library is void, and will automatically terminate your rights under this License. However, parties who have received copies, or rights, from you under this License will not have their licenses terminated so long as such parties remain in full compliance.

9. You are not required to accept this License, since you have not signed it. However, nothing else grants you permission to modify or distribute the Library or its derivative works. These actions are prohibited by law if you do not accept this License. Therefore, by modifying or distributing the Library (or any work based on the Library), you indicate your acceptance of this License to do so, and all its terms and conditions for copying, distributing or modifying the Library or works based on it.

10. Each time you redistribute the Library (or any work based on the Library), the recipient automatically receives a license from the original licensor to copy, distribute, link with or modify the Library subject to these terms and conditions. You may not impose any further restrictions on the recipients' exercise of the rights granted herein. You are not responsible for enforcing compliance by third parties with this License.

11. If, as a consequence of a court judgment or allegation of patent infringement or for any other reason (not limited to patent issues), conditions are imposed on you (whether by court order, agreement or otherwise) that contradict the conditions of this License, they do not excuse you from the conditions of this

License. If you cannot distribute so as to satisfy simultaneously your obligations under this License and any other pertinent obligations, then as a consequence you may not distribute the Library at all. For example, if a patent license would not permit royalty-free redistribution of the Library by all those who receive copies directly or indirectly through you, then the only way you could satisfy both it and this License would be to refrain entirely from distribution of the Library. If any portion of this section is held invalid or unenforceable under any particular circumstance, the balance of the section is intended to apply, and the section as a whole is intended to apply in other circumstances. It is not the purpose of this section to induce you to infringe any patents or other property right claims or to contest validity of any such claims; this section has the sole purpose of protecting the integrity of the free software distribution system which is implemented by public license practices. Many people have made generous contributions to the wide range of software distributed through that system in reliance on consistent application of that system; it is up to the author/donor to decide if he or she is willing to distribute software through any other system and a licensee cannot impose that choice. This section is intended to make thoroughly clear what is believed to be a consequence of the rest of this License.

12. If the distribution and/or use of the Library is restricted in certain countries either by patents or by copyrighted interfaces, the original copyright holder who places the Library under this License may add an explicit geographical distribution limitation excluding those countries, so that distribution is permitted only in or among countries not thus excluded. In such case, this License incorporates the limitation as if written in the body of this License.

13. The Free Software Foundation may publish revised and/or new versions of the Lesser General Public License from time to time. Such new versions will be similar in spirit to the present version, but may differ in detail to address new problems or concerns. Each version is given a distinguishing version number. If the Library specifies a version number of this License which applies to it and "any later version", you have the option of following the terms and conditions either of that version or of any later version published by the Free Software Foundation. If the Library does not specify a license version number, you may choose any version ever published by the Free Software Foundation.

14. If you wish to incorporate parts of the Library into other free programs whose distribution conditions are incompatible with these, write to the author to ask for permission. For software which is copyrighted by the Free Software Foundation, write to the Free Software Foundation; we sometimes make exceptions for this. Our decision will be guided by the two goals of preserving the free status of all derivatives of our free software and of promoting the sharing and reuse of software generally.

No warranty

15. BECAUSE THE LIBRARY IS LICENSED FREE OF CHARGE, THERE IS NO WARRANTY FOR THE LIBRARY, TO THE EXTENT PERMITTED BY APPLICABLE LAW. EXCEPT WHEN OTHERWISE STATED IN WRITING THE COPYRIGHT HOLDERS AND/OR OTHER PARTIES PROVIDE THE LIBRARY "AS IS" WITHOUT WARRANTY OF ANY KIND, EITHER EXPRESSED OR IMPLIED, INCLUDING, BUT NOT LIMITED TO, THE IMPLIED WARRANTIES OF MERCHANTABILITY AND FITNESS FOR A PARTICULAR PURPOSE. THE ENTIRE RISK AS TO THE QUALITY AND PERFORMANCE OF THE LIBRARY IS WITH YOU. SHOULD THE LIBRARY PROVE DEFECTIVE, YOU ASSUME THE COST OF ALL NECESSARY SERVICING, REPAIR OR CORRECTION.

16. IN NO EVENT UNLESS REQUIRED BY APPLICABLE LAW OR AGREED TO IN WRITING WILL ANY COPYRIGHT HOLDER, OR ANY OTHER PARTY WHO MAY MODIFY AND/OR REDISTRIBUTE THE LIBRARY AS PERMIT-TED ABOVE, BE LIABLE TO YOU FOR DAMAGES, INCLUDING ANY GENERAL, SPECIAL, INCIDENTAL OR CONSEQUENTIAL DAMAGES ARISING OUT OF THE USE OR INABILITY TO USE THE LIBRARY (INCLUDING BUT NOT LIMITED TO LOSS OF DATA OR DATA BEING RENDERED INACCURATE OR LOSSES SUSTAINED BY YOU OR THIRD PARTIES OR A FAILURE OF THE LIBRARY TO OPERATE WITH ANY OTHER SOFTWARE), EVEN IF SUCH HOLDER OR OTHER PARTY HAS BEEN ADVISED OF THE POSSIBILITY OF SUCH DAMAGES.

END OF TERMS AND CONDITIONS

How to apply these terms to your new libraries

If you develop a new library, and you want it to be of the greatest possible use to the public, we recommend making it free software that everyone can redistribute and change. You can do so by permitting redistribution under these terms (or, alternatively, under the terms of the ordinary General Public License).

To apply these terms, attach the following notices to the library. It is safest to attach them to the start of each source file to most effectively convey the exclusion of warranty; and each file should have at least the "copyright" line and a pointer to where the full notice is found. <one line to give the library's name and a brief idea of what it does.> Copyright © <year> <name of author> This library is free software; you can redistribute it and/or modify it under the terms of the GNU Lesser General Public License as published by the Free Software Foundation; either version 2.1 of the License, or (at your option) any later version. This library is distributed in the hope that it will be useful, but WITHOUT ANY WARRANTY; without even the implied warranty of MERCHANTABILITY or FITNESS FOR A PARTICULAR PURPOSE. See the GNU Lesser General Public License for more details. You should have received a copy of the

GNU Lesser General Public License along with this library; if not, write to the Free Software Foundation, Inc., 59 Temple Place, Suite 330, Boston, MA 02111-1307 USA. Also add information on how to contact you by electronic and paper mail. You should also get your employer (if you work as a programmer) or your school, if any, to sign a "copyright disclaimer" for the library, if necessary. Here is a sample; alter the names:

Yoyodyne, Inc., hereby disclaims all copyright interest in the library 'Frob' (a library for tweaking knobs) written by James Random Hacker.

<signature of Ty Coon>, 1 April 1990

Ty Coon, President of Vice

That's all there is to it!

GNU Free Documentation License

Version 1.1, March 2000

Copyright © 2000 Free Software Foundation, Inc.

59 Temple Place, Suite 330, Boston, MA 02111-1307 USA

Everyone is permitted to copy and distribute verbatim copies of this license document, but changing it is not allowed.

0. Preamble

The purpose of this License is to make a manual, textbook, or other written document "free" in the sense of freedom: to assure everyone the effective freedom to copy and redistribute it, with or without modifying it, either commercially or noncommercially. Secondarily, this License preserves for the author and publisher a way to get credit for their work, while not being considered responsible for modifications made by others.

This License is a kind of "copyleft", which means that derivative works of the document must themselves be free in the same sense. It complements the GNU General Public License, which is a copyleft license designed for free software.

We have designed this License in order to use it for manuals for free software, because free software needs free documentation: a free program should come with manuals providing the same freedoms that the software does. But this License is not limited to software manuals; it can be used for any textual work, regardless of subject matter or whether it is published as a printed book. We recommend this License principally for works whose purpose is instruction or reference.

1. Applicability and definitions

This License applies to any manual or other work that contains a notice placed by the copyright holder saying it can be distributed under the terms of this License. The

"Document", below, refers to any such manual or work. Any member of the public is a licensee, and is addressed as "you".

A "Modified Version" of the Document means any work containing the Document or a portion of it, either copied verbatim, or with modifications and/or translated into another language.

A "Secondary Section" is a named appendix or a front-matter section of the Document that deals exclusively with the relationship of the publishers or authors of the Document to the Document's overall subject (or to related matters) and contains nothing that could fall directly within that overall subject. (For example, if the Document is in part a textbook of mathematics, a Secondary Section may not explain any mathematics.) The relationship could be a matter of historical connection with the subject or with related matters, or of legal, commercial, philosophical, ethical, or political position regarding them.

The "Invariant Sections" are certain Secondary Sections whose titles are designated, as being those of Invariant Sections, in the notice that says that the Document is released under this License.

The "Cover Texts" are certain short passages of text that are listed, as Front-Cover Texts or Back-Cover Texts, in the notice that says that the Document is released under this License.

A "Transparent" copy of the Document means a machine-readable copy, represented in a format whose specification is available to the general public, whose contents can be viewed and edited directly and straightforwardly with generic text editors or (for images composed of pixels) generic paint programs or (for drawings) some widely available drawing editor, and that is suitable for input to text formatters or for automatic translation to a variety of formats suitable for input to text formatters. A copy made in an otherwise Transparent file format whose markup has been designed to thwart or discourage subsequent modification by readers is not Transparent. A copy that is not "Transparent" is called "Opaque".

Examples of suitable formats for Transparent copies include plain ASCII without markup, Texinfo input format, LaTeX input format, SGML or XML using a publicly available DTD, and standard-conforming simple HTML designed for human modification. Opaque formats include PostScript, PDF, proprietary formats that can be read and edited only by proprietary word processors, SGML or XML for which the DTD and/or processing tools are not generally available, and the machine-generated HTML produced by some word processors for output purposes only.

The "Title Page" means, for a printed book, the title page itself, plus such following pages as are needed to hold, legibly, the material this License requires to appear in the title page. For works in formats which do not have any title page as such, "Title Page" means the text near the most prominent appearance of the work's title, preceding the beginning of the body of the text.

2. Verbatim copying

You may copy and distribute the Document in any medium, either commercially or noncommercially, provided that this License, the copyright notices, and the license notice saying this License applies to the Document are reproduced in all copies, and that you add no other conditions whatsoever to those of this License. You may not use technical measures to obstruct or control the reading or further copying of the copies you make or distribute. However, you may accept compensation in exchange for copies. If you distribute a large enough number of copies you must also follow the conditions in section 3.

You may also lend copies, under the same conditions stated above, and you may publicly display copies.

3. Copying in quality

If you publish printed copies of the Document numbering more than 100, and the Document's license notice requires Cover Texts, you must enclose the copies in covers that carry, clearly and legibly, all these Cover Texts: Front-Cover Texts on the front cover, and Back-Cover Texts on the back cover. Both covers must also clearly and legibly identify you as the publisher of these copies. The front cover must present the full title with all words of the title equally prominent and visible. You may add other material on the covers in addition. Copying with changes limited to the covers, as long as they preserve the title of the Document and satisfy these conditions, can be treated as verbatim copying in other respects.

If the required texts for either cover are too voluminous to fit legibly, you should put the first ones listed (as many as fit reasonably) on the actual cover, and continue the rest onto adjacent pages.

If you publish or distribute Opaque copies of the Document numbering more than 100, you must either include a machine-readable Transparent copy along with each Opaque copy, or state in or with each Opaque copy a publicly-accessible computer-network location containing a complete Transparent copy of the Document, free of added material, which the general network-using public has access to download anonymously at no charge using public-standard network protocols. If you use the latter option, you must take reasonably prudent steps, when you begin distribution of Opaque copies in quantity, to ensure that this Transparent copy will remain thus accessible at the stated location until at least one year after the last time you distribute an Opaque copy (directly or through your agents or retailers) of that edition to the public.

It is requested, but not required, that you contact the authors of the Document well before redistributing any large number of copies, to give them a chance to provide you with an updated version of the Document.

4. Modifications

You may copy and distribute a Modified Version of the Document under the conditions of sections 2 and 3 above, provided that you release the Modified Version under precisely this License, with the Modified Version filling the role of the Document, thus licensing distribution and modification of the Modified Version to whoever possesses a copy of it. In addition, you must do these things in the Modified Version:

A. Use in the Title Page (and on the covers, if any) a title distinct from that of the Document, and from those of previous versions (which should, if there were any, be listed in the History section of the Document). You may use the same title as a previous version if the original publisher of that version gives permission.

B. List on the Title Page, as authors, one or more persons or entities responsible for authorship of the modifications in the Modified Version, together with at least five of the principal authors of the Document (all of its principal authors, if it has less than five).

C. State on the Title page the name of the publisher of the Modified Version, as the publisher.

D. Preserve all the copyright notices of the Document.

E. Add an appropriate copyright notice for your modifications adjacent to the other copyright notices.

F. Include, immediately after the copyright notices, a license notice giving the public permission to use the Modified Version under the terms of this License, in the form shown in the Addendum below.

G. Preserve in that license notice the full lists of Invariant Sections and required Cover Texts given in the Document's license notice.

H. Include an unaltered copy of this License.

I. Preserve the section entitled "History", and its title, and add to it an item stating at least the title, year, new authors, and publisher of the Modified Version as given on the Title Page. If there is no section entitled "History" in the Document, create one stating the title, year, authors, and publisher of the Document as given on its Title Page, then add an item describing the Modified Version as stated in the previous sentence.

J. Preserve the network location, if any, given in the Document for public access to a Transparent copy of the Document, and likewise the network locations given in the Document for previous versions it was based on. These may be placed in the "History" section. You may omit a network location for a work that was published at least four years before the Document itself, or if the original publisher of the version it refers to gives permission.

K.   In any section entitled "Acknowledgements" or "Dedications", preserve the section's title, and preserve in the section all the substance and tone of each of the contributor acknowledgements and/or dedications given therein.

L.   Preserve all the Invariant Sections of the Document, unaltered in their text and in their titles. Section numbers or the equivalent are not considered part of the section titles.

M.   Delete any section entitled "Endorsements". Such a section may not be included in the Modified Version.

N.   Do not retitle any existing section as "Endorsements" or to conflict in title with any Invariant Section.

If the Modified Version includes new front-matter sections or appendices that qualify as Secondary Sections and contain no material copied from the Document, you may at your option designate some or all of these sections as invariant. To do this, add their titles to the list of Invariant Sections in the Modified Version's license notice. These titles must be distinct from any other section titles.

You may add a section entitled "Endorsements", provided it contains nothing but endorsements of your Modified Version by various parties—for example, statements of peer review or that the text has been approved by an organization as the authoritative definition of a standard.

You may add a passage of up to five words as a Front-Cover Text, and a passage of up to 25 words as a Back-Cover Text, to the end of the list of Cover Texts in the Modified Version. Only one passage of Front-Cover Text and one of Back-Cover Text may be added by (or through arrangements made by) any one entity. If the Document already includes a cover text for the same cover, previously added by you or by arrangement made by the same entity you are acting on behalf of, you may not add another; but you may replace the old one, on explicit permission from the previous publisher that added the old one.

The author(s) and publisher(s) of the Document do not by this License give permission to use their names for publicity for or to assert or imply endorsement of any Modified Version.

5. Combining documents

You may combine the Document with other documents released under this License, under the terms defined in section 4 above for modified versions, provided that you include in the combination all of the Invariant Sections of all of the original documents, unmodified, and list them all as Invariant Sections of your combined work in its license notice.

The combined work need only contain one copy of this License, and multiple identical Invariant Sections may be replaced with a single copy. If there are multiple Invariant Sections with the same name but different contents, make the title of each such section unique by adding at the end of it, in parentheses, the name of the original author or publisher of that section if known, or else a unique number. Make the same adjustment to the section titles in the list of Invariant Sections in the license notice of the combined work.

In the combination, you must combine any sections entitled "History" in the various original documents, forming one section entitled "History"; likewise combine any sections entitled "Acknowledgements", and any sections entitled "Dedications". You must delete all sections entitled "Endorsements."

6. Collections of documents

You may make a collection consisting of the Document and other documents released under this License, and replace the individual copies of this License in the various documents with a single copy that is included in the collection, provided that you follow the rules of this License for verbatim copying of each of the documents in all other respects.

You may extract a single document from such a collection, and distribute it individually under this License, provided you insert a copy of this License into the extracted document, and follow this License in all other respects regarding verbatim copying of that document.

7. Aggregation with independent works

A compilation of the Document or its derivatives with other separate and independent documents or works, in or on a volume of a storage or distribution medium, does not as a whole count as a Modified Version of the Document, provided no compilation copyright is claimed for the compilation. Such a compilation is called an "aggregate", and this License does not apply to the other self-contained works thus compiled with the Document, on account of their being thus compiled, if they are not themselves derivative works of the Document.

If the Cover Text requirement of section 3 is applicable to these copies of the Document, then if the Document is less than one quarter of the entire aggregate, the Document's Cover Texts may be placed on covers that surround only the Document within the aggregate. Otherwise they must appear on covers around the whole aggregate.

8. Translation

Translation is considered a kind of modification, so you may distribute translations of the Document under the terms of section 4. Replacing Invariant Sections with translations requires special permission from their copyright holders, but you may include translations of some or all Invariant Sections in addition to the original versions of these Invariant Sections. You may include a translation of this License provided that you also include the original English version of this License. In case of a disagreement between the translation and the original English version of this License, the original English version will prevail.

9. Termination

You may not copy, modify, sublicense, or distribute the Document except as expressly provided for under this License. Any other attempt to copy, modify, sublicense or distribute the Document is void, and will automatically terminate your rights under this License. However, parties who have received copies, or rights, from you under this License will not have their licenses terminated so long as such parties remain in full compliance.

10. Future revisions of this license

The Free Software Foundation may publish new, revised versions of the GNU Free Documentation License from time to time. Such new versions will be similar in spirit to the present version, but may differ in detail to address new problems or concerns. See http://www.gnu.org/copyleft/.

Each version of the License is given a distinguishing version number. If the Document specifies that a particular numbered version of this License "or any later version" applies to it, you have the option of following the terms and conditions either of that specified version or of any later version that has been published (not as a draft) by the Free Software Foundation. If the Document does not specify a version number of this License, you may choose any version ever published (not as a draft) by the Free Software Foundation.

Addendum: How to use this license for your documents

To use this License in a document you have written, include a copy of the License in the document and put the following copyright and license notices just after the title page:

Copyright © YEAR YOUR NAME.

Permission is granted to copy, distribute and/or modify this document under the terms of the GNU Free Documentation License, Version 1.1 or any later version published by the Free Software Foundation; with the Invariant Sections being LIST THEIR TITLES, with the Front-Cover Texts being LIST, and with the Back-Cover Texts being LIST. A copy of the license is included in the section entitled "GNU Free Documentation License".

If you have no Invariant Sections, write "with no Invariant Sections" instead of saying which ones are invariant. If you have no Front-Cover Texts, write "no Front-Cover Texts" instead of "Front-Cover Texts being LIST"; likewise for Back-Cover Texts.

If your document contains nontrivial examples of program code, we recommend releasing these examples in parallel under your choice of free software license, such as the GNU General Public License, to permit their use in free software.

The BSD License

The following is a BSD license template. To generate your own license, change the values of OWNER, ORGANIZATION and YEAR from their original values as given here, and substitute your own.

Note: The advertising clause in the license appearing on BSD Unix files was officially rescinded by the Director of the Office of Technology Licensing of the University of California on July 22 1999. He states that clause 3 is "hereby deleted in its entirety."

Note the new BSD license is thus equivalent to the MIT License, except for the no-endorsement final clause.

<OWNER> = Regents of the University of California

<ORGANIZATION> = University of California, Berkeley

<YEAR> = 1998

In the original BSD license, the first occurrence of the phrase "COPYRIGHT HOLDERS AND CONTRIBUTORS" in the disclaimer read "REGENTS AND CONTRIBUTORS".

Here is the license template:

Copyright © <YEAR>, <OWNER>

All rights reserved.

Redistribution and use in source and binary forms, with or without modification, are permitted provided that the following conditions are met:

* Redistributions of source code must retain the above copyright notice, this list of conditions and the following disclaimer.

* Redistributions in binary form must reproduce the above copyright notice, this list of conditions and the following disclaimer in the documentation and/or other materials provided with the distribution.

* Neither the name of the <ORGANIZATION> nor the names of its contributors may be used to endorse or promote products derived from this software without specific prior written permission.

THIS SOFTWARE IS PROVIDED BY THE COPYRIGHT HOLDERS AND CONTRIBUTORS "AS IS" AND ANY EXPRESS OR IMPLIED WARRANTIES, INCLUDING, BUT NOT LIMITED TO, THE IMPLIED WARRANTIES OF MERCHANTABILITY AND FITNESS FOR A PARTICULAR PURPOSE ARE DISCLAIMED. IN NO EVENT SHALL THE REGENTS OR CONTRIBUTORS BE LIABLE FOR ANY DIRECT, INDIRECT, INCIDENTAL, SPECIAL, EXEMPLARY, OR

CONSEQUENTIAL DAMAGES (INCLUDING, BUT NOT LIMITED TO, PROCUREMENT OF SUBSTITUTE GOODS OR SERVICES; LOSS OF USE, DATA, OR PROFITS; OR BUSINESS INTERRUPTION) HOWEVER CAUSED AND ON ANY THEORY OF LIABILITY, WHETHER IN CONTRACT, STRICT LIABILITY, OR TORT (INCLUDING NEGLIGENCE OR OTHERWISE) ARISING IN ANY WAY OUT OF THE USE OF THIS SOFTWARE, EVEN IF ADVISED OF THE POSSIBILITY OF SUCH DAMAGE.

Netscape Public License

Version 1.0

1. Definitions.

1.1. "Contributor" means each entity that creates or contributes to the creation of Modifications.

1.2. "Contributor Version" means the combination of the Original Code, prior Modifications used by a Contributor, and the Modifications made by that particular Contributor.

1.3. "Covered Code" means the Original Code or Modifications or the combination of the Original Code and Modifications, in each case including portions thereof.

1.4. "Electronic Distribution Mechanism" means a mechanism generally accepted in the software development community for the electronic transfer of data.

1.5. "Executable" means Covered Code in any form other than Source Code.

1.6. "Initial Developer" means the individual or entity identified as the Initial Developer in the Source Code notice required by Exhibit A.

1.7. "Larger Work" means a work which combines Covered Code or portions thereof with code not governed by the terms of this License.

1.8. "License" means this document.

1.9. "Modifications" means any addition to or deletion from the substance or structure of either the Original Code or any previous Modifications. When Covered Code is released as a series of files, a Modification is:

A.   Any addition to or deletion from the contents of a file containing Original Code or previous Modifications.

B.   Any new file that contains any part of the Original Code or previous Modifications.

1.10. "Original Code" means Source Code of computer software code which is described in the Source Code notice required by Exhibit A as Original Code, and which, at the time of its release under this License is not already Covered Code governed by this License.

1.11. "Source Code" means the preferred form of the Covered Code for making modifications to it, including all modules it contains, plus any associated interface definition files, scripts used to control compilation and installation of an Executable, or a list of source code differential comparisons against either the Original Code or another well known, available Covered Code of the Contributor's choice. The Source Code can be in a compressed or archival form, provided the appropriate decompression or de-archiving software is widely available for no charge.

1.12. "You" means an individual or a legal entity exercising rights under, and complying with all of the terms of, this License or a future version of this License issued under Section 6.1. For legal entities, "You" includes any entity which controls, is controlled by, or is under common control with You. For purposes of this definition, "control" means (a) the power, direct or indirect, to cause the direction or management of such entity, whether by contract or otherwise, or (b) ownership of fifty percent (50%) or more of the outstanding shares or beneficial ownership of such entity.

2. Source code license.

2.1. The initial developer grant.

The Initial Developer hereby grants You a world-wide, royalty-free, non-exclusive license, subject to third party intellectual property claims:

(a)   to use, reproduce, modify, display, perform, sublicense and distribute the Original Code (or portions thereof) with or without Modifications, or as part of a Larger Work; and

(b)   under patents now or hereafter owned or controlled by Initial Developer, to make, have made, use and sell ("Utilize") the Original Code (or portions thereof), but solely to the extent that any such patent is reasonably necessary to enable You to Utilize the Original Code (or portions thereof) and not to any greater extent that may be necessary to Utilize further Modifications or combinations.

2.2. Contributor grant.

Each Contributor hereby grants You a world-wide, royalty-free, non-exclusive license, subject to third party intellectual property claims:

(a)   to use, reproduce, modify, display, perform, sublicense and distribute the Modifications created by such Contributor (or portions thereof) either on an unmodified basis, with other Modifications, as Covered Code or as part of a Larger Work; and

(b)   under patents now or hereafter owned or controlled by Contributor, to Utilize the Contributor Version (or portions thereof), but solely to the extent that any such patent is reasonably necessary to enable You to Utilize the Contributor Version (or portions thereof), and not to any greater extent that may be necessary to Utilize further Modifications or combinations.

3. Distribution obligations.

3.1. Application of license.

The Modifications which You create or to which You contribute are governed by the terms of this License, including without limitation Section 2.2. The Source Code version of Covered Code may be distributed only under the terms of this License or a future version of this License released under Section 6.1, and You must include a copy of this License with every copy of the Source Code You distribute. You may not offer or impose any terms on any Source Code version that alters or restricts the applicable version of this License or the recipients' rights hereunder. However, You may include an additional document offering the additional rights described in Section 3.5.

3.2. Availability of source code.

Any Modification which You create or to which You contribute must be made available in Source Code form under the terms of this License either on the same media as an Executable version or via an accepted Electronic Distribution Mechanism to anyone to whom you made an Executable version available; and if made available via Electronic Distribution Mechanism, must remain available for at least twelve (12) months after the date it initially became available, or at least six (6) months after a subsequent version of that particular Modification has been made available to such recipients. You are responsible for ensuring that the Source Code version remains available even if the Electronic Distribution Mechanism is maintained by a third party.

3.3. Description of modifications.

You must cause all Covered Code to which you contribute to contain a file documenting the changes You made to create that Covered Code and the date of any change. You must include a prominent statement that the Modification is derived, directly or indirectly, from Original Code provided by the Initial Developer and including the name of the Initial Developer in (a) the Source Code, and (b) in any notice in an Executable version or related documentation in which You describe the origin or ownership of the Covered Code.

3.4. Intellectual property matters

(a) Third Party Claims.
   If You have knowledge that a party claims an intellectual property right in particular functionality or code (or its utilization under this License), you must include a text file with the source code distribution titled "LEGAL" which describes the claim and the party making the claim in sufficient detail that a recipient will know whom to contact. If you obtain such knowledge after You make Your Modification available as described in Section 3.2, You shall promptly modify the LEGAL file in all copies You make available thereafter and shall take other steps (such as notifying appropriate mailing lists or newsgroups) reasonably calculated to inform those who received the Covered Code that new knowledge has been obtained.

(b) Contributor APIs.
   If Your Modification is an application programming interface and You own or control patents which are reasonably necessary to implement that API, you must also include this information in the LEGAL file.

3.5. Required notices.

You must duplicate the notice in Exhibit A in each file of the Source Code, and this License in any documentation for the Source Code, where You describe recipients' rights relating to Covered Code. If You created one or more Modification(s), You may add your name as a Contributor to the notice described in Exhibit A. If it is not possible to put such notice in a particular Source Code file due to its structure, then you must include such notice in a location (such as a relevant directory file) where a user would be likely to look for such a notice. You may choose to offer, and to charge a fee for, warranty, support, indemnity or liability obligations to one or more recipients of Covered Code. However, You may do so only on Your own behalf, and not on behalf of the Initial Developer or any Contributor. You must make it absolutely clear than any such warranty, support, indemnity or liability obligation is offered by You alone, and You hereby agree to indemnify the Initial Developer and every Contributor for any liability incurred by the Initial Developer or such Contributor as a result of warranty, support, indemnity or liability terms You offer.

3.6. Distribution of executable versions.

You may distribute Covered Code in Executable form only if the requirements of Section 3.1–3.5 have been met for that Covered Code, and if You include a notice stating that the Source Code version of the Covered Code is available under the terms of this License, including a description of how and where You have fulfilled the obligations of Section 3.2. The notice must be conspicuously included in any notice in an Executable version, related documentation or collateral in which You describe recipients' rights relating to the Covered Code. You may distribute the Executable version of Covered Code under a license of Your choice, which may contain terms different from this License, provided that You are in compliance with the terms of this License and that the license for the Executable version does not attempt to limit or alter the recipient's rights in the Source Code version from the rights set forth in this License. If You distribute the Executable version under a different license You must make it absolutely clear that any terms which differ from this License are offered by You alone, not by the Initial Developer or any Contributor. You hereby agree to indemnify the Initial Developer and every Contributor for any liability incurred by the Initial Developer or such Contributor as a result of any such terms You offer.

3.7. Larger works.

You may create a Larger Work by combining Covered Code with other code not governed by the terms of this License and distribute the Larger Work as a single product. In such a case, You must make sure the requirements of this License are fulfilled for the Covered Code.

4. Inability to comply due to statute or regulation.

If it is impossible for You to comply with any of the terms of this License with respect to some or all of the Covered Code due to statute or regulation then You must: (a) comply with the terms of this License to the maximum extent possible; and (b) describe the limitations and the code they affect. Such description must be included in the LEGAL file described in Section 3.4 and must be included with all distributions of the Source Code. Except to the extent prohibited by statute or regulation, such description must be sufficiently detailed for a recipient of ordinary skill to be able to understand it.

5. Application of this license.

This License applies to code to which the Initial Developer has attached the notice in Exhibit A, and to related Covered Code.

6. Versions of the license.

6.1. New versions.

Netscape Communications Corporation ("Netscape") may publish revised and/or new versions of the License from time to time. Each version will be given a distinguishing version number.

6.2. Effect of new versions.

Once Covered Code has been published under a particular version of the License, You may always continue to use it under the terms of that version. You may also choose to use such Covered Code under the terms of any subsequent version of the License published by Netscape. No one other than Netscape has the right to modify the terms applicable to Covered Code created under this License.

6.3. Derivative works.

If you create or use a modified version of this License (which you may only do in order to apply it to code which is not already Covered Code governed by this License), you must (a) rename Your license so that the phrases "Mozilla", "MOZILLAPL", "MOZPL", "Netscape", "NPL" or any confusingly similar phrase do not appear anywhere in your license and (b) otherwise make it clear that your version of the license contains terms which differ from the Mozilla Public License and Netscape Public License. (Filling in the name of the Initial Developer, Original Code or Contributor in the notice described in Exhibit A shall not of themselves be deemed to be modifications of this License.)

7. Disclaimer of warranty.

COVERED CODE IS PROVIDED UNDER THIS LICENSE ON AN "AS IS" BASIS, WITHOUT WARRANTY OF ANY KIND, EITHER EXPRESSED OR IMPLIED, INCLUDING, WITHOUT LIMITATION, WARRANTIES THAT THE COVERED CODE IS FREE OF DEFECTS, MERCHANTABLE, FIT FOR A PARTICULAR PURPOSE OR NON-INFRINGING. THE ENTIRE RISK AS TO THE QUALITY AND PERFORMANCE OF THE COVERED CODE IS WITH YOU. SHOULD ANY COVERED CODE PROVE DEFECTIVE IN ANY RESPECT, YOU (NOT THE INITIAL DEVELOPER OR ANY OTHER CONTRIBUTOR) ASSUME THE COST OF ANY NECESSARY SERVICING, REPAIR OR CORRECTION. THIS DISCLAIMER OF WARRANTY CONSTITUTES AN ESSENTIAL PART OF THIS LICENSE. NO USE OF ANY COVERED CODE IS AUTHORIZED HEREUNDER EXCEPT UNDER THIS DISCLAIMER.

8. Termination.

This License and the rights granted hereunder will terminate automatically if You fail to comply with terms herein and fail to cure such breach within 30 days of becoming aware of the breach. All sublicenses to the Covered Code which are properly granted shall survive any termination of this License. Provisions which, by their nature, must remain in effect beyond the termination of this License shall survive.

9. Limitation of liability.

UNDER NO CIRCUMSTANCES AND UNDER NO LEGAL THEORY, WHETHER TORT (INCLUDING NEGLIGENCE), CONTRACT, OR OTHERWISE, SHALL THE INITIAL DEVELOPER, ANY OTHER CONTRIBUTOR, OR ANY DISTRIBUTOR OF COVERED CODE, OR ANY SUPPLIER OF ANY OF SUCH PARTIES, BE LIABLE TO YOU OR ANY OTHER PERSON FOR ANY INDIRECT, SPECIAL, INCIDENTAL, OR CONSEQUENTIAL DAMAGES OF ANY CHARACTER INCLUDING, WITHOUT LIMITATION, DAMAGES FOR LOSS OF GOODWILL, WORK STOPPAGE, COMPUTER FAILURE OR MALFUNCTION, OR ANY AND ALL OTHER COMMERCIAL DAMAGES OR LOSSES, EVEN IF SUCH PARTY SHALL HAVE BEEN INFORMED OF THE POSSIBILITY OF SUCH DAMAGES. THIS LIMITATION OF LIABILITY SHALL NOT APPLY TO LIABILITY FOR DEATH OR PERSONAL INJURY RESULTING FROM SUCH PARTY'S NEGLIGENCE TO THE EXTENT APPLICABLE LAW PROHIBITS SUCH LIMITATION. SOME JURISDICTIONS DO NOT ALLOW THE EXCLUSION OR LIMITATION OF INCIDENTAL OR CONSEQUENTIAL DAMAGES, SO THAT EXCLUSION AND LIMITATION MAY NOT APPLY TO YOU.

10. U.S. government end users.

The Covered Code is a "commercial item," as that term is defined in 48 C.F.R. 2.101 (Oct. 1995), consisting of "commercial computer software" and "commercial computer software documentation," as such terms are used in 48 C.F.R. 12.212 (Sept. 1995). Consistent with 48 C.F.R. 12.212 and 48 C.F.R. 227.7202-1 through 227.7202-4 (June 1995), all U.S. Government End Users acquire Covered Code with only those rights set forth herein.

11. Miscellaneous.

This License represents the complete agreement concerning subject matter hereof. If any provision of this License is held to be unenforceable, such provision shall be reformed only to the extent necessary to make it enforceable. This License shall be governed by California law provisions (except to the extent applicable law, if any, provides otherwise), excluding its conflict-of-law provisions. With respect to disputes in which at least one party is a citizen of, or an entity chartered or registered to do business in, the United States of America: (a) unless otherwise agreed in writing, all disputes relating to this License (excepting any dispute relating to intellectual property rights) shall be subject to final and binding arbitration, with the losing party paying all costs of arbitration; (b) any arbitration relating to this Agreement shall be held in Santa Clara County, California, under the auspices of JAMS/EndDispute; and (c) any litigation relating to this Agreement shall be subject to the jurisdiction of the Federal Courts of the Northern

District of California, with venue lying in Santa Clara County, California, with the losing party responsible for costs, including without limitation, court costs and reasonable attorneys fees and expenses. The application of the United Nations Convention on Contracts for the International Sale of Goods is expressly excluded. Any law or regulation which provides that the language of a contract shall be construed against the drafter shall not apply to this License.

12. Responsibility for claims.

Except in cases where another Contributor has failed to comply with Section 3.4, You are responsible for damages arising, directly or indirectly, out of Your utilization of rights under this License, based on the number of copies of Covered Code you made available, the revenues you received from utilizing such rights, and other relevant factors. You agree to work with affected parties to distribute responsibility on an equitable basis.

Amendments

Additional Terms applicable to the Netscape Public License.

I. Effect.
    These additional terms described in this Netscape Public License—
    Amendments shall apply to the Mozilla Communicator client code and to all
    Covered Code under this License.

II. "Netscape's Branded Code" means Covered Code that Netscape distributes
    and/or permits others to distribute under one or more trademark(s) which are
    controlled by Netscape but which are not licensed for use under this License.

III. Netscape and logo.
    This License does not grant any rights to use the trademark "Netscape", the
    "Netscape N and horizon" logo or the Netscape lighthouse logo, even if such
    marks are included in the Original Code.

IV. Inability to Comply Due to Contractual Obligation.
    Prior to licensing the Original Code under this License, Netscape has licensed
    third party code for use in Netscape's Branded Code. To the extent that
    Netscape is limited contractually from making such third party code available
    under this License, Netscape may choose to reintegrate such code into Covered
    Code without being required to distribute such code in Source Code form, even
    if such code would otherwise be considered "Modifications" under this License.

V. Use of Modifications and Covered Code by Initial Developer.

V.1. In General.
    The obligations of Section 3 apply to Netscape, except to the extent specified in
    this Amendment, Section V.2 and V.3.

V.2. Other Products.

Netscape may include Covered Code in products other than the Netscape's Branded Code which are released by Netscape during the two (2) years following the release date of the Original Code, without such additional products becoming subject to the terms of this License, and may license such additional products on different terms from those contained in this License.

V.3. Alternative Licensing.

Netscape may license the Source Code of Netscape's Branded Code, including Modifications incorporated therein, without such additional products becoming subject to the terms of this License, and may license such additional products on different terms from those contained in this License.

VI. Arbitration and Litigation.

Notwithstanding the limitations of Section 11 above, the provisions regarding arbitration and litigation in Section 11(a), (b) and (c) of the License shall apply to all disputes relating to this License.

Exhibit A.

"The contents of this file are subject to the Netscape Public License Version 1.0 (the "License"); you may not use this file except in compliance with the License. You may obtain a copy of the License at http://www.mozilla.org/NPL/

Software distributed under the License is distributed on an "AS IS" basis, WITHOUT WARRANTY OF ANY KIND, either express or implied. See the License for the specific language governing rights and limitations under the License.

The Original Code is Mozilla Communicator client code, released March 31, 1998.

The Initial Developer of the Original Code is Netscape Communications Corporation. Portions created by Netscape are Copyright © 1998 Netscape Communications Corporation. All Rights Reserved.

Contributor(s): _____."

[NOTE: The text of this Exhibit A may differ slightly from the text of the notices in the Source Code files of the Original Code. This is due to time constraints encountered in simultaneously finalizing the License and in preparing the Original Code for release. You should use the text of this Exhibit A rather than the text found in the Original Code Source Code for Your Modifications.]

Mozilla Public License

Version 1.1

1. Definitions.

1.0.1. "Commercial Use" means distribution or otherwise making the Covered Code available to a third party.

1.1. "Contributor" means each entity that creates or contributes to the creation of Modifications.

1.2. "Contributor Version" means the combination of the Original Code, prior Modifications used by a Contributor, and the Modifications made by that particular Contributor.

1.3. "Covered Code" means the Original Code or Modifications or the combination of the Original Code and Modifications, in each case including portions thereof.

1.4. "Electronic Distribution Mechanism" means a mechanism generally accepted in the software development community for the electronic transfer of data.

1.5. "Executable" means Covered Code in any form other than Source Code.

1.6. "Initial Developer" means the individual or entity identified as the Initial Developer in the Source Code notice required by Exhibit A.

1.7. "Larger Work" means a work which combines Covered Code or portions thereof with code not governed by the terms of this License.

1.8. "License" means this document.

1.8.1. "Licensable" means having the right to grant, to the maximum extent possible, whether at the time of the initial grant or subsequently acquired, any and all of the rights conveyed herein.

1.9. "Modifications" means any addition to or deletion from the substance or structure of either the Original Code or any previous Modifications. When Covered Code is released as a series of files, a Modification is:

A. Any addition to or deletion from the contents of a file containing Original Code or previous Modifications.

B. Any new file that contains any part of the Original Code or previous Modifications.

1.10. "Original Code" means Source Code of computer software code which is described in the Source Code notice required by Exhibit A as Original Code, and which, at the time of its release under this License is not already Covered Code governed by this License.

1.10.1. "Patent Claims" means any patent claim(s), now owned or hereafter acquired, including without limitation, method, process, and apparatus claims, in any patent Licensable by grantor.

1.11. "Source Code" means the preferred form of the Covered Code for making modifications to it, including all modules it contains, plus any associated interface definition files, scripts used to control compilation and installation of an Executable, or source code differential comparisons against either the Original Code or another well known, available Covered Code of the Contributor's choice. The Source Code can be in a compressed or archival form, provided the appropriate decompression or de-archiving software is widely available for no charge.

1.12. "You" (or "Your") means an individual or a legal entity exercising rights under, and complying with all of the terms of, this License or a future version of this License issued under Section 6.1. For legal entities, "You" includes any entity which controls, is controlled by, or is under common control with You. For purposes of this definition, "control" means (a) the power, direct or indirect, to cause the direction or management of such entity, whether by contract or otherwise, or (b) ownership of more than fifty percent (50%) of the outstanding shares or beneficial ownership of such entity.

2. Source code license.

2.1. The initial developer grant.

The Initial Developer hereby grants You a world-wide, royalty-free, non-exclusive license, subject to third party intellectual property claims:

(a) under intellectual property rights (other than patent or trademark) Licensable by Initial Developer to use, reproduce, modify, display, perform, sublicense and distribute the Original Code (or portions thereof) with or without Modifications, and/or as part of a Larger Work; and

(b) under Patents Claims infringed by the making, using or selling of Original Code, to make, have made, use, practice, sell, and offer for sale, and/or otherwise dispose of the Original Code (or portions thereof).

(c) the licenses granted in this Section 2.1(a) and (b) are effective on the date Initial Developer first distributes Original Code under the terms of this License.

(d) Notwithstanding Section 2.1(b) above, no patent license is granted: (1) for code that You delete from the Original Code; (2) separate from the Original Code; or (3) for infringements caused by: (i) the modification of the Original Code or (ii) the combination of the Original Code with other software or devices.

2.2. Contributor grant.

Subject to third party intellectual property claims, each Contributor hereby grants You a world-wide, royalty-free, non-exclusive license

(a) under intellectual property rights (other than patent or trademark) Licensable by Contributor, to use, reproduce, modify, display, perform, sublicense and distribute the Modifications created by such Contributor (or portions thereof) either on an unmodified basis, with other Modifications, as Covered Code and/or as part of a Larger Work; and

(b) under Patent Claims infringed by the making, using, or selling of Modifications made by that Contributor either alone and/or in combination with its Contributor Version (or portions of such combination), to make, use, sell, offer for sale, have made, and/or otherwise dispose of: (1) Modifications made by that Contributor (or portions thereof); and (2) the combination of Modifications made by that Contributor with its Contributor Version (or portions of such combination).

(c) the licenses granted in Sections 2.2(a) and 2.2(b) are effective on the date Contributor first makes Commercial Use of the Covered Code.

(d) Notwithstanding Section 2.2(b) above, no patent license is granted: (1) for any code that Contributor has deleted from the Contributor Version; (2) separate from the Contributor Version; (3) for infringements caused by: (i) third party modifications of Contributor Version or (ii) the combination of Modifications made by that Contributor with other software (except as part of the Contributor Version) or other devices; or (4) under Patent Claims infringed by Covered Code in the absence of Modifications made by that Contributor.

3. Distribution obligations.
3.1. Application of license.

The Modifications which You create or to which You contribute are governed by the terms of this License, including without limitation Section 2.2. The Source Code version of Covered Code may be distributed only under the terms of this License or a future version of this License released under Section 6.1, and You must include a copy of this License with every copy of the Source Code You distribute. You may not offer or impose any terms on any Source Code version that alters or restricts the applicable version of this License or the recipients' rights hereunder. However, You may include an additional document offering the additional rights described in Section 3.5.

3.2. Availability of source code.

Any Modification which You create or to which You contribute must be made available in Source Code form under the terms of this License either on the same media as an

Executable version or via an accepted Electronic Distribution Mechanism to anyone to whom you made an Executable version available; and if made available via Electronic Distribution Mechanism, must remain available for at least twelve (12) months after the date it initially became available, or at least six (6) months after a subsequent version of that particular Modification has been made available to such recipients. You are responsible for ensuring that the Source Code version remains available even if the Electronic Distribution Mechanism is maintained by a third party.

3.3. Description of modifications.

You must cause all Covered Code to which You contribute to contain a file documenting the changes You made to create that Covered Code and the date of any change. You must include a prominent statement that the Modification is derived, directly or indirectly, from Original Code provided by the Initial Developer and including the name of the Initial Developer in (a) the Source Code, and (b) in any notice in an Executable version or related documentation in which You describe the origin or ownership of the Covered Code.

3.4. Intellectual property matters

(a) Third Party Claims.
     If Contributor has knowledge that a license under a third party's intellectual property rights is required to exercise the rights granted by such Contributor under Sections 2.1 or 2.2, Contributor must include a text file with the Source Code distribution titled "LEGAL" which describes the claim and the party making the claim in sufficient detail that a recipient will know whom to contact. If Contributor obtains such knowledge after the Modification is made available as described in Section 3.2, Contributor shall promptly modify the LEGAL file in all copies Contributor makes available thereafter and shall take other steps (such as notifying appropriate mailing lists or newsgroups) reasonably calculated to inform those who received the Covered Code that new knowledge has been obtained.

(b) Contributor APIs.
     If Contributor's Modifications include an application programming interface and Contributor has knowledge of patent licenses which are reasonably necessary to implement that API, Contributor must also include this information in the LEGAL file.

(c) Representations.
     Contributor represents that, except as disclosed pursuant to Section 3.4(a) above, Contributor believes that Contributor's Modifications are Contributor's original creation(s) and/or Contributor has sufficient rights to grant the rights conveyed by this License.

3.5. Required notices.

You must duplicate the notice in Exhibit A in each file of the Source Code. If it is not possible to put such notice in a particular Source Code file due to its structure, then You must include such notice in a location (such as a relevant directory) where a user would be likely to look for such a notice. If You created one or more Modification(s) You may add your name as a Contributor to the notice described in Exhibit A. You must also duplicate this License in any documentation for the Source Code where You describe recipients' rights or ownership rights relating to Covered Code. You may choose to offer, and to charge a fee for, warranty, support, indemnity or liability obligations to one or more recipients of Covered Code. However, You may do so only on Your own behalf, and not on behalf of the Initial Developer or any Contributor. You must make it absolutely clear than any such warranty, support, indemnity or liability obligation is offered by You alone, and You hereby agree to indemnify the Initial Developer and every Contributor for any liability incurred by the Initial Developer or such Contributor as a result of warranty, support, indemnity or liability terms You offer.

3.6. Distribution of executable versions.

You may distribute Covered Code in Executable form only if the requirements of Section 3.1–3.5 have been met for that Covered Code, and if You include a notice stating that the Source Code version of the Covered Code is available under the terms of this License, including a description of how and where You have fulfilled the obligations of Section 3.2. The notice must be conspicuously included in any notice in an Executable version, related documentation or collateral in which You describe recipients' rights relating to the Covered Code. You may distribute the Executable version of Covered Code or ownership rights under a license of Your choice, which may contain terms different from this License, provided that You are in compliance with the terms of this License and that the license for the Executable version does not attempt to limit or alter the recipient's rights in the Source Code version from the rights set forth in this License. If You distribute the Executable version under a different license You must make it absolutely clear that any terms which differ from this License are offered by You alone, not by the Initial Developer or any Contributor. You hereby agree to indemnify the Initial Developer and every Contributor for any liability incurred by the Initial Developer or such Contributor as a result of any such terms You offer.

3.7. Larger works.

You may create a Larger Work by combining Covered Code with other code not governed by the terms of this License and distribute the Larger Work as a single product. In such a case, You must make sure the requirements of this License are fulfilled for the Covered Code.

4. Inability to comply due to statute or regulation.

If it is impossible for You to comply with any of the terms of this License with respect to some or all of the Covered Code due to statute, judicial order, or regulation then You must: (a) comply with the terms of this License to the maximum extent possible; and (b) describe the limitations and the code they affect. Such description must be included in the LEGAL file described in Section 3.4 and must be included with all distributions of the Source Code. Except to the extent prohibited by statute or regulation, such description must be sufficiently detailed for a recipient of ordinary skill to be able to understand it.

5. Application of this license.

This License applies to code to which the Initial Developer has attached the notice in Exhibit A and to related Covered Code.

6. Versions of the license.

6.1. New Versions.

Netscape Communications Corporation ("Netscape") may publish revised and/or new versions of the License from time to time. Each version will be given a distinguishing version number.

6.2. Effect of New Versions.

Once Covered Code has been published under a particular version of the License, You may always continue to use it under the terms of that version. You may also choose to use such Covered Code under the terms of any subsequent version of the License published by Netscape. No one other than Netscape has the right to modify the terms applicable to Covered Code created under this License.

6.3. Derivative Works.

If You create or use a modified version of this License (which you may only do in order to apply it to code which is not already Covered Code governed by this License), You must (a) rename Your license so that the phrases "Mozilla", "MOZILLAPL", "MOZPL", "Netscape", "MPL", "NPL" or any confusingly similar phrase do not appear in your license (except to note that your license differs from this License) and (b) otherwise make it clear that Your version of the license contains terms which differ from the Mozilla Public License and Netscape Public License. (Filling in the name of the Initial Developer, Original Code or Contributor in the notice described in Exhibit A shall not of themselves be deemed to be modifications of this License.)

7. Disclaimer of warranty.

COVERED CODE IS PROVIDED UNDER THIS LICENSE ON AN "AS IS" BASIS, WITHOUT WARRANTY OF ANY KIND, EITHER EXPRESSED OR IMPLIED, INCLUDING, WITHOUT LIMITATION, WARRANTIES THAT THE COVERED CODE IS FREE OF DEFECTS, MERCHANTABLE, FIT FOR A PARTICULAR PURPOSE OR NON-INFRINGING. THE ENTIRE RISK AS TO THE QUALITY AND PERFORMANCE OF THE COVERED CODE IS WITH YOU. SHOULD ANY COVERED CODE PROVE DEFECTIVE IN ANY RESPECT, YOU (NOT THE INITIAL DEVELOPER OR ANY OTHER CONTRIBUTOR) ASSUME THE COST OF ANY NECESSARY SERVICING, REPAIR OR CORRECTION. THIS DISCLAIMER OF WARRANTY CONSTITUTES AN ESSENTIAL PART OF THIS LICENSE. NO USE OF ANY COVERED CODE IS AUTHORIZED HEREUNDER EXCEPT UNDER THIS DISCLAIMER.

8. Termination.

8.1. This License and the rights granted hereunder will terminate automatically if You fail to comply with terms herein and fail to cure such breach within 30 days of becoming aware of the breach. All sublicenses to the Covered Code which are properly granted shall survive any termination of this License. Provisions which, by their nature, must remain in effect beyond the termination of this License shall survive.

8.2. If You initiate litigation by asserting a patent infringement claim (excluding declaratory judgment actions) against Initial Developer or a Contributor (the Initial Developer or Contributor against whom You file such action is referred to as "Participant") alleging that:

(a) such Participant's Contributor Version directly or indirectly infringes any patent, then any and all rights granted by such Participant to You under Sections 2.1 and/or 2.2 of this License shall, upon 60 days notice from Participant terminate prospectively, unless if within 60 days after receipt of notice You either: (i) agree in writing to pay Participant a mutually agreeable reasonable royalty for Your past and future use of Modifications made by such Participant, or (ii) withdraw Your litigation claim with respect to the Contributor Version against such Participant. If within 60 days of notice, a reasonable royalty and payment arrangement are not mutually agreed upon in writing by the parties or the litigation claim is not withdrawn, the rights granted by Participant to You under Sections 2.1 and/or 2.2 automatically terminate at the expiration of the 60 day notice period specified above.

(b) any software, hardware, or device, other than such Participant's Contributor Version, directly or indirectly infringes any patent, then any rights granted to You by such Participant under Sections 2.1(b) and 2.2(b) are revoked effective as of the date You first made, used, sold, distributed, or had made, Modifications made by that Participant.

8.3. If You assert a patent infringement claim against Participant alleging that such Participant's Contributor Version directly or indirectly infringes any patent where such claim is resolved (such as by license or settlement) prior to the initiation of patent infringement litigation, then the reasonable value of the licenses granted by such Participant under Sections 2.1 or 2.2 shall be taken into account in determining the amount or value of any payment or license.

8.4. In the event of termination under Sections 8.1 or 8.2 above, all end user license agreements (excluding distributors and resellers) which have been validly granted by You or any distributor hereunder prior to termination shall survive termination.

9. Limitation of liability.

UNDER NO CIRCUMSTANCES AND UNDER NO LEGAL THEORY, WHETHER TORT (INCLUDING NEGLIGENCE), CONTRACT, OR OTHERWISE, SHALL YOU, THE INITIAL DEVELOPER, ANY OTHER CONTRIBUTOR, OR ANY DISTRIBUTOR OF COVERED CODE, OR ANY SUPPLIER OF ANY OF SUCH PARTIES, BE LIABLE TO ANY PERSON FOR ANY INDIRECT, SPECIAL, INCIDENTAL, OR CONSEQUENTIAL DAMAGES OF ANY CHARACTER INCLUDING, WITHOUT LIMITATION, DAMAGES FOR LOSS OF GOODWILL, WORK STOPPAGE, COMPUTER FAILURE OR MALFUNCTION, OR ANY AND ALL OTHER COMMERCIAL DAMAGES OR LOSSES, EVEN IF SUCH PARTY SHALL HAVE BEEN INFORMED OF THE POSSIBILITY OF SUCH DAMAGES. THIS LIMITATION OF LIABILITY SHALL NOT APPLY TO LIABILITY FOR DEATH OR PERSONAL INJURY RESULTING FROM SUCH PARTY'S NEGLIGENCE TO THE EXTENT APPLICABLE LAW PROHIBITS SUCH LIMITATION. SOME JURISDICTIONS DO NOT ALLOW THE EXCLUSION OR LIMITATION OF INCIDENTAL OR CONSEQUENTIAL DAMAGES, SO THIS EXCLUSION AND LIMITATION MAY NOT APPLY TO YOU.

10. U.S. government end users.

The Covered Code is a "commercial item," as that term is defined in 48 C.F.R. 2.101 (Oct. 1995), consisting of "commercial computer software" and "commercial computer software documentation," as such terms are used in 48 C.F.R. 12.212 (Sept. 1995). Consistent with 48 C.F.R. 12.212 and 48 C.F.R. 227.7202-1 through 227.7202-4 (June 1995), all U.S. Government End Users acquire Covered Code with only those rights set forth herein.

11. Miscellaneous.

This License represents the complete agreement concerning subject matter hereof. If any provision of this License is held to be unenforceable, such provision shall be reformed only to the extent necessary to make it enforceable. This License shall be governed by California law provisions (except to the extent applicable law, if any, provides otherwise), excluding its conflict-of-law provisions. With respect to disputes in which at least one party is a citizen of, or an entity chartered or registered to do business in the United States of America, any litigation relating to this License shall be subject to the jurisdiction of the Federal Courts of the Northern District of California, with venue lying in Santa Clara County, California, with the losing party responsible for costs, including without limitation, court costs and reasonable attorneys' fees and expenses. The application of the United Nations Convention on Contracts for the International Sale of Goods is expressly excluded. Any law or regulation which provides that the language of a contract shall be construed against the drafter shall not apply to this License.

12. Responsibility for claims.

As between Initial Developer and the Contributors, each party is responsible for claims and damages arising, directly or indirectly, out of its utilization of rights under this License and You agree to work with Initial Developer and Contributors to distribute such responsibility on an equitable basis. Nothing herein is intended or shall be deemed to constitute any admission of liability.

13. Multiple-licensed code.

Initial Developer may designate portions of the Covered Code as "Multiple-Licensed". "Multiple-Licensed" means that the Initial Developer permits you to utilize portions of the Covered Code under Your choice of the NPL or the alternative licenses, if any, specified by the Initial Developer in the file described in Exhibit A.

EXHIBIT A—Mozilla Public License.

"The contents of this file are subject to the Mozilla Public License Version 1.1 (the "License"); you may not use this file except in compliance with the License. You may obtain a copy of the License at

http://www.mozilla.org/MPL/

Software distributed under the License is distributed on an "AS IS" basis, WITHOUT WARRANTY OF ANY KIND, either express or implied. See the License for the specific language governing rights and limitations under the License.

The Original Code is _____.

The Initial Developer of the Original Code is _____
Portions created by
_____ are Copyright © _____.
All Rights Reserved.
Contributor(s): _____ .
Alternatively, the contents of this file may be used under the terms of the _____
license (the "[_____] License"), in which case the provisions of [_____] License are
applicable instead of those above. If you wish to allow use of your version of this file
only under the terms of the [_____] License and not to allow others to use your version
of this file under the MPL, indicate your decision by deleting the provisions above
and replace them with the notice and other provisions required by the [_____] License.
If you do not delete the provisions above, a recipient may use your version of this file
under either the MPL or the [_____] License."

[NOTE: The text of this Exhibit A may differ slightly from the text of the notices
in the Source Code files of the Original Code. You should use the text of this Exhibit
A rather than the text found in the Original Code Source Code for Your Modifications.]

Quick Reference for Choosing a Free Software License, version 0.9.9.1, 2002-01-05

License	hackers like to code under it	combine with proprietary and redistribute	combine with GPLed code and redistribute	must share source of redistributed version contribution	must include patent license with contribution
X11/BSD-new	Y	Y	Y	N	N
GNU LGPL	Y	Y	Y	Y	Y
GNU GPL	1	N	Y	Y	Y
Mozilla PL 1.1	2	Y	N3	Y	N

News

Try the interactive version, hacked by Peter Lowe <pgl@mini.instinct.org>. It allows you
to choose which kind of bias the table will reflect. http://yoyo.org/~pgl/lqr/.

Key:

- "1" Some members of the community refuse to accept GPLed source code into
  their projects, although other members of the community strongly prefer

GPLed source code over other licenses. Contrast with code under BSD-new and LGPL, which nobody refuses to accept.

- "2" I have never heard anyone proclaim that they prefer the MPL nor that they eschew it. Contrast this with X11/BSD-new and LGPL, which many people have told me that they prefer, and with the GPL, which many people have told me that they prefer and many people have told me that they eschew.

- "3" MPL 1.1 can be specifically amended to allow combining with GPL, according to the FSF's license list.

Explanations of columns:

- "hackers like to accept code under it"—I intend this to mean whether members of the community like to use source code under this license, instead of whether members of the community like to create new source code under this license. This is because I'm assuming that readers have already created their own source codes, and I'm assuming that they want their source codes to be used as widely possible by members of the open source/free software community. The difference between these two meanings of "likes it" is shown up by the case of the GPL: a hypothetical open source/free software hacker may prefer to create source code under the GPL, but may prefer to use source code licensed to her under a license that permits her to combine the licensed source code with proprietary source code. My opinion that people like to receive source code under a given license is obviously subjective (maybe the community doesn't really like The Frobozz Public License, but my biased perspective makes me think that they do), but it is a very important factor when deciding what license to use. If you feel that my summary above is inaccurate, please let me know.

- "combine with proprietary and redistribute"—Is it legal to accept code from its author under the terms of this license, combine it with proprietary code, and ship the resulting application to a third person without giving them freely licensed source code of the proprietary part?

- "combine with GPLed code and redistribute"—Is it legal to accept code from its author under the terms of this license, combine it with GPLed code, and ship the resulting application to a third person?

- "must share source of redistributed version"—Does this license forbid the recipient of the source code from modifying it and shipping his modified version to a third party without giving them the source?

- "must include patent license with contribution"—Does this license require that if the recipient combines the code with his own contribution and then ships the resulting combined app, that he must contribute a license to any patents that he holds that would restrict usage of the resulting app?

Disclaimers
This is not legal advice

I am not a lawyer, and this is not legal advice. I do not accept any responsibility or liability for the consequences of any actions you may take after reading this document.

(Note: some lawyers have already written to me to suggest that this document looks like legal advice, and that this could get me into trouble. While I sincerely appreciate their help, I am unsure how to proceed. Apparently the only way to be safe against the accusation of having given "legal advice" is to write with such ambiguity and obfuscation that nobody can learn anything from what you've written. Presumably this culture of fear increases the demand for lawyers' services. I value speaking plainly, and I feel that plain discussion of software licenses is much needed. In particular, this document would be useless if all specifics were removed in favor of cautious generalities. Therefore, I simply reiterate that I am not a lawyer and that I am not acting as one in describing my understanding of the law in simple terms.)

Bugs

There are probably incorrect statements in this document—I have already discovered several such "bugs" from earlier versions. If you see one, please inform me so that I can fix it.

My goal in writing this document is to provide information for people who are choosing a free software license for their own projects. My goal in this document is not advocacy.

Bias

Nonetheless, my biases will inevitably show through in places. One prominent example of my bias is that I arranged it so that the answer is "Y" for all the features that I personally like. For example, in the case of "Must share source of redistributed version", I could have called it "Can redistribute proprietary version", and NOTed all the values, but I wanted to be able to scan across a row counting "Y"s as good and "N"s as bad. If you think that allowing recipients of your code to alter the code and ship proprietary versions is good, then I suggest you make a copy of the table, remove the "Not" from that column heading, and NOT all the values in that column. Then it will be easier for you to read with your value-judging eyes. Peter Lowe <pgl@mini.instinct.org> has written an interactive web page that does this for you: http://yoyo.org/~pgl/lqr/

An even more insidious example of my bias is what I've omitted. I tried to pick only the licenses which free software/open source hackers might seriously be considering using.

Moreover, I have deliberately omitted licenses which are "overshadowed" by another license which has substantially similar characteristics but is more widely known and used. The goal of this document is to help people choose a license for their own code, not to provide a map of all extant licenses, and I assume that authors prefer a widely known and used license over an equivalent but obscure one, or (gack!) inventing Yet Another Free Software License of their own.

A widely questioned omission is the Artistic License under which Perl is distributed. While it is a widely used and liked license, it doesn't seem to have substantial technical differences to the X11/BSD-new license. The salient difference seems to be that the Artistic License makes your having a copy of the Perl source code contingent on your refraining from publishing a modified version without source code and calling that modified version "Perl". A similar, but not identical effect could be achieved by getting a trademark on the name "Perl", in the way that Linus Torvalds has a trademark on "Linux". While the issue of branding is very important in general, this particular feature of the Artistic License doesn't motivate me to include it in this table.

I would like to create a companion piece—a larger table with more rows (to include other licenses which are widely used, good, or have other interesting characteristics) and more columns (to explain those characteristics).

Issues
What about public domain?

According to these messages from the license-discuss mailing list: [1, 2, 3, 4, 5], it is not possible to voluntarily place your software into the public domain under United States law. There is a common myth that one can do so simply by creating a work and writing "This software/work/text is hereby placed in the public domain.", but that does not have the legal effect that it is commonly believed to have. For example, it might later be possible for you to assert your ownership over the code and forbid others to use it. Also, it might be possible for a user to sue you as the author of the code.

If you want your source code to be usable in that way, then you should consider using the X11 or modified BSD licenses, which add only the restrictions that the copyright notice and disclaimer of warranty remain intact.

The license does not restrict the copyright holder!

The most common misunderstanding about software licenses is that giving someone else a copy of your source code under a license restricts what you are allowed to do with your source code. The truth is, if you write some code, and give it to someone else under the terms of License X, or publish it so that anyone may use it under the terms of License X, this does not subject you to the terms of License X! You are the author of the code, and you hold the copyright, and giving someone permission to use the code does not restrict you to using the code in only the way that that person is allowed to use it!

Now it may be that some licenses do contain clauses which constrain the original author. But the important myth that I wish to dispel is the notion that giving someone permission to use your source code automatically restricts how you may use your source code. For example, if I give you permission to make copies of a book that I wrote, but only if you stand on your head while doing so, this does not mean that I must stand on my head whenever I make copies of my book.

But what about patches?

However, there is a catch. Suppose you publish your code under License X, and then another person writes a patch that fixes bugs and adds features, and sends you the patch, and you add the patch to your own source tree and publish a new version. Now, what rights do you have to the contents of the patch? And how did including the patch into your source code affect your rights to the source code?

This is a murky area. People who have thought about it seem to be of the opinion that if the patch is sufficiently small and simple, then it has no legal effect, but that if it is a large and complex patch, that you need permission from the author of the patch (who is, naturally, the holder of the copyright to the patch) before you can "combine" the patch with your source code and ship the resulting "derived work".

But suppose that you and the author of the patch didn't discuss the matter? Now it gets really murky. It might be the case that the author of the patch could later sue you for having used his patch in a way that he didn't want, but on the other hand a court might rule that by sending the patch to you, it was understood that he was giving you the right to use it. Most actual hackers seem to assume that submitters of patches are automatically granting the recipient a license to use the patch and to use the combined work derived from combining the patch with the original source tree. As far as I know, this assumption is not supported by any legal fact.

This appears to be an open issue to me and I hope that the community, especially the legally trained members of the community, will speak up.

Explanations of rows:

Please use the FSF's list of free software licenses and opensource.org's list of open source licenses to find out more about these licenses.

- "X11/BSD-new" is listed on the FSF's site as "The X11 license" and "The modified BSD license". The modified BSD license is listed on the opensource.org site as "The BSD license". The opensource.org site does not include the X11 license, but it does list "The MIT license", which is very similar to X11/BSD-new, except that X11/BSD-new forbid the recipient from using the name of the author to endorse or promote products, and the MIT license does not.

- "GNU LGPL" is listed on the FSF's site as "The GNU Lesser General Public License (or GNU LGPL for short)". It is listed on the opensource.org site as "The GNU Library or 'Lesser' Public License (LGPL)".

- "GNU GPL" is listed on the FSF's site as "The GNU General Public License (or GNU GPL for short)". It is listed on the opensource.org site as "The GNU General Public License (GPL)".

- "Mozilla PL 1.1" is listed on the FSF's site as "The Mozilla Public License (MPL)". It is listed on the opensource.org site as "The Mozilla Public License 1.1 (MPL 1.1)".

Other resources

An up-to-date and accurate list of free software/open source licenses is maintained by the FSF. It is a useful reference even if you do not share the FSF's values with respect to source licenses. If this document and the FSF's list disagree on a point of fact or a point of law, then it is very likely due to a bug in this document and I would like to know about it.

opensource.org hosts a mailing list specifically about this issue. You can browse the archives. They also have a list of licenses that meet the Open Source Definition. As of this writing the list on opensource.org appears to be less up-to-date and comprehensive than the list on the FSF's site.

Based on "license_quick_ref.html", originally written by Zooko in 2001 and posted to "http://zooko.com/license_quick_ref.html".

written in 2001 by Zooko; You may copy and use this document in unmodified form. Alternatively, you may copy and use this document in modified form, provided that you remove this line (that begins: 'written in 2001 by Zooko...') and retain the line above (that begins: 'Based on "license_quick_ref.html"...').

—Zooko O'Whielacronx

ENDNOTES

Introduction

[1] <store.yahoo.com/modernhumoriststore/mp3poster.html>.

[2] It may seem as though I give the open source movement—and its chief evangelists, like Eric Raymond—short shrift in this book. If that's the case, it's only because *Commonspace: Beyond Virtual Community*, the companion volume to this book, deals with both open source and Raymond's philosophy at great length.

[3] <www.cnn.com/2001/TECH/industry/04/19/ibm.guerilla.idg/>.

PART I FREE
Chapter 1   Give it away now

[1] Mark Surman and Darren Wershler-Henry, *Commonspace: Beyond Virtual Community*. (Toronto: FT.com, 2001), 109–110.

[2] Garrett Hardin, "The Tragedy of the Commons," *Science*, 162 (1968):1243–1248, <dieoff.org/page95.htm>.

[3] <www.tuxedo.org/~esr/writings/magic-cauldron/>.

[4] <www.itworld.com/Tech/2427/ITW2676/>.

[5] <www.bartleby.com/61/23/P0482300.html>.

[6] Marcel Mauss, *The Gift: The Form and Reason for Exchange in Archaic Societies*, Trans. W.D. Halls. (London: Routledge, 1990), 36.

[7] Jacques Derrida, *Given Time: I. Counterfeit Money*. [1991]. Trans. Peggy Kamuf. (Chicago: University of Chicago Press, 1992), 7.

[8] Mauss, 68.

[9] Mauss, 69.

[10] Georges Bataille, *The Accursed Share, Volume One: Consumption*. Trans. Robert Hurley. (New York: Zone Books, 1988), 23.

[11] Ibid, 24.

[12] Ibid, 25–26.

[13] Ibid, 172.

[14] Ibid, 181.

[15] Steve McCaffery, *North of Intention: Critical Writings 1973–1986*. (New York/Toronto: Roof Books/Nightwood Editions, 1986), 203.

[16] Derrida, 7.

[17] McCaffery, 219.

[18] Bataille, 69.

¹⁹ Ibid, 70.

²⁰ Ibid, 73.

²¹ Ibid, 77.

Chapter 2   The road to copyleft

¹ <www.tuxedo.org/~esr/jargon/html/entry/Share-and-enjoy!.html>.

² <www.theunderdogs.org/faq.php#e1>.

³ <www.spa.org/piracy/copyright/24hr.asp>.

⁴ <www.cnet.com/techtrends/0-1544321-7-2409520.html?tag=st.sr.1544321-7-2409521.back2.1544321-7-2409520>.

⁵ <www.internettrash.com/users/corn_am_i/>.

⁶ <www.adventurecollective.com/articles/feature%2Dabandonwarez.htm>.

⁷ <www.theunderdogs.org/faq.php#a4>.

⁸ <mivox.com/essays/text/petition.html>.

⁹ <www.cnet.com/techtrends/0-1544321-7-2409522.html?tag=st.sr.1544321-7-2409520.txt.1544321-7-2409522>.

¹⁰ <www.freewarehof.org/sstory.html>.

¹¹ <www.jsonline.com/news/state/may00/katz21052000a.asp>.
    <www.computeraddicts.com/pkzip.htm>.

¹² <www.oreilly.com/ask_tim/amazon_patent.html>.

¹³ < www.vjolt.net/vol5/issue3/v5i3a11-Ravicher.html>.

¹⁴ <www.gnu.org/copyleft/copyleft.html#WhatIsCopyleft>.

¹⁵ <www.gnu.org/gnu/thegnuproject.html>.

¹⁶ Malaclypse the Younger [Kerry Wendel Thornley]. *Principia Discordia, OR How I Found Goddess And What I Did To Her When I Found Her*, 5th edition. (San Francisco: Loompanics Unlimited, 1979).

¹⁷ <www.gnu.org/copyleft/copyleft.html>.

¹⁸ <www.vjolt.net/vol5/issue3/v5i3a11-Ravicher.html>.

¹⁹ Ibid.

²⁰ Robert P. Merges, 'The End of Friction? Property Rights and Contract in the "Newtonian" World of On-Line Commerce,' 12 *Berkeley Tech. L.J.*, 115.

²¹ <www.linuxplanet.com/linuxplanet/reports/2000/1/>.

²² Ibid.

²³ Ibid.

²⁴ Ibid.

[25] Peter Wayner, *Free for All: How Linux and the Free Software Movement Undercut the High-Tech Titans*. (New York: HarperBusiness, 2000), 43.

[26] <www.gnu.org/licenses/license-list.html#OriginalBSD>.

[27] Wayner, 44.

[28] <www.oreillynet.com/cs/weblog/view/wlg/526>.

[29] <linux.oreillynet.com/pub/a/linux/2001/08/15/free_software.html>.

[30] <noframes.linuxjournal.com/articles/currents/0032.html>.

[31] <www.gnu.org/licenses/license-list.html>.

[32] <www.theregister.co.uk/content/4/22749.html>.

[33] <www.microsoft.com/presspass/exec/craig/05-03sharedsource.asp>.

[34] <www.microsoft.com/business/licensing/ssfaq.asp>.

[35] <www.theregister.co.uk/content/archive/18742.html>.

[36] <http://www2.usermagnet.com/cox/index.html>.

[37] <www.computerworld.com/storyba/0,4125,NAV47_STO64507,00.html>.

PART 2   ... AS IN SPEECH

[1] <www.gnu.org/philosophy/why-free.html>.

Chapter 3   All your base are belong to us

[1] <www.planettribes.com/allyourbase/index.shtml>.

[2] <db.gamefaqs.com/console/genesis/file/zero_wing.txt>.

[3] <www.theregister.co.uk/content/2/17419.html>.

[4] < www.ecommercetimes.com/perl/story/10222.html>.

[5] Andy Oram, ed. *Peer-to-Peer: Harnessing the Power of Disruptive Technologies*. (Sebastopol: O'Reilly & Associates, 2001), 13–14.

[6] <www.eetimes.com/story/OEG20011211S0054>.

[7] <news.cnet.com/news/0-1003-200-5851009.html?tag=tp_pr>.

[8] <news.bbc.co.uk/hi/english/business/newsid_1448000/1448347.stm>.

[9] <news.cnet.com/news/0-1003-200-5067906.html>.

[10] <www.satirewire.com/news/0106/xpbug.shtml>.

[11] <news.cnet.com/news/0-1003-200-5067906.html>.

[12] <www.theregister.co.uk/content/2/17419.html>.

[13] <www.wired.com/wired/archive/9.05/broadband.html>.

[14] <broadband.ic.gc.ca/english/>.

[15] <news.cnet.com/news/0-1004-200-6157676.html?ptag=cd_pr>.

16 <news.cnet.com/news/0-1004-200-7339605.html?tag=lh>.

17 <www.wired.com/wired/archive/9.05/broadband.html?pg=3&topic=
   &topic_set=>.

18 <www.theregister.co.uk/content/2/17419.html>.

19 <attrition.org/quotes/msoft.html>.

20 <bbspot.com/News/2000/4/MS_Buys_Evil.html>.

21 <www.smh.com.au/icon/0105/09/news6.html>.

22 <archives.seattletimes.nwsource.com/cgi-bin/texis/web/vortex/
   display?slug=micrprivacy080&date=20010408>.

23 Ibid.

24 <www.zdnet.com/zdnn/stories/news/0,4586,2766045,00.html>.

25 <www.itworld.com/Net/3564/IWD010405hnpassport/>.

26 <www.theregister.co.uk/content/4/18002.html>.

27 <www.passport.com/Consumer/TermsOfUse.asp>.

28 <www.theregister.co.uk/content/4/18165.html>.

29 <scriptingnews.userland.com/stories/storyReader$1254>.

30 <public.wsj.com/sn/y/SB991862595554629527.html>.

31 <davenet.userland.com/2001/06/18/integrityInWebwriting>.

32 <news.cnet.com/news/0-1003-200-6399150.html>.

33 <www.theregister.co.uk/content/4/20033.html>.

34 <www.salon.com/tech/feature/2001/07/10/microsoft_school/index.html>.

35 <www.zdnet.com/zdnn/stories/news/0,4586,2803078,00.html>.

36 <www.theregister.co.uk/content/2/18589.html>.

37 <www.theregister.co.uk/content/4/19195.html>.

38 <seattlep-i.nwsource.com/business/24393_reward24.shtml>.

39 <www.landfield.com/isn/mail-archive/2001/Apr/0087.html>.

40 <www.zdnet.com/intweek/stories/news/0,4164,2766045,00.html>.

41 <www.sfgate.com/cgi-bin/article.cgi?f=/news/archive/2001/08/08/
   financial2044EDT0375.DTL&type=tech_article>.

42 <www.theregister.co.uk/content/4/20937.html>.

43 <slashdot.org/article.pl?sid=01/08/09/1254204&mode=thread>.

44 <www.tech-report.com/onearticle.x/2938>.

45 <news.cnet.com/news/0-1003-200-5903000.html>.

46 <www.zdnet.com/zdnn/stories/news/0,4586,2815189,00.html>.

47 <www.tuxedo.org/~esr/jargon/html/entry/FUD.html>.

[48] <www.geocities.com/SiliconValley/Hills/9267/fuddef.html>.

[49] <www.opensource.org/halloween/halloween1.html>.

[50] <www.opensource.org/halloween/halloween1.html>.

[51] <www.nytimes.com/library/tech/98/11/biztech/articles/03memo.html>.

[52] <content.techweb.com/wire/story/TWB20010110S0006>.

[53] <www.theregister.co.uk/content/1/12266.html>.

[54] <news.cnet.com/investor/news/newsitem/0-9900-1028-4825719-RHAT.html?tag=ltnc>.

[55] <www.zdnet.com/eweek/stories/general/0,11011,2687872,00.html>.

[56] <slashdot.org/articles/01/02/15/1825221.shtml>.

[57] <www.suntimes.com/output/tech/cst-fin-micro01.html>.

[58] <ars.userfriendly.org/cartoons/?id=20010604>.

[59] <news.cnet.com/news/0-1003-200-6322264.html?tag=tp_pr>.

[60] <www.opensource.org/halloween/halloween1.html>.

[61] <davenet.userland.com/1996/05/23/embraceextend>.

[62] <www.opensource.org/halloween/halloween1.html>.

Chapter 4 'A stark moral choice'

[1] <www.gnu.org/gnu/manifesto.html>.

[2] <www.blinkenlights.com/classiccmp/gateswhine.html>.

[3] <www.gnu.org/gnu/thegnuproject.html>.

[4] Ibid.

[5] <www.gnu.org/gnu/manifesto.html>.

[6] <www.gnu.org/gnu/thegnuproject.html>.

[7] <www.gnu.org/philosophy/luispo-rms-interview.html>.

[8] <www.gnu.org/gnu/why-gnu-linux.html>.

[9] Ibid.

[10] <www.gnu.org/gnu/why-gnu-linux.html>.

[11] <news.bbc.co.uk/hi/english/sci/tech/newsid_1507000/1507326.stm>.

[12] <www.linuxplanet.com/linuxplanet/opinions/3328/1/>.

[13] <www.netscape.com/newsref/pr/newsrelease558.html>.

[14] <www.opensource.org/docs/history.html>.

[15] <gazette.euskal-linux.org/issue28/raymond.html>.

[16] Tim O'Reilly, 'Remaking the Peer-to-Peer Meme' in Andy Oram, ed. *Peer to Peer: Harnessing the Power of Disruptive Technologies.* (Sebastopol: O'Reilly & Associates, 2001), 38.

[17] O'Reilly, 42, 44.

[18] Ibid, 43-45.

[19] Ibid, 41-47.

[20] <www.newsforge.com/article.pl?sid=01/05/10/028220&mode=nested>.

[21] <news.cnet.com/news/0-1003-200-6954900.html>.

[22] <theregister.co.uk/content/20099.html>.

[23] <mail.gnome.org/archives/gnome-hackers/2001-July/msg00037.html>.

[24] <www.dotgnu.org>.

[25] <www.infoworld.com/articles/hn/xml/01/09/26/010926hnpassriup.xml>.

[26] <www.zdnet.co.uk/itweek/analysis/2001/31/enterprise/open-source/>.

[27] <www.infoworld.com/articles/hn/xml/01/09/26/010926hnpassriup.xml>.

PART 3   ... AND BEER
Chapter 5   Bait and switch

[1] <emoglen.law.columbia.edu/publications/lu-12.html>.

[2] <www.negativland.com/minidis.html>.

[3] <www.sims.berkeley.edu/~pam/papers/digdilsyn.pdf>.

[4] <www.speculations.com/kick.htm>.

[5] Ibid.

[6] <www.speculations.com/timp.htm>.

[7] <www.ironminds.com/ironminds/issues/010430/cafe.shtml>.

[8] <www.stephenking.com/nyt_oped_120100.html>.

[9] <slashdot.org/features/00/11/30/1238204.shtml>.

[10] <www.stephenking.com/sk_120400_2.html>.

[11] <www.siliconvalley.com/docs/news/tech/003067.htm>.

[12] <slashdot.org/features/00/11/30/1238204.shtml>.

[13] <caselaw.lp.findlaw.com/scripts/getcase.pl?court=US&vol=000&invol=00-201&friend=usatoday>.

[14] <www.wired.com/news/politics/0,1283,42538,00.html>.

[15] <www.toad.com/gnu/whatswrong.html>.

[16] <www.spacedaily.com/news/robot-01h.html>.

[17] <www.sdmi.org/pr/OL_Sept_6_2000.htm>.

[18] <www2.linuxjournal.com/cgi-bin/frames.pl/articles/misc/0022.html>.

[19] <www.cs.princeton.edu/sip/sdmi/sdmimessage.txt>.

[20] <www.riaa.org/PR_Story.cfm?id=407>.

[21] <www.cs.princeton.edu/sip/sdmi/riaaletter.html>.

[22] <www.eff.org/Legal/Cases/Felten_v_RIAA/>.

[23] <www.eff.org/Legal/Cases/Felten_v_RIAA/20010813_eff_felten_pr.html>.

[24] <www.publiclibraryofscience.org/plosLetter.shtml>.

[25] <www.publiclibraryofscience.org/plosFAQ.htm#faq5>.

[26] <news.cnet.com/news/0-1005-200-5125655.html>.

[27] <www.internetnews.com/ec-news/article/0,,4_785031,00.html>.

[28] <www.kuro5hin.org/story/2001/7/25/103136/121>.

[29] <www.everything2.com/index.pl?node=Everything%20FAQ&lastnode_id=
    792908>.

Chapter 6   Introducing P2P

[1] <www.openp2p.com/pub/a/p2p/2001/03/27/orwant_security.html>.

[2] <www.openp2p.com/pub/a/p2p/2000/11/24/shirky1-whatisp2p.html>.

[3] <www.openp2p.com/pub/a/p2p/2000/11/24/shirky1-whatisp2p.html?page=2>.

[4] <www.openp2p.com/pub/a/p2p/2000/11/24/shirky1-whatisp2p.html>.

[5] <www.openp2p.com/pub/a/p2p/2000/11/24/shirky1-whatisp2p.html?page=2>.

[6] <www.zdnet.com/zdnn/stories/news/0,4586,2704598,00.html>.

[7] <www.openp2p.com/pub/a/p2p/2001/03/27/orwant_security.html>.

[8] <www.openp2p.com/pub/a/p2p/2001/03/27/orwant_security.html>.

[9] <www.wired.com/news/technology/0%2C1282%2C47365%2C00.html>.

[10] <www.msnbc.com/news/594462.asp?cp1=1>.

[11] <www.msnbc.com/news/594462.asp?cp1=1>.

[12] <www.arl.org/info/frn/copy/primer.html>.

[13] < www.anti-dmca.org/dmca-index.html>.

[14] <www.ybp.com/yrm/trialogue/1099/1099reflc.htm>.

[15] <www.thestandard.com/article/0,1902,22914,00.html>.

[16] <www.thestandard.com/article/0,1902,22914,00.html>.

[17] <www.thestandard.com/article/0,1902,22914,00.html?body_page=2>.

[18] <www.nytimes.com/library/tech/00/07/cyber/cyberlaw/21law.html>
    <www.linuxworld.com/linuxworld/lw-2000-01/lw-01-dvd-interview.html>.

[19] <www.linuxworld.com/linuxworld/lw-2000-01/lw-01-dvd-interview.html>.

[20] <www.eff.org/IP/Video/DVD_Updates/20000720_dvd_update.html>.

[21] <www.linuxworld.com/linuxworld/lw-2000-01/lw-01-dvd-interview.html>.

[22] <www.lovdata.no/all/tl-19610512-002-029.html#39I>; English translation at <www.lemuria.org/DeCSS/norwegianlaw.txt>.

[23] <www.theregister.co.uk/content/6/17164.html>.

[24] <www.lemuria.org/DeCSS/decss.html>.

[25] <www-2.cs.cmu.edu/~dst/DeCSS/Gallery/index.html>.

[26] <www.salon.com/tech/feature/2000/09/13/touretzky/index1.html>.

[27] <www.sciencemag.org/cgi/content/full/293/5537/2028>.

[28] <eon.law.harvard.edu/openlaw/DVD/NY/appeal/000126-cryptographers-amicus.html>.

[29] <news.cnet.com/news/0-1005-201-6545588-0.html>.

[30] <www.techlawjournal.com/courts/kathleenr/Default.htm>.

[31] <www.eff.org/IP/DMCA/US_v_Sklyarov/us_v_sklyarov_faq.html>.

[32] <www.eff.org/IP/DMCA/US_v_Sklyarov/20011213_eff_pr.html>.

[33] <www.eff.org/IP/DMCA/US_v_Sklyarov/us_v_sklyarov_faq.htm>.

[34] <www.eff.org/IP/DMCA/US_v_Sklyarov/20010717_eff_sklyarov_pr.html>.

[35] <www.adobe.com/aboutadobe/pressroom/pressreleases/200107/20010723dcma.html>.

[36] <www.thestandard.com/newsletters/display/0,2098,100-1236,00.html>.

[37] <news.cnet.com/news/0-1005-200-3345604.html>.

[38] <news.cnet.com/news/0-1005-200-4672411.html?tag=rltdnws>.

[39] <www.cnn.com/2001/LAW/02/12/napster.decision.03/>.

[40] <www.wired.com/news/business/0,1367,42677,00.html>.

[41] <news.cnet.com/news/0-1005-200-5784848.html?tag=bplst>.

[42] <www.thestandard.com/article/0,1902,26900,00.html>.

[43] <www.theregister.co.uk/content/6/19487.html>.

[44] <www.theregister.co.uk/content/6/20428.html>.

[45] <www.zdnet.com/zdnn/stories/news/0,4586,5097347,00.html?chkpt=zdnnp1tp02>.

Chapter 7 Life after Napster

[1] <www.eff.org/IP/P2P/Napster/20010227_P2P_Copyright_White_Paper.html>.

[2] <www.eff.org/IP/P2P/Napster/20010227_P2P_Copyright_White_Paper.html>.

[3] <www.zdnet.com/zdnn/stories/news/0,4586,2687120,00.html>.

[4] <news.cnet.com/news/0-1005-200-1945948.html?tag=rltdnws>.

[5] <news.cnet.com/news/0-1005-200-1945948.html?tag=rltdnws>.

[6] <www.theregister.co.uk/content/7/19665.html>.

[7] <www.thestandard.com/article/0,1902,24573,00.html>.

[8] <www.arancidamoeba.com/mrr/problemwithmusic.html>.

[9] <www.salon.com/tech/feature/2000/06/14/love/index4.html>.

[10] <www.salon.com/tech/feature/2001/06/01/digital_music/index.html>.

[11] <news.cnet.com/news/0-1004-200-6674297.html>.

[12] <www.theregister.co.uk/content/4/19603.html>.

[13] <www.assntrends.com/archive0804.htm>.

[14] <www.wired.com/news/mp3/0,1285,47296,00.html>.

[15] <news.cnet.com/news/0-1005-200-5936091.html>.

[16] < www.ntk.net>.

[17] <www.newscientist.com/news/news.jsp?id=ns99991367>

[18] <news.cnet.com/news/0-1005-200-7299321.html>.

[19] <news.cnet.com/news/0-1014-201-7311791-0.html>.

[20] <news.cnet.com/news/0-1014-201-7311791-1.html?tag=unkn>.

[21] <news.cnet.com/news/0-1005-201-7320279-0.html?tag=tp_pr>.

[22] <newsbytes.com/news/01/165959.html>.

[23] <www.theregister.co.uk/content/6/18132.html>

[24] <www.thenation.com/doc.mhtml?i=20010312&s=moglen>.

[25] <slashdot.org/features/00/12/28/1653257.shtml>.

[26] <www.pbs.org/cringely/pulpit/pulpit20010208.html>.

[27] Andy Oram, ed. *Peer-to-Peer: Harnessing the Power of Disruptive Technologies.* (Sebastopol: O'Reilly & Associates, 2001), 98.

[28] <www.openp2p.com/lpt/a/705>.

[29] <www.geek.com/news/geeknews/2001sep/gee20010907007748.htm>.

[30] <www.theregister.co.uk/content/6/23137.html>.

[31] <www.mp3newswire.net/stories/2001/expire.html>.

[32] <www.theregister.co.uk/content/4/23387.html>.

[33] <www.siliconvalley.com/docs/news/svfront/cd121701.htm>.

[34] Raoul Vaniegem, *The Revolution of Everyday Life*, Trans. Donald Nicholson-Smith. (London: Rebel Press/Left Bank Books, 1994), 81.

Conclusion

[1] <www.newsbytes.com/news/01/169823.html>.

[2] Ibid.

[3] <news.bbc.co.uk/hi/english/sci/tech/newsid_1556000/1556097.stm>.

[4] <www.newsbytes.com/news/01/170342.html>.

[5] <news.cnet.com/news/0-1005-200-7642356.html?tag=mn_hd>.

[6] <www.newsbytes.com/news/01/171616.html>.

[7] <www.politechbot.com/docs/hollings.090701.html>.

[8] <www.wired.com/news/politics/0,1283,46655,00.html>.

[9] <www.zdnet.com/zdnn/stories/news/0,4586,5098618,00.html>.

[10] <news.cnet.com/news/0-1275-210-7632187-1.html?tag=bt_bh>.

[11] Ibid.

[12] <www.infoworld.com/articles/hn/xml/00/12/12/001212hnibmlin.xml>.

[13] Ibid.

[14] Ibid.

[15] <www.wired.com/wired/archive/9.10/linux.html?pg=3&topic=&topic_set=>.

[16] <www.silicon.com/bin/bladerunner?30REQEVENT=&REQAUTH=
21046&14001REQSUB=REQINT1=48777>.

[17] <www.wininformant.com/Articles/Index.cfm?ArticleID=23086>.

[18] <www.interesting-people.org/archives/interesting-people/200110/
msg00380.html>.

[19] <web.siliconvalley.com/content/sv/2001/10/26/opinion/dgillmor/weblog/tbl.htm>.

[20] <news.cnet.com/news/0-1005-200-7660935.html?tag=mn_hd>.

[21] <www.wired.com/news/technology/0,1282,48105-2,00.html>.

[22] <www.usdoj.gov/opa/pr/2001/November/01_at_569.htm>.

[23] <www.nytimes.com/2001/11/01/technology/01SOFT.html>.

[24] <web.siliconvalley.com/content/sv/2001/11/02/opinion/dgillmor/weblog/
index.htm#msft>.

[25] <www.wired.com/ncws/antitrust/0,1551,48118,00.html>.

[26] <www.theregister.co.uk/content/4/22647.html>.

[27] <www.pbs.org/cringely/pulpit/pulpit20020103.html>.

[28] <www.oreilly.com/catalog/opensources/book/linus.html>.

[29] <www.theregister.co.uk/content/55/22613.html>.

[30] <dailynews.yahoo.com/h/cn/20011102/tc/
movie_industry_dealt_dvdcracking_blow_1.html>.

[31] David Brin, 'Getting Our Priorities Straight.' Peter Ludlow, ed. *Crypto Anarchy, Cyberstates, and Pirate Utopias.* (Cambridge: MIT Press), 2001.

[32] Ibid, 30.

Afterword

[1] <www.dell.com/linux>.

[2] <www.thestandard.com/article/0,1902,27280,00.html>.

[3] <www.zdnet.com/zdnn/stories/news/0,4586,2640108,00.html>.

[4] < www.sun.com/smi/Press/sunflash/2000-07/sunflash.20000719.1.html>.

[5] <www.acm.org/cacm/AUG96/antimac.htm>.

[6] <www.advogato.org/article/130.html>.

[7] <primates.helixcode.com/~miguel/bongo-bong.html>.

[8] <www.linuxplanet.com/linuxplanet/opinions/3387/1/>.

[9] <www.netslaves.com/comments/983976069.shtml>.

[10] <tuxedo.org/~esr/writings/cathedral-bazaar/cathedral-bazaar/x305.html>.

[11] <gartner11.gartnerweb.com/public/static/hotc/hc00083186a.html>.

[12] Neal Stephenson, *In the Beginning ... Was the Command Line.* (New York: Avon, 1999), 81–82.

[13] Ibid, 84.

[14] Ibid, 84.

[15] <slashdot.org/article.pl?sid=01/07/18/1445233&mode=thread>.

[16] <www.linuxplanet.com/linuxplanet/opinions/3328/3/>.

[17] <slashdot.org/article.pl?sid=01/08/05/2356243&mode=thread>.

[18] <news.bbc.co.uk/hi/english/business/newsid_1161000/1161921.stm>.

[19] < www.embedded-linux.org/qa.php3#Q7>.

[20] <www.newsforge.com/article.pl?sid=01/08/10/1441239>.

BIBLIOGRAPHY OF PRINT WORKS

Bataille, Georges. *The Accursed Share, Volume One: Consumption.* Trans. Robert Hurley. New York: Zone Books, 1988.

Bataille, Georges, et al. *Encyclopedia Acephalica.* London: Atlas Press, 1995.

Brin, David. 'Getting Our Priorities Straight.' Ludlow, Peter, ed. *Crypto Anarchy, Cyberstates, and Pirate Utopias.* Cambridge: MIT Press, 2001.

Derrida, Jacques. *Given Time: I. Counterfeit Money.* [1991]. Trans. Peggy Kamuf. Chicago: University of Chicago Press, 1992.

Malaclypse the Younger [Kerry Wendel Thornley]. *Principia Discordia, OR How I Found Goddess And What I Did To Her When I Found Her.* 5th edition. San Francisco: Loompanics Unlimited, 1979.

Mauss, Marcel. *The Gift: The Form and Reason for Exchange in Archaic Societies.* [1950]. Trans. W.D. Halls. London: Routledge, 1990.

McCaffery, Steve. *North of Intention: Critical Writings 1973–1986.* New York/Toronto: Roof Books/Nightwood Editions, 1986.

Oram, Andy, ed. *Peer-to-Peer: Harnessing the Power of Disruptive Technologies.* Sebastopol: O'Reilly & Associates, 2001.

Stephenson, Neal. *In the Beginning ... Was the Command Line.* New York: Avon, 1999.

Surman, Mark, and Darren Wershler-Henry. *Commonspace: Beyond Virtual Community.* Toronto: FT.com, 2000.

Vaniegem, Raoul. *The Revolution of Everyday Life.* Trans. Donald Nicholson-Smith. London: Rebel Press/Left Bank Books, 1994.

Wayner, Peter. *Free for All: How Linux and the Free Software Movement Undercut the High-Tech Titans.* New York: HarperBusiness, 2000.

INDEX

Security Systems Standards
     and Certification Act
     (SSCA), 162–163
SEGA Genesis, 48
SETI@home, 116–117, 119
shared control, 182–183
Shared Source, 36, 37–43
shareware, 15, 19–22
Sharrard, Jeremy, 151
Shirky, Clay, 115–116, 117
Siegler, Joakim, 182
Silicon Alley Reporter, 6
Sinnreich, Aram, 139, 150
SirCam virus, 43
Skylarov, Dmitri, 134–135
Slashdot, 72, 112, 176, 188
Slemko, Marc, 167
Smart Tags, 62–64
Software & Information
     Industry Association, 55
software licenses
     enterprise agreements, 54
     Free Software. See Free
          Software licenses
     group licensing, 64–66
     legal interpretations, 25–26
     OEM license, 66
     pay as you go, 54–55
software ownership, 24–26
Solaris, 178
Sony Music, 136
SourceForge, 86
Special Libraries Association,
     103–104
Speedera, 56
spyware, 144
Stallman, Richard M., 23, 26,
     33, 75, 77, 79–81, 173
StarOffice, 66, 164, 177–179
Stephenson, Neal, 187–188
Stiennon, Richard, 60
Streambox, 105–106
Sturtz, David, 73
Sullivan, Brendan, 170
Sun Microsystems, 65–66, 87,
     164, 177–178, 180
SunnComm, 148, 150
Surman, Mark, 4
Surrealism, 9
System Enhancement, 21

T
Taito, 48
TCP/IP protocol, 31
Tech Report, 68
Third Voice, 63
Time, 104
Toaplan, 48
Torvalds, Linus, 32, 78
Touretzky, David S., 130
"Tragedy of the Commons,"
     4–5
Tribute to Jim Reeves (Pride),
     148
Trott, Bob, 61
Tucows, 20
2600, 130, 132

U
UC Berkeley, 32
Ulrich, Lars, 136
Universal Music, 136
     see also Vivendi Universal
University Microfilms, 104
Unix, 31
Unix/Linux ideal, 183–184
Usenix Security Conference,
     108
User Friendly, 72
UseTheSource.com, 64

V
VA Linux Systems, 86
Vaidhyanathan, Siva, 119–120
Valloppillil, Vinod, 70
Verance Corporation, 107
Visse, Bob, 167
Vivendi Universal, 137, 149,
     157
von Lohmann, Fred, 140, 141

W
W3C Validator Service,
     166–167
warez, 15, 16
Warner Music Group, 136, 138
Wayner, Peter, 31
Web
     annotation, 63
     retagging, 63
     services, 53, 86

Webnoize, 161
Weiss, Amy, 148
"What's Wrong with Copy
     Protection" (Gilmore), 104
Wikipedia, 111, 112
WikiWiki, 112
Wilcox, John, 62
Windows
     alternatives to, 175–177
     Blue Screen of Death
          (BSOD), 174–175
Winer, Dave, 63, 73
WIPO Copyright Treaty, 16
World Intellectual Property
     Organization, 122
"Writing as a General
     Economy" (McCaffery),
     10–11

X
Ximian, 86, 175, 182, 183
XML, 62–64

Y
Yahoo!, 50

Z
ZDNet, 60, 68
Zero Wing, 47–48
Zeropaid, 155
zip file compression format, 21